MARTIN BARBER was a senior UN official and has extensive experience in humanitarian affairs and peace operations – both at UN headquarters and in the field. He served as Director of the United Nations Mine Action Service (UNMAS) at UN headquarters in New York from 2000 until his retirement from the UN in 2005. Previously, he was chief of policy development and advocacy in the UN Office for the Coordination of Humanitarian Affairs (OCHA).

From 1996 to 1998, Barber was Deputy Special Representative of the UN Secretary-General in the UN Mission in Bosnia and Herzegovina (UNMIBH), Sarajevo. From 1989 to 1996, he worked with the UN Office for Coordination of Humanitarian Assistance to Afghanistan (UNOCHA) in Islamabad, Pakistan, serving as UN Humanitarian Coordinator for Afghanistan in 1995 to 1996. From 1975 to 1982 he served with the Office of the UN High Commissioner for Refugees (UNHCR) in Laos and Thailand. Between 1982 and 1989, he was Director of the British Refugee Council, London. From 2010 to 2013, he served as Senior Adviser in the Office for the Coordination of Foreign Aid in the government of the United Arab Emirates.

Barber is now a consultant and analyst working on humanitarian issues. He holds a doctorate in Southeast Asian Sociology from the University of Hull and is an Honorary Fellow of the University of Edinburgh. In 2006, he was made an OBE for services to de-mining.

'*Blinded by Humanity* is an engaging examination of the UN's efforts to accomplish its humanitarian aims and political goals, which at times may seem at cross purposes. Martin Barber's wide experience and frank analysis will interest UN watchers and humanitarian activists alike because it provides valuable insights on how to make the UN a more effective instrument for peace, security and human rights.'

Kofi Annan, former Secretary-General of the United Nations

'Sometimes understanding humanitarian work and the workings of the UN seems insurmountably complex. Martin Barber's book is an essential tool to break through the complexities and understand various aspects of humanitarian assistance and the UN.'

Jody Williams, Winner, with the International Campaign to
Ban Landmines (ICBL), of the Nobel Peace Prize, 1997

'Every humanitarian, and new recruit to the UN, would benefit from reading (this book).'

Lord Malloch-Brown, former Deputy Secretary-General
of the UN and Administrator of the
UN Development Programme (UNDP)

'Humanitarian efforts are too often dominated either by academics with no practical experience or practitioners unguided by research. Martin Barber has managed to combine the two in this valuable merger of real-life experience and knowledge.'

Jan Egeland, Secretary General of the Norwegian Refugee Council
and former Emergency Relief Coordinator

'A fascinating read that will be of great interest to all those concerned with how the UN and the UN system actually work.'

Mats Berdal, Professor of Security and Development,
King's College London

BLINDED BY HUMANITY

INSIDE THE UN'S HUMANITARIAN OPERATIONS

MARTIN BARBER

Lesley

With best wishes

M

I.B. TAURIS

LONDON · NEW YORK

First published in 2015 by I.B.Tauris & Co Ltd
6 Salem Road, London W2 4BU
175 Fifth Avenue, New York NY 10010
www.ibtauris.com

Distributed in the United States and Canada Exclusively by Palgrave Macmillan
175 Fifth Avenue, New York NY 10010

ISBN: 978 1 78453 067 9
eISBN: 978 0 85773 806 6

A full CIP record for this book is available from the British Library
A full CIP record is available from the Library of Congress

Library of Congress Catalog Card Number: available

Typeset by Saxon Graphics Ltd., Derby
Printed and bound by CPI Group (UK) Ltd, Croydon, CR0 4YY

CONTENTS

For William and Tom

ILLUSTRATIONS

Figures

Plates

5   Afghan refugee returning home from Pakistan, 2002. Photo courtesy of UNHCR/P. Benetar.

6   New Afghan refugees at Roghani camp near Chaman in Pakistan, December 2001 (Also cover photo). Photo courtesy of United Nations/ Luke Powell.

7   UN High Commissioner for Refugees Sadruddin Aga Khan and his wife Princess Catherine visit Lao people displaced by the war being resettled in the Plain of Jars, September 1975. Photo courtesy of UNHCR/J. Becket.

8   UN Coordinator Sadruddin Aga Khan leads high-level delegation to Afghanistan and Pakistan – Islamabad, October 1990.
(l–r: author; Benon Sevan, Personal Representative of the Secretary-General; James Ingram, executive director, WFP; Thorvald Stoltenberg, UN High Commissioner for Refugees; Sadruddin; President of Pakistan, Ghulam Ishaq Khan, and Foreign Minister, Sahabzada Yaqub Ali Khan.) Author photo.

9   Bosnia and Herzegovina – destruction in Derventa region, 1998. Photo courtesy of UNHCR/A. Hollmann.

10   Bomb destroys part of UN headquarters in Baghdad, killing UN Special Representative Sergio Vieira de Mello and 21 others, 19 August 2003. Photo courtesy of United Nations/AP photo.

11   Unexploded ordnance awaiting destruction in Laos. Photo courtesy of Ian Mansfield.

12   Mine detection dog and handler in Afghanistan. Photo courtesy of MDC Kabul.

13   Princess Diana visits UN Mine Action Coordination Centre in Sarajevo, 17 August 1997. Photo by permission of AP.

14   A de-miner in Lebanon uses a detector to locate hidden mines or bombs. Photo courtesy of Sean Sutton/MAG.

15   The author bids farewell to Secretary-General Kofi Annan upon retirement from the UN, 2 August 2005. Photo courtesy of United Nations/Eakinder Debebe.

ACKNOWLEDGEMENTS

There are several people, no longer alive, who I wish could read this book, and who, in one way or another, have helped me to write it. The first of these was my father, Philip, who showed me that life is more fulfilling if you are ready to question received wisdom. I hope he would have enjoyed reading this. Then come those whose lives were cut short by accident, illness or terrorism and who have influenced the way I think and work. These include Jacques Cuénod, Darryl Han, Sergio Vieira de Mello, Jacques Mouchet and Sadruddin Aga Khan. I am glad that David Lockwood who played a major part in the events described in Chapter 4, was able to read and comment on the manuscript before his death in January 2012.

Among the living, I owe a particular debt to two people for their encouragement and support during the writing of this book. Professor Mats Berdal of Kings College, London has encouraged, advised and supported me every step of the way. Nicholas Morris, formerly of UNHCR, and a friend for 35 years, read every chapter as soon as I sent it to him, offered trenchant comments and, when necessary, pushed me to keep going.

I am greatly indebted to Mark Malloch-Brown, who pops up in these pages from Chapter 2 onwards, for his kind Foreword and for his extremely valuable comments on the drafts of Chapters 2, 9 and 10.

I am also extremely grateful to a number of former colleagues who kindly read most or all of the manuscript and offered valuable insights. These include Randolph Kent, Frederick Lyons, Jeff Crisp and Robert England. Other former colleagues kindly read early drafts of individual chapters and in some cases saved me from factual inaccuracies and errors of interpretation. These include Everett Ressler, Alan Phillips, Bob Eaton and Ian Mansfield. Of course, any errors that remain are entirely my responsibility.

A number of family, friends and former colleagues have helped in different ways with the publication of the book. These include my sons, William and Tom, my sister, Sarah Backhouse, Teresa Francis, Sultan Al Shamsi, Mohammed Azam Chaudhry, Julia Chatellier, Helena Fraser, John Flanagan, David Harland, Susan Hopper, Bruce Jones, Rashid Khalikov, Francesco Mancini, Ian Mansfield, Ian Marvin, Ross Mountain, Yvon Orand and Hansjoerg Strohmeyer.

Everybody who works in the United Nations relies on colleagues for everything they do. I remain indebted to an enormous number of past and current staff members of the UN system, as well as to counterparts and interlocutors in governments, NGOs, the media and representatives of the communities affected by disaster. I cannot possibly name all of them. However, there are a few, not already mentioned, that I feel I must acknowledge, for their support and guidance at critical stages in my career. They are Amphay Doré, Jean-Marie Guéhenno, Iqbal Riza and. Zia Rizvi.

There is one group of unsung heroes in UN operations, without whose courage and professionalism we would not get anywhere – the drivers. They are often required to wait many hours and then to drive safely on dangerous roads; we all owe our lives to people like Amir Ali Khan, who drove me in Pakistan for seven years.

At I.B.Tauris, my editors, Lester Crook and Joanna Godfrey have guided me expertly through the process of publication with able support from Cécile Rault, Katherine Tulloch and Antonia Leslie. Rob Brown and his team at Saxon Graphics have worked quickly and efficiently to get it into print.

But my greatest debt is to my family: to Keolila, my partner for 28 years, who cheerfully accepted the constant disruptions that are part of this type of life, and to William and Tom, who had less choice in the matter, but have given me great joy and wonderful support.

FOREWORD

Martin Barber was of 'the Indo-Chinese Refugee' generation – as was I. There was an earlier group of humanitarian workers who were the 'Biafra generation' and others followed, drawn into humanitarian work by Afghanistan, the Horn of Africa, Central America and later still the Bosnian conflict and the Great Lakes region of Africa and now Syria. Each stimulated an outpouring of sympathy – and each led young men and women to postpone more orthodox careers to go and help. We came as idealists anxious to save victims from the terrible inhumanity of conflict. We came to save lives.

When it was over – and for Martin that was many decades later – we were forced to a reckoning: had we achieved what we set out to do? Each of us had our own moment of truth when the head finally controlled the heart and we came to realise that our apparently simple acts of charity often had unintended consequences. That things are never simple and that relief workers must have the modesty to listen and learn – and not presume things are ever straightforward as Martin concludes at the end of his book. This is the story of his own journey of self-discovery. It is one that every humanitarian and new recruit to the UN would benefit from reading.

He writes: 'If there is one message that I would pass on to young people wanting to do good in the world, it is this: be passionate, but know your world. Everybody can have good intentions, and indeed, most people do. If you fail to understand the context in which you are working and the people you are working with, and if you do not assess, with infinite care, the likely impact of your actions on them, you may find that you will do more harm than good.'

Admittedly, Martin was hardly the callow innocent that I was when I arrived to work for him in Thailand in 1979. He was already a veteran of VSO in Laos and subsequent post-graduate field work in social anthropology in the region. He had exactly the enviable local knowledge that many of us lacked.

But as his career took him on to Pakistan and Afghanistan, to Bosnia and elsewhere he, like the rest of us, had to learn how little he knew. Perhaps because he had started at such an advantage in Indo-China, doubting that the mass resettlement of Vietnamese, Lao and Cambodians in the US and the West would be the straightforward panacea that was anticipated, he brought a much stronger caution and critical judgement to humanitarian work from a much earlier stage than most of us.

This is his story of a lifetime's witness of unintended consequences. But those early years in Laos and then Thailand gave him the other critical qualification for a humanitarian career: passion. Without passion, that scepticism that is so useful in the world of the UN with all its compromises, quickly descends into cynicism. Those of us who stuck at this did so because, like Martin, early on a flame was lit that never extinguished: he cared. As this book, which charts his personal journey from Laos to Abu Dhabi, so eloquently shows, his is a humanitarianism that balances head and heart.

Lord Malloch-Brown

PREFACE

War and refugees were recurring themes of my childhood. My father often admitted that his service in the British Army during World War II had been the most interesting years of his life. He liked to talk about the places he had been while in uniform, the people he had met, the amusing and tragic events that he had witnessed.

One of his favourite stories concerned my birth. In February 1945, he was in Holland with his battery of anti-aircraft gunners when he received the news of my birth. He was staying with a local family. That evening, he told them his news. 'Oh, Major Barber, what wonderful news', cried Mrs Vadenburg. 'And to think that you haven't been home for two years!' Mr Vadenburg quickly corrected his wife. My parents always assured me that my father had indeed been involved in my conception.

In civilian life my father, like his father and grandfather before him, was a chartered accountant. He had taken the job reluctantly, because his father wanted at least one of his sons to follow in his footsteps. His three elder brothers had all declined. My father would have preferred to be a publisher.

In 1949, to the delight of my mother, a Londoner, my father got a job in London, and we moved south from Sheffield. In his spare time, my father soon became involved with a charity called the British Council for Aid to Refugees (BCAR), initially as its honorary treasurer, and later as chairman. He would often tell us stories of the refugees from Eastern Europe who had come to Britain after the war, and also of the extraordinary ladies who gave of their time and money to help them. My uncle Adam was himself one of those refugees, from Poland. One Christmas Day, previously a strictly family affair, we were joined for lunch by a young refugee from Bulgaria, whose story, told in halting English, made a lasting impression.

So, it seemed quite natural that the first thing I should do after leaving school was to join a work camp organised by the United Nations Association (UNA) of the UK in southern Austria. The aim of the camp was to help a Romanian refugee family to build their new home in a village outside Klagenfurt.

The energy of the Romanian, and his gratitude for the help we were giving him, seemed limitless. He got up at four every morning to milk the cows on the farm where he worked. When he had finished work on the farm, he would come over to the building site. While we were straining to push the heavy barrows of bricks up the wooden planks to the bricklayer, he would run up singing lustily. He had known what it was to have absolutely nothing – as German speakers his family had been forced out of their home in Romania – but now he had been given a chance. He was unstoppable.

St Andrews University, on the east coast of Scotland, was a quiet and rather conservative place in the 1960s. I joined the Debating Society and found that I enjoyed the cut and thrust of argument. I took part in debating competitions in Dublin and Glasgow. This opened my eyes to the great issues that would consume Western Europe in 1968.

In 1966, during the summer vacation, I took part in another UNA work camp, this time in north-western Greece, close to the Albanian border. We installed a piped water system in a village where, for hundreds of years, families had got all their water from the village spring and carried it back to their houses in buckets. As the project progressed, we would have the pleasure of inviting village families to turn on the tap in their gardens for the first time. Then the pancakes would come out, the ouzo would flow and work would stop for the day. But then, the next day, when we had to turn off the supply while we installed the tap in the next house, old ladies would rush up to our camp to complain furiously that they had no water. How were they supposed to live without water? With the arrival of a modern convenience, the memory of centuries of hard work can be so quickly erased.

With these experiences, I could not imagine following my father into his accountancy firm. Indeed, he did his best to dissuade me from doing so. He had no desire to impose on me the burden that he had taken on from his father. So, in 1968, I applied to go out into the world with Voluntary Service Overseas (VSO), a British volunteering charity.

A two-year volunteer assignment, even in a country as captivating as Laos, does not lead inevitably to a career in an international organisation. Even after another two years in Laos doing research for my doctorate in social anthropology, I might well have returned to an academic career in the UK. But in late 1974, I was invited to join the UN High Commissioner for Refugees' (UNHCR) groundbreaking programme for internally displaced people in Laos, and the decision to accept was not difficult.

Forty years later, after a career working with people caught up in some of the twentieth century's most intractable conflicts, I have had the opportunity to reflect. The years have brought a rich feast of experience, from tantalising glimpses of what might have been, to the very worst that we humans can do to each other, as well as the best. While I celebrate the achievements and the friendships crafted in shared experience, the nagging question remains: could we, should we have done better?

In 2006, I was invited to offer a course at the University of Edinburgh on 'The United Nations and Complex Emergencies', for 36 final-year students of politics, international relations and social anthropology. The experience forced me to refine my thinking on some of the most difficult issues in the humanitarian field, but it also confronted me with the fact that there are few books about this field written by practitioners. There is plenty of academic work; particular operations have been analysed in depth, but when my students asked where they could find out what it was like to have a career in this field, there seemed to be little on offer. So, I decided to try and fill the gap.

While describing life working for the UN in various situations, in this book I also look at a broad set of questions: how effective have international organisations been in bringing peace and comfort to people affected by conflict? How did the UN perform? And, based on the lessons it has learned since 1975, how might the UN improve its capacity to help people affected by conflict in the twenty-first century?

Through the lens of my own involvement in specific operations, I examine the work of the United Nations in humanitarian assistance, aid to refugees, peacekeeping, peacebuilding and mine action (de-mining), with a particular focus on Laos, Afghanistan and Bosnia-Herzegovina, the countries where I worked. The book analyses recent policy developments intended to improve the quality and effectiveness of the UN's work in these fields, and it assesses the extent to which recent reforms are likely to make the UN a more effective partner for countries emerging from conflict.

Working for the United Nations in countries consumed by conflict can be both exhilarating and frustrating. The exhilaration comes from the unique legitimacy and prestige of the UN, its ability to bring people together from all parts of the world to focus on a desperate problem affecting people in one place, and to make a real difference. The frustrations come from the reverse side of the coin. The diversity that can achieve wonders can also breed misunderstandings and failure. When a global organisation fails to deliver, people suffer.

A colleague once said that there are two types of people who work for the United Nations: those who feel it is a privilege to work for the global organisation, and those who spend their time worrying about what the UN owes them. Colleagues in the first group were more congenial and interesting, since they were always searching for ways to improve the performance of their organisation. This book is a personal effort to celebrate the achievements of the United Nations in countries in conflict, while honestly setting out and analysing its weaknesses. It is intended both as a contribution to the historical record and an objective assessment of where changes are needed.

To be successful, leaders of United Nations operations in countries emerging from conflict need to work in partnership with a daunting range of organisations and individuals. These include: the host government, its ministries and local authorities; rebel groups that have to be persuaded to join the political process or allow the passage of humanitarian aid; representatives of affected communities; military officers, whether from the warring parties or international peacekeeping forces; the governments of donor countries that fund the operations; a plethora of international and regional organisations, from the World Bank and the agencies of the UN system to the International Committee of the Red Cross (ICRC); a myriad of non-governmental organisations (NGOs), both national and international; journalists from the affected country and around the world; commercial companies keen to contribute equipment and services to the effort; and, of course, the individual women and men recruited to work on the operation, with their own needs, skills, hopes and fears.

It is small wonder that coordinators of such operations can have a significant impact on the success or failure of the enterprise, or that it is notoriously difficult to find people capable of fulfilling the task effectively. The leadership of UN operations, its nature, requirements and challenges is a particular focus of this book.

The material in the following pages comes from three sources: the literature on UN operations; interviews and correspondence with former colleagues and present staff of the UN system; and my own documents, notes and recollections.

The book is organised chronologically. The introduction provides background to three main areas of my work: protection and assistance for refugees, coordination of humanitarian response and peacekeeping. It also points to some of the striking similarities in the recent histories of Laos, Afghanistan and Bosnia and Herzegovina.

Chapter 1 is about Laos between 1968 and 1977. It introduces some of the issues developed in the two following chapters, about refugees in Thailand and in Europe. Chapter 2 is about the arrival in Thailand of refugees from Laos, Vietnam and Cambodia between 1975 and 1981. It looks particularly at when and how resettlement in Western countries became the solution of choice. Chapter 3 is about the reception of refugees and asylum-seekers in Britain between 1981 and 1988. It tackles questions about asylum, refugee law and economic migration.

Chapter 4 is about Afghanistan. It looks at how the UN handled the crisis there, from the departure of Soviet troops in 1989 until 1996. It considers issues of coordination and the response to landmines, and asks if there are lessons that still have to be learned, and which could help the international community in Afghanistan today. Chapter 5 looks at the international community's response to the crisis in Bosnia and Herzegovina, with a focus on the period between 1996 and 1998, immediately after the end of the war.

Chapter 6 takes us to the Headquarters of the UN in New York and looks at the first term of Kofi Annan as Secretary-General from 1997 to 2001. It examines the reforms that he introduced to the UN's humanitarian and peacekeeping operations. Then, Chapter 7 examines the story of the remarkable international response to the problem of anti-personnel landmines. Chapter 8 offers a brief look at an often neglected feature of international aid, the contribution of Gulf Arab donors.

Chapter 9 is about the 'coordination' of humanitarian operations, the focus of so much of the work I have been involved in, and now the responsibility of a large office in the UN Secretariat. Chapter 10 is a concluding essay that bears the title of the book. It identifies seven 'blind spots' that, in my view, constrain international organisations in their efforts to bring help to those in need and to bring peace and prosperity to troubled countries. It asks whether the United Nations is prepared for the operational challenges of the twenty-first century. Has the UN learned how to respond quickly and effectively in an emergency; how to find, train and support good leaders; how to make the parts of the UN system work effectively together; and how to empower people in affected countries to take the lead in the recovery of their own societies? Or does the UN remain, in some areas, obstinately blind to its own shortcomings, as well as to practical ways of addressing them?

The book is intended to be accessible to the general reader with an interest in the United Nations, but it is aimed particularly at students of international relations and humanitarian affairs, not as a textbook, but as general reading, to add the flavour of real life to their studies. If the brightest young people aspire to join the United Nations, the future of this unique global institution will be assured. If this book is also of interest to academics, diplomats, policy makers and United Nations and NGO colleagues, I shall of course be delighted.

INTRODUCTION

Before launching into the main narrative, I felt it would be important to set the scene briefly and give some background to the three principal UN activities that feature in the story – the aid to refugees, the coordination of humanitarian response in emergencies, and peacekeeping operations. I have also included a short essay on the shared experiences of Laos, Afghanistan and Bosnia in the second half of the twentieth century, and I have introduced one of the central themes of the book under the heading, 'Good intentions are not enough'.

The United Nations and refugees

Who is a refugee, and what are his or her rights? These questions continue to stir debate today, more than 60 years after the adoption in 1951 of the Convention relating to the Status of Refugees.

Consultations leading up to the adoption of the 1951 Convention were all based on definitions limited in time and space. When the Convention was agreed, it defined a refugee as a person who:

> As a result of events occurring before 1 January 1951, and owing to well-founded fear of being persecuted for reasons of race, religion, nationality, membership of a particular social group or political opinion is outside the country of his nationality and is unable, or, owing to such fear unwilling to avail himself of the protection of that country [...] and is unwilling to return to it.

Not only did the Convention restrict refugee status to the victims of events before 1951, but it limited those events to what had happened in Europe. It was the process of de-colonisation in Africa in the 1960s which would generate the next major refugee emergencies. Operating under its Statute, which, unlike the Convention, did not restrict the definition of a refugee in time and space, the Office of the UN High Commissioner for Refugees (UNHCR) offered to help. The process towards universalisation of the refugee definition, and of the institution established to protect and assist refugees, had begun. In 1967, a Protocol was adopted which extended the provisions of the 1951 Convention in time and space, to cover all persons anywhere who met the definition of a refugee.

The key provision of the Convention and Protocol, which imposes a binding obligation on states, is that refugees may not under any circumstances be forced to return to the country of their nationality against their will. This is the principle of *non-refoulement*. States ratifying the Convention and Protocol agree to keep on their soil people who are able to demonstrate that they meet the criteria for refugee status. It is hardly surprising that a few states were reluctant to accede to the 1967 Protocol and some took many years to do so. Many of those states that did accede might have thought twice about it, if they could have foreseen developments in international travel over the next 40 years, and the ease with which people who manage to escape persecution in their home country could show up in countries on another continent.

In Chapter 3, I take a closer look at what happened when principles established for the protection of refugees in Europe were deemed to apply, unchanged, to people leaving Africa and arriving in Europe, or leaving Asia and arriving in America.

Coordination of humanitarian response

In the 1980s, when I was at the British Refugee Council (BRC), it had become obvious that the UN lacked the capacity to coordinate the response of its own agencies to humanitarian crises. As an NGO working with refugees, we could see that the UN's work with refugees was well organised, because UNHCR had clear responsibility to lead the international effort. However, when people were displaced within their own countries as a result of conflict, nobody knew who was in charge of the international response. At the BRC, we campaigned for the UN Secretary-General to assign responsibility for assisting internally displaced persons to an existing UN agency or to create a new office to take it on. We were rebuffed, but our intervention and those of many other bodies, had an effect. When the Geneva Accords of 1988 brought to an end the Soviet occupation of Afghanistan, Secretary-General Perez de Cuellar asked his former rival for the job and ex-UN High Commissioner for refugees, Prince Sadruddin Aga Khan, to become the UN coordinator of economic and humanitarian assistance programmes relating to Afghanistan (UNOCA), with his headquarters in Geneva. The appointment of Sadruddin for Afghanistan was one of a number of *ad hoc* responses to the challenge of coordinating the international effort in emergencies.

Eventually, in 1991, the General Assembly adopted resolution 46/182, which created the post of Emergency Relief Coordinator (ERC) at the UN headquarters in New York. It also asked the ERC to chair a new Inter-Agency Standing Committee (IASC), bringing together not only the UN family of agencies, but also the Red Cross and Red Crescent movements and international NGOs. This represented an extraordinary turn-around. From a situation only 20 years earlier when the UN's role in international humanitarian response to emergencies had been limited, quite deliberately, to natural disasters, the United Nations, in the person of the Emergency Relief Coordinator, was being asked to lead the whole international effort to respond to what were now called 'complex emergencies'.

The first ERC, Jan Eliasson of Sweden, and his brand-new Department of Humanitarian Affairs (DHA), had a difficult beginning. They were up against the free spirits of the UN Children's Fund (UNICEF), UNHCR and World Food Programme (WFP), who were not used to being 'coordinated' by a department in New York. Initially, most of DHA's senior staff in New York were not seasoned humanitarian workers, but had been transferred from economic units of the Secretariat. Although some had come on secondment from the UN agencies, the agencies' lack of enthusiasm for the whole enterprise meant that they did not always send their best staff to take up these posts.

DHA's difficulties were further compounded by the fact that its headquarters was split between New York and Geneva. While staff in New York had never worked together before, the team in Geneva, based around the staff of the old UN Office for Disaster Relief Coordination (UNDRO), had been working solely on natural disasters, and would need time to adapt to the new environment of complex emergencies. In Chapter 6, I look in detail at the transformation of DHA into the Office for the Coordination of Humanitarian Affairs (OCHA) in 1997, and the brief, but pivotal reign as ERC of Sergio Vieira de Mello.

In 2006, just 15 years after the establishment of DHA, the General Assembly did another extraordinary thing; it set up a fund, the Central Emergency Response Fund (CERF), with an annual target of US$450 million, and put it entirely in the hands of the ERC. From being a non-player in the world of humanitarian relief, the UN Secretariat had become not only the chief coordinator, but also the principal source of rapid funding in the immediate aftermath of a rapid-onset disaster.

Keeping the peace

The end of the Cold War, bringing with it an unprecedented period of consensus in the Security Council, saw a flurry of new peacekeeping initiatives, for which the UN Secretariat was completely unprepared. Although the operations in Namibia, Mozambique and Cambodia were concluded without too many disasters, the period between 1993 and 1995 saw the ignominious withdrawals from Somalia and Haiti, the genocide in Rwanda and the massacre of 8,000 Bosnian men and boys at Srebrenica. When Kofi Annan took office as Secretary-General of the United Nations on 1 January 1997, many people predicted that UN peacekeeping would not recover. They could not have been more wrong. Chapter 6 looks in detail at how the reputation of UN peacekeeping was substantially restored.

This brief account of how the United Nations deals with the three principal components of crisis response – support for refugees, coordination of humanitarian aid and peacekeeping – has told three quite separate stories. Since 2000, and the publication of the Report of the Panel on UN Peace Operations, chaired by Lakhdar Brahimi, the three strands have been brought closer together, culminating in the creation of a number of 'multi-dimensional peace operations', in which a deputy special representative of the Secretary-General is given responsibility for coordinating both humanitarian and recovery action from within a peacekeeping mission. Chapter 9 offers a short essay on this phenomenon, looking at the pros and cons of this arrangement.

The Great Game – twentieth-century style

The three war-torn countries where I worked between 1975 and 1998, although separated by thousands of miles, have a lot in common. Laos, Afghanistan and Bosnia and Herzegovina are all land-locked and mountainous. They each contain several distinct ethnic groups, which have close ties to larger populations of the same ethnicity in neighbouring countries. They all could be said to have got 'caught in the cross-fire' of wider conflicts between their larger neighbours, backed by the great powers. They all exported a substantial part of their populations as refugees. As one writer on Laos put it, they were either 'buffer-states or battle-grounds'. Tragically, in the second half of the twentieth century, they all became both.

At one level it is easy to see what the three countries had in common. The competition for influence in Central and South Asia between Russia and Britain in the nineteenth century became known as the Great Game. Similar games were played out in Southeast Asia between Britain and France and later between the United States and the Soviet Union, and in the Balkans between Western Europe and the Ottoman Empire. In all three cases, the rival powers could not see any great benefit from ruling these countries, but they felt they had to prevent their rivals from doing so. Instability in these countries was preferable to peace under the influence of one's enemies.

The game was played in very similar ways in each case. The powers exploited the natural fault lines of ethnic rivalry or dynastic succession, or both. Local leaders ambitious for power were encouraged to press their claims by force of arms if necessary, with the backing of the great powers or their local proxies. Long-simmering resentment at perceived injustice found a sympathetic ear with the generous outsiders.

In Laos, the minority hill tribes had for centuries been kept out of the productive lowlands by the dominant ethnic Lao. Modern education opportunities and jobs in the administration went predominantly to the Lao. The pro-communist Pathet Lao (Lao Nation) movement found it easy to recruit among the hill tribes by articulating this injustice.

In Afghanistan, the Pushtoon kings from Kandahar had retained their control over the Tajik and Uzbek communities in the north in part by settling landless Pushtoon families from the south on some of the most productive land in the northern valleys. Sponsors of opposition to the status quo had little difficulty in tapping the rich seams of historical resentment.

In Bosnia, the Serbs viewed the Muslim Bosniacs in a similar fashion to the Lao hill tribes' view of the ethnic Lao in the lowlands. The Muslims, with Turkish support, had taken over the most productive land in the valleys and pushed the Serbs up into the hills. In Serb eyes, the Muslims kept for themselves the best opportunities in education and employment and looked down on the Serbs as uncultured peasants.

Seen in this way, the three countries were, and to differing degrees still are, volatile powder kegs waiting to explode again. In each case, their best days in history coincided with the rule of a strong leader able to keep the lid on internal opposition. In Laos, this means going back to King Souligna Vongsa at the end of the seventeenth and start of the eighteenth centuries. In Afghanistan, King Zahir Shah and his advisors managed to balance the competing pressures for 40 years from 1933 to 1973, and in the case of Bosnia and Herzegovina, Marshal Tito held it together as part of Yugoslavia after his exploits in World War II, until his death in 1980 released all the latent tensions and hostilities.

When considering the recent history of Laos, Afghanistan and Bosnia it is interesting to look at how Switzerland managed to avoid the same fate during the great wars of the twentieth century in Europe. In simple terms, it had by then acquired a mature set of national institutions which enabled it to adopt a policy of neutrality and then stick to it. Its constitution guarantees that its different communities (French, German and Italian) need a substantial degree of control over their own lives. In other words, the highly decentralised cantonal system is key to the strength of Switzerland as a diverse, multi-ethnic and multi-lingual society, capable of resisting pressures from outside to turn in on itself by demonising members of the other ethnic and linguistic groups.

While Laos, Afghanistan and Bosnia show many similarities in the history of their descent into internal conflict, the story could hardly be more different in the roadmaps they have each chosen, as they seek to emerge from it. The Bosnian constitution, negotiated at Dayton, Ohio in 1995, is closest to the Swiss model. The distinct identities of the Muslim Bosniacs, the Catholic Croats and the Orthodox Serbs are recognised in the structure of the 12 cantons of the Federation of Bosniacs and Croats, and the Serb Republic within a decentralised state.

Since the Pathet Lao took over in 1975, the Lao People's Democratic Republic has been a one-party state. But this national structure has not prevented continuous debate within the party about how the country should be governed. The fact that the party leadership is predominantly from the communities that were historically marginalised has helped to even out the opportunities for education and employment. The party is increasingly able to ensure that the provincial and district leadership teams represent all the major ethnicities present in the province. In the 35 years of its rule, the party has gradually decentralised and encouraged local branches to seek out talented cadres by listening to the opinions of local party members.

Of course, the children of the top leaders enjoy a privileged lifestyle in Vientiane, and corruption can be found at all levels of society, but historical imbalances have been substantially corrected, and the playing field is more level than it was. Even if Laos is not the parliamentary democratic paradise that Western politicians might wish for, it has found a measure of stability and increasing levels of prosperity that some of its neighbouring democracies are beginning to envy.

Afghanistan has not chosen either of these paths. It has not decentralised and it has not sought to correct historical inequities. On the contrary, the Constitution of 2003 put all the powers of patronage into the hands of a president elected by universal suffrage, which obliges candidates to make deals with regional power-brokers who can deliver the votes.

I will return to this theme in Chapter 4, on Afghanistan, when I look at why the international effort to restore stability has so far failed, and is likely to continue to fail, unless changes are made to the strategy that reflect the country's history and learn the lessons of twentieth-century conflicts in the countries with which Afghanistan shares so many historical features.

Good intentions are not enough

While this book features a large cast of organisational and individual characters, they can be considered in two broad groups: first the refugees and displaced persons, the orphans, widows and those disabled by bullets or maimed by landmines, those who have lost their homes, their livelihoods and sometimes their mental health from exposure to war; and then, on the other side, the army of institutions and individuals who want to help.

We shall meet these two protagonists, the needy and the helpers, in all kinds of different settings; but running through these encounters will be a simple idea: good motivation without competence is not enough, or, more simply, the 'why' cannot be divorced from the 'how'. Too often the most basic admonition to 'Do no harm!' is overlooked and actions are justified not because of the impact they will have on those in need, but by the satisfaction they bring to those who give. It has been a central focus of my career to promote the marriage of the motivation – to bring help to those who suffer – with the professional competence required to do the job effectively.

Lao People's Democratic Republic

Printing date: April 2014
Sources: UNHCR - UNJLC - UNSDI-T
Feedback: mapping@unhcr.org
Filename: LAO_InsetMap_Publication.worr

⊛   Capital

•   Towns of Interest

━━━   International boundary

The boundaries and names shown and the designations used on this map do not imply official endorsement or acceptance by the United Nations.

Figure 1   Map of Lao People's Democratic Republic.

1

STARTING OUT

In Laos

The panel of interviewers at Queens College, Dundee in April 1968 was intimidating. In the middle sat the director of Voluntary Service Overseas (VSO). He was leafing through a voluminous binder.

'Would you like to go to Rwanda?'

'What would I be doing?'

'Teaching English at a Roman Catholic School.'

'Would I be expected to support the school's religion?'

'They won't expect you to teach religion, but they might not be too happy if you were actively opposed.'

I said that might be a problem. The director resumed leafing through his binder.

'Would you like to go to Thakkek?'

'I don't think I know where that is.'

'It's in Laos.'

'Er, yes. But, isn't there a war going on there? Won't my parents be worried?'

The director said that the war was in the countryside, that Thakkek was on the Mekong River, and that if there was any problem, I would be able to take a boat across the river and find safety in Thailand.

This interview took place during my final term studying French and German at St Andrews University in Scotland. On the basis of the explanation about evacuation, I persuaded my parents that this would be a great first job.

When the formal offer came, it was for a post as an English language teacher at the Lycée in Luang Prabang. The map seemed to indicate that, while the town was indeed on the Mekong River, at that point both sides of the river are in Laos. I kept this information to myself.

Arrival

At the end of July 1968, eight young British volunteers flew via Bangkok to Vientiane, the administrative capital of Laos, to work for VSO. We all spent two months in intensive Lao language training. We were introduced to the slow relaxed pace of life. We found the good French restaurants, the cheap Vietnamese noodle stalls and the cafes overlooking the Mekong, where we could enjoy a beer and watch the sun go down after a day studying Lao.

Lao is a monosyllabic, tonal language, closely related to Thai. Those with a musical ear have an advantage. For example, the word sounding like '*nah*' can mean 'aunt', 'rice-field' or 'in front of', depending on the tone applied. There is plenty of room for misunderstanding. I had always enjoyed singing and found I took to the new language more readily than some of my colleagues.

After the language training, I took a Royal Air Lao flight to Luang Prabang. The aircraft was a World War II vintage DC3. It was the height of the rainy season and the memory of that first view of the lush tropical jungle and spectacular mountains during the one-hour flight has remained with me.

Luang Prabang, the royal capital of Laos, was then a town of perhaps 30,000 inhabitants lying on the left bank of the Mekong River, at its junction with the Nam Khane. It is dominated by a conically shaped hill, Phou Si, with a small Buddhist temple at the top. From there, the whole town is spread out below, including the modest but charming Royal Palace.

Luang Prabang seemed an idyllic place. The pace of life was slow. In late September it was coming into the best season of the year. The rains were finishing, vegetation was lush, the heat was subsiding and cool breezes began to blow off the Mekong in the evenings. Surrounded by mountains, the town's buildings were a happy blend of French colonial, traditional wooden Lao houses raised off the ground on stilts, colourful Buddhist temples and Chinese merchants' shop-houses along the main street. Every evening pairs of teenage boys and girls on bicycles and motorbikes would ride slowly around the town, the drivers allowing their pillion passengers to flirt with each other as they rode along. Today Luang Prabang, which looks largely unchanged since the 1960s, is a UNESCO World Heritage Site and is a favourite destination for student backpackers.

Context

In 1968, throughout Indo-China (Laos, Cambodia and Vietnam), France and the United States were competing for influence over the national elites. In Laos, national leaders all spoke French. Even when they spoke Lao, their conversation was peppered with French words. The Lycée where I taught offered the only complete secondary education in the north of the country. Its students came mainly from elite families, with a few very bright children of poor farmers, including some from ethnic minority hill tribes, who had made their way through the primary school system.

I lived in a comfortable two-storey house with wooden shutters, just opposite the only hotel in town. Every day I drove out to the Lycée on my 80 cc Suzuki motorbike. Most of the year I would arrive covered in dust. The coating of dust would be thicker if my ride coincided with the arrival of the rich kids in their chauffeur-driven Mercedes. Some students travelled on motorbikes or bicycles. The poorest walked.

Among my students at the Lycée was a bright member of the Hmong hill tribe. One day he came to my house to discuss his future options. I asked him about his home village. How far away was it? Oh, it was very far, many days' walk. Was it in Laos? Oh no, not at all. So we went to the map of Laos and he told me which road he took from Luang Prabang, where the bus stopped and where he started to walk. We ended up with my finger right in the middle of northern Laos. So, look, your village is in Laos, I said. Oh no, it's Hmong. My student, one of the best educated young people of his tribe, had no concept of a national entity consisting of land within defined borders. For him, Laos was the city of Luang Prabang, the main roads and the villages inhabited by Lao speakers, but where he lived was Hmong territory.

In Luang Prabang, the small French-educated Lao elite ran the provincial administration, the police and the military. There were Chinese merchants and Vietnamese technicians. There was a USAID (US Agency for International Development) mission, which housed the US Central Intelligence Agency (CIA) team supporting the Royal Lao government's military operations against the communist rebels, known as the Pathet Lao. The remainder of the population consisted of ethnic Lao families, many of whom had recently been farmers in nearby villages and had migrated into town, often to escape the war.

Buddhism

I was keen to learn more about the religion of these beautiful, polite, smiling and apparently happy people and the saffron-robed Buddhist monks who lived in the many charming temples (*wat*). When I was introduced to Amphay Doré, I got my chance. Amphay was doing research into the origins and history of the Lao people. He travelled between Paris, Vientiane and Luang Prabang and was hugely knowledgeable about the Lao, their religion and their culture. And he was generous with his time. His family had a traditional Lao-style wood and bamboo house on the outskirts of the town and he would invite me there to talk about the Lao and about Buddhism.

In Laos, as in Thailand and Cambodia, the Theravada Buddhism of Sri Lanka had meshed with the Brahmin Hindu traditions of kingship and ancient local animist spirit cults into a religious tradition that was both rigorous and flexible. It was rigorous in the demands of discipline that it made on its monks; a barefoot quest for food from the population immediately after dawn, no meals after midday, regular chanting sessions and spartan living conditions. But it was flexible in accommodating non-Buddhist beliefs and traditions.

Amphay had a wonderfully calm, but confident attitude to Lao culture. The key lessons that he taught me, which would be reinforced in 1974 when I spent a month as a monk in one of Luang Prabang's temples, were the search for a harmonious existence, the inevitability of suffering and death, respect for all living things, the concepts of *meta* and *karuna*, loosely translatable as 'compassion', and the need to remain detached from material and ephemeral things and feelings. Of course, there is much more than that to Buddhism and Lao culture, but these are the core elements that have stayed with me and influenced my approach to life.

Geography and history

A land-locked country of some 3 million people in the late 1960s – the population in 2012 was estimated at just over 6.5 million – Laos is bordered by Myanmar, China, Vietnam, Cambodia and Thailand. The country had been part of French Indo-China from the beginning of the twentieth century until 1954, when it became an independent constitutional monarchy, with a king based in Luang Prabang and a government and administration in Vientiane.

About half the population of Laos is of Lao ethnicity. The other 50 per cent is made up of people speaking over 70 different languages. The present Lao government, seeking to use the word 'Lao' to denote nationality rather than ethnicity, has found a simple way to distinguish between the three principal ethnic groupings. The *Lao Lum* ('the low Lao') are the ethnic Lao living in the lowlands. The *Lao Kang* ('the middle Lao') are the highland Mon-Khmer peoples living on the lower slopes of the mountains, and the *Lao Sung* ('the high Lao') are the Sinitic groups such as the Hmong and Yao living on the upper slopes and mountain tops.

Almost immediately after independence, Laos was sucked into the Indo-China Wars, pitting first the French and then the Americans against the nationalist/communist North Vietnamese movement led by Ho Chi Minh. In 1962 Laos found itself briefly at the centre of international attention, when US President John F. Kennedy grappled with this sideshow to the Vietnam War. A Geneva Conference ratified a ceasefire, which quickly broke down. The war spluttered on, much of it in secret. Worst affected were people living in the mountains in the north and east of the country and along the so-called 'Ho Chi Minh trail', a long network of routes, partly in Laos and partly in Vietnam, running north–south down the Annamite chain of mountains, which separate eastern Laos from central Vietnam. The 'trail' was used by the North Vietnamese to bring supplies from the north to the south.

In 1968, the prime minister of the Royal Lao Government was Prince Souvanna Phouma, the elder half-brother of Prince Souphanouvong, one of the leaders of the pro-communist Pathet Lao. This family rivalry was mirrored in many Lao families across the country. Many young idealists, disgusted by the wealth and corruption of the royalist elite, and by its apparent disregard for the welfare of ordinary people, had gone off to join the Pathet Lao in the jungle.

While the divisions in Lao families represented genuine disagreements about the way forward for the country, Lao military officers on both sides tried to prosecute the war in a civilised way, as far as possible. Unit commanders on one side might find themselves confronting former colleagues from school or military college on the other. They would negotiate informal ceasefires, while recognising the need to fire off the occasional artillery barrage into the jungle, so that superior officers would be impressed with their zeal for combat. On one occasion, in Sayaboury, a cow fell victim to such a barrage. The villagers were outraged by the carelessness of the opposing forces and demanded reparations. Eventually, a few chickens changed hands, and honour was satisfied.

This 'civilised' war between Lao brothers was in sharp contrast to the other, 'secret' war in Laos between forces backed by the CIA, and consisting mainly of Hmong tribesmen, and Pathet Lao tribal forces, heavily reinforced by North Vietnamese troops. For these Hmong and other hill tribes in provinces close to the Vietnamese border, the war was devastating. The Hmong tribes were split between those backed by the CIA, which supported the Royal Government, and those supported by the North Vietnamese. In the Hmong heartlands, terrible battles killed, injured or displaced thousands of families. The fact that the Hmong grew valuable opium poppies simply raised the stakes and made the fight fiercer.

Similarly, the Mon-Khmer hill tribes living in villages in the mountains of eastern and southern Laos, who had been virtually untouched by any previous attempts at modernisation, suddenly found themselves caught up in the fight between high-altitude American bombers and Vietnamese on bicycles for control of their ancestral lands, which had become part of the Ho Chi Minh trail.

The United States Air Force dropped more tons of bombs on Laos in the 1960s than were used in the whole of World War II by all sides. Thousands of ordinary people lost their lives, limbs or livelihoods, and tens of thousands were uprooted from their homes, because of decisions taken by people on the other side of the world, who would never have to see the consequences of those decisions. Even today, people living in the Lao countryside are losing their lives and limbs to the detonation of unexploded munitions dropped more than 40 years ago.

As my VSO colleagues and I settled into our jobs, we began to understand that as VSO teachers we were substitutes for the troops that the British prime minister, Harold Wilson, wisely refused to send to Vietnam. I would discover much later that the British Embassy in Vientiane had struggled unsuccessfully throughout the 1960s and early 1970s to persuade the Americans to moderate some of their more self-destructive policies, which would lead inexorably to defeat in Vietnam and ignominious departure from Cambodia and Laos in 1975.

War and identity

Living in Luang Prabang while a war was being fought in the surrounding countryside was a strange experience. For most of the time we were unaffected by what was happening. We could ignore the T-28s, single-engine bombers that took off with bombs strapped under their wings and returned without them. We accepted without question the limits on our freedom of movement around the town – 20 kilometres on the road to the south, no more than 10 kilometres in most other directions. But then a column of destitute Hmong tribespeople would walk through the town fleeing from the fighting, looking for somewhere to set up a temporary camp; or a colleague working at the hospital would report a particularly large group of wounded soldiers and villagers being brought in for treatment.

In the face of the appalling things happening in their country, how did the Lao themselves react? I suspect that the best answer is, 'Much like almost everybody does, all over the world'. They felt anger, but soon discovered there was little to be gained from it. They felt compassion for the victims, but they had few resources to share with them. Above all, they felt confusion – why was this happening to their country? And because their politicians seemed to be pawns of bigger powers whose leaders were so remote, they felt powerless to do anything about it. The compassionate Buddhist Lao were not better or worse equipped to cope with this disaster than the Muslim Afghans or the Catholic Croats of Bosnia. Life goes on, and we all adapt. Tendencies towards fatalism are reinforced.

Laos, Afghanistan and Bosnia are all, in one sense, intermittently successful experiments in multi-ethnic co-habitation. But they were infected with the bi-polar disease of the second half of the twentieth century and it wreaked terrible destruction on them. For the people of Laos, Vietnam and Cambodia, 1975 would be the fateful year. For Laos and Vietnam, it brought the end of the war, the victory of communism and the start of a great refugee exodus. For Cambodia, it would bring Year Zero, Pol Pot and genocide.

First departure and return

In June 1970, after two years with VSO in Luang Prabang, I said my goodbyes. But my anguish at having to leave this enchanting country was tempered by a lifeline. During induction for VSOs at the University of Hull, Professor Mervyn Jaspan, the director of the Centre for Southeast Asian Studies, had taken a particular interest in those of us going to Laos. It was a country with which the Centre had no ties. He encouraged us to keep in touch with the Centre. I did so, and he offered me the chance to do a one-year B.Phil programme in the social anthropology of Southeast Asia, which might then lead to the chance to do research in Laos for a doctoral degree. So, in September 1970 I travelled to Hull, on the east coast of England, to study anthropology, with a focus on Southeast Asia.

Social anthropology is about how communities with a defined linguistic, cultural and geographical identity organise their lives, in terms of family and social relations, their economy and their political interaction with the outside world. For my dissertation I studied the work of a French anthropologist, Georges Condominas, who had worked in Vietnam and Laos, and whose book about a hill tribe in South Vietnam carried the title which sums up the core message of anthropology, *L'Exotique est Quotidien,* 'the exotic is everyday', or more simply, the reality of a person's daily life is normal routine for him or her, however extraordinary or 'exotic' it may seem to people from a different culture.

I am still surprised by how long it took me to work out what Condominas meant by this title. At one level it is blindingly obvious; of course children all over the world are 'socialised' to consider their lives, their language, their customs as 'normal', just what ordinary people do. But it is as though there is something in our make-up that doesn't want to admit this obvious fact. We find it hard to imagine ourselves in the shoes (or the bare feet) of a member of a primitive tribe in the Vietnamese jungle or the Amazon rainforest.

I returned to Laos in September 1972 to carry out my research and to teach part-time at the Royal Institute of Law and Administration. My research was focussed on two communities, one within the urban area of Vientiane and one in the countryside. I identified a large well-established village of about a hundred families some 50 kilometres north of Vientiane, and a district on the north-west edge of Vientiane city, inhabited mainly by the families of civil servants, police and military officers. From 1972 to 1974, I divided my time between the two communities and the law school, carrying out family surveys and collecting information about social relations in the village and town. The experience deepened my appreciation of Lao society and culture. In a city like Vientiane, Lao families were able to keep up many of their traditional practices, but it was in the rural villages that these traditions affected every aspect of people's daily lives.

First aid project

In the summer of 1973, Professor Jaspan announced that he would like to visit me, meet my contacts at the Institute and travel with me to Luang Prabang, to see the legendary royal capital. In Luang Prabang, we did the sights and then I offered to take him to Xieng Ngeun, the district town 20 kilometres south on the road to Vientiane. It would give him a chance to see rural Laos.

As we approached Xieng Ngeun in our rented jeep, we saw a mass of people in a field on our right. We learned that they were from villages in the mountains to the south and had been displaced by an outbreak of fighting. There were perhaps 2,000 of them. It was the rainy season, the ground was sodden, and the people had no adequate shelter, little food and apparently no medical help. The children looked malnourished and many were suffering from malaria. Professor Jaspan was appalled.

This was the last stop on his trip, and on his way home to England he set out to draw attention to the plight of these people. He gave interviews to the BBC, wrote letters to the local newspapers in Hull and lobbied the British government and major charities to do something.

A few weeks later, I received a message that Save the Children (UK) had decided to divert a medical team from Vietnam to help the displaced at Xieng Ngeun. Would I travel to Luang Prabang with the administrator, ahead of the team's arrival, so that the doctor and nurse could hit the ground running?

Major 'Spots' Leppard was one of the great characters of the Indo-China conflict. He appears in a number of books about the period as a military attaché and agent of British intelligence. By the time I met him, he was working for Save the Children. He and I travelled up to Luang Prabang to prepare the ground for the team's arrival. The first thing we did was to drive down to Xieng Ngeun to see the displaced people. But they had gone. There was no sign of them at all. On enquiry we learned that some days earlier, an informal agreement had been reached with the local Pathet Lao commander and the people had returned to their villages in the area under Pathet Lao control. There would be no way for the medical team to reach them.

'Spots' told me it was too late to turn the medical team around. Supplies and equipment had already arrived in Vientiane, and the team was on its way. We would have to find something else for them to do. We did, but it was not enough to keep them fully occupied. A medical team had been withdrawn from an area of Vietnam where they could not keep pace with demand and brought to an 'emergency' in Laos, which was over by the time they arrived. Save the Children had raised money for the operation in good faith, but without good judgement. The operation had been a mistake. There would be many times in the future when I would recall this story, either to myself, or in discussions with colleagues anxious for a quick fix or a high-profile gesture which would show the world that we were 'doing something', even if what we were doing was a diversion, more for show, for publicity, than to meet a defined and realistic objective. It was an early introduction to the idea that good intentions are not enough.

Second transition

Before returning to Britain to write up my thesis I went back to Luang Prabang to spend a month as a Buddhist monk in a forest temple on the outskirts of the city. Before the ordination ceremony, all my hair was shaved off, and I exchanged my clothes for the white robe of an aspirant. After the ceremony I was dressed in the saffron robe of a monk and given a bowl with which to conduct the daily quest for alms. At the temple I became the most junior of a dozen monks. The timeless rhythms of the ascetic Buddhist monastic life took over – sleeping on a mat on the hard floor, the pre-dawn quest for food from the local population, the hours of chanting, the periods of instruction from the senior monk, the fasting every day from midday onwards and the sessions of meditation. In addition to the regular *samadhi* meditation, I spent ten days in *vipassana*. This meant being left entirely alone in my cell, with no contact with the other monks, except when the abbot came to see me, which he did about once every three days. To experience the solitude of intense meditation and the discipline of the monastic life is at times frightening, but profoundly enriching. There is probably not another single month in my life that has had such an important impact on me.

When I left the temple, and returned to Vientiane in December 1974, another series of events combined to prolong my association with Laos. The peace agreement between the royalist government and the Pathet Lao provided for the return to their villages of people displaced during the conflict. The UN High Commissioner for Refugees (UNHCR) had been approached to help with the process and had sent a team of staff to develop a plan.

Arriving back in Vientiane, I picked up my mail. There was a letter from my father telling me about UNHCR's announcement of their programme in Indo-China. 'Maybe there's a job for you there some day?' he had written. Within hours Martin Griffiths at UNICEF had also told me about the UNHCR operation and I had run into Werner Blatter, a Swiss, formerly with the Red Cross in Vientiane, who told me that he was now part of the UNHCR team. He invited me to meet his boss.

A few days later I flew back to London, knowing that there was a chance that I would soon be back in Laos, for a third time. After two days of interviews with UNHCR in Geneva, I was offered a job as an associate programme officer in UNHCR's regional office for Indo-China, in Vientiane. Why was I selected? I think simply because I spoke fluent French, on which they tested me, and good Lao, which they took on trust, and knew the country well. I was in the right place at the right time.

UNHCR

My first reaction on joining the United Nations was astonishment. I recall quite vividly the sense of awe with which I realised that I was now employed by the world's only global organisation and that they would be paying me for the privilege of working for them in the country I loved.

Overnight, my income had multiplied by ten. I was no longer required to eke out my existence on the modest VSO allowance or an equally miserly research grant. This induced the first of what would be a series of losing battles with my conscience over the ethics of being well paid in very poor countries for doing work that I considered essentially charitable.

I was extraordinarily fortunate in the team that I joined. The UN did not then provide induction training to its professional staff. You were expected to know what you needed to know and to learn the rest on the job. This has only recently begun to change. During my time in the UN I watched as new recruits sank or swam depending heavily on the quality and experience of their first boss. Those who happened to join a large overworked team, run by a manager of limited experience or unsympathetic manner, might easily acquire a view of the UN that was partial or negative, and might never really learn the basics of their agency's role and history. But if, as I did, you have a first boss of great experience, who has the time and inclination to share that knowledge and experience, you gain a priceless start in the long process of learning and acclimatisation.

Jacques Cuénod, UNHCR's first regional representative for Indo-China, based in Vientiane, was a Swiss national, with an English mother and English wife. He had spent most of the previous ten years representing UNHCR in some of the most intractable refugee crises in Africa. He was excited to be in a new part of the world and eager to learn more about the people. He believed passionately in the principles of refugee law and relished the chance to share his enthusiasm.

Cuénod set up the UNHCR office in a pleasant colonial-style villa in the centre of Vientiane. He took a spacious office on the ground floor and I was given what had once been a bedroom on the first floor. It was simply furnished, air-conditioned and it was perfect.

Darryl Han, a brilliant young Burmese, who was to die tragically young a few years later in a car accident in Geneva, was Cuénod's deputy. His quiet, thoughtful manner allied to a streak of sometimes fierce determination and his knowledge of regional politics made him an ideal complement to Cuénod. As the events of 1975 unfolded in neighbouring Vietnam, Cuénod and Han spent more and more time in Hanoi and Saigon, and Han became a rare visitor to Vientiane.

The events unfolding in Indo-China were at the top of the agenda for UNHCR. The High Commissioner at the time was Prince Sadruddin Aga Khan, uncle of the Aga Khan and a future candidate for the post of UN Secretary-General. Sadruddin's chef de cabinet was a young Pakistani, Zia Rizvi, educated at the Sorbonne and equally fluent in French and English. With a reputation for brilliance and arrogance, he visited us several times in Laos and would play a major part in shaping the course of my career in the UN.

This was the cast of senior characters in my UNHCR world. Alongside and in support we gradually assembled a team of international and Lao staff, who would work together over the next two years and more on the programme to help Lao families displaced by the war to return to their original homes.

Return to villages

The 1974 ceasefire between the royalists and the Pathet Lao had divided the territory into royalist-administered and Pathet Lao-administered areas, while the capital itself was jointly administered. A national coalition government was formed, in which each side had half the ministries, and each deputy minister was from the other side.

The war had left the royalists in control of the major cities along the Mekong River, and strips of countryside along the river varying in width from just a few kilometres to about 60 kilometres to the north of Vientiane. The rest of the country was under the control of the Pathet Lao. As the war had ground on, and the area controlled by the Royal Lao government progressively shrank, more and more families had fled their villages on the frontlines and sought sanctuary in and around the major Mekong towns. There, some had been taken in by relatives, others had found jobs, but many had lived on handouts from charities in shanty towns on the outskirts of the cities.

At the request of its Mixed Commission on Refugees and Displaced Persons, the Lao Coalition Government asked UNHCR to help facilitate the return of these people to their villages. Although they were not, in a legal sense, refugees, since they had not left their country of origin, and UNHCR had never undertaken such a programme before, Sadruddin agreed to the request; thus began UNHCR's long and difficult involvement in the question of internally displaced persons (IDPs).

Immediately on returning to Vientiane in February 1975, I was involved in discussions with the Coalition Government on the mechanics of the planned returns. Although the two sides met formally in the Mixed Commission, they did not trust each other, and the Pathet Lao in particular insisted on separate meetings with UNHCR. This was a bit of a problem, since none of their representatives spoke English or French, they had no interpreters and they would not accept an interpreter from the Vientiane side. I was therefore pressed into service. At the first meeting I quickly discovered that the Pathet Lao spoke a different version of the Lao language to that I was used to in Vientiane. Several times I had to ask them to repeat and then explain words that I had never heard before. The Pathet Lao had developed a new vocabulary of socialist jargon. Everybody was a 'comrade', *sahai*. Soon this vocabulary would be in use by officials all over the country.

Although the people to benefit from UNHCR's programme could not be classified as refugees, UNHCR decided to apply the same principles as would have been applied for refugee return. UNHCR would need to be satisfied that people were returning voluntarily and that they had been provided with sufficient information about what they could expect on their return home.

After the overall arrangements had been agreed in Vientiane, we moved out to the provincial capitals to organise the returns from each one to the rural areas in the Pathet Lao zone. By far the most challenging of the return movements was that from Vientiane to the Plain of Jars in Xieng Khouang province to the north. This would have to be undertaken by air to the dirt landing strip outside the small town of Phonesavanh. But what sort of aircraft could we use? The remaining Air America planes at Vientiane airport were not acceptable to the Pathet Lao, and communist-world aircraft would not be easily acceptable to the royalists. In the end, both sides agreed to allow an Australian Air Force DC3, an Aeroflot Antonov and a Royal Air Lao DC3 to make up our fleet. I was assigned to negotiate with the Aeroflot representative. He liked to meet early. He spoke no English and I speak no Russian, so we communicated in Lao. I would arrive at eight, and he would serve hard boiled eggs and vodka for breakfast.

So, we had our transport, but would people decide to go? Looking back nearly 40 years later, one thing still bothers me. We did not do enough to find out what conditions would be like for people choosing to return. We had extremely limited access to Pathet Lao areas. We made a visit of a few hours to the Plain of Jars, but that was after the return movements had already begun. We had no way of verifying the optimistic statements of the Pathet Lao officials that we met there. And most of all, we did not appreciate the extent of the dangers facing the returnees from unexploded cluster munitions, known as 'bombees', littering the province. Cluster bombs were dropped from American aircraft in canisters usually containing about 200 individual bomblets, each the size of a soft-drink can. The bomblets were supposed to explode on hitting the ground, but up to a quarter of them failed to do so, settling on or just below the surface waiting silently for a person or animal to come along and set them off. In 2008, the Convention on Cluster Munitions was adopted, finally banning the type of weapon that so polluted the countryside of Laos, as well as Afghanistan and Bosnia. The Convention became binding international law in August 2010, 50 years after these weapons were first deployed in Indo-China.

In recent years, because of my work in Afghanistan and with the UN Mine Action Service, and what I now know about the extent of contamination in Laos, I have had many opportunities to think back to that time. For a long time, I even managed to convince myself that we had not known that unexploded ordnance was a particular threat. But, going back over old reports, it is clear that we did know about the problem, although perhaps not about its extent. But we were unable to do anything about it. Incredibly, there would be no significant humanitarian mine clearance and awareness programmes anywhere in the world until another 15 years had passed and the UN began its humanitarian operations in 1989 in Afghanistan.

As international NGOs, particularly the Quakers and Mennonites, obtained better access in the early 1980s to some of the areas where returnees had settled in Xieng Khouang province, they became fully aware of the dangers facing the returnees. Their calls for help from the US government, which had dropped the bombs, and which could have provided information about drop zones and weapon types, fell on deaf ears.

As with so many programmes of voluntary return, this one started slowly. But a trickle of families arriving at Vientiane airport soon became a flood. Many families found the decision very difficult. Some arrived at the airport still undecided. Fathers, mothers and children argued and cried while sitting in the waiting area. Sometimes we would suggest that they come back the following day. In at least one case that I witnessed, a couple could not agree, and one partner got on the plane, while the other stayed behind.

The issue of the 'voluntary' nature of return, and how to ensure that people were not coerced into staying or returning by political pressure or false propaganda, is a major theme of the next two chapters of this book. My UNHCR colleagues and I would argue and agonise over it. The arguments were never fully settled.

In Laos in 1975, the Pathet Lao were themselves somewhat ambivalent about the return to villages programme. On the one hand, they wanted more people in the areas under their control. On the other, they were wary of the impact that the returnees would have on the population that had remained in their villages throughout the war. Perhaps they would bring in decadent capitalist ideas. In this they were expressing a concern similar to those that I would meet later in Afghanistan and Bosnia; how can we prevent those who stayed at home and suffered throughout the war from feeling resentful and antagonistic towards those who had left for the safety of the cities or a foreign country? Will those returning be reluctant to adapt to new realities and think they can just return to their original homes and pick up where they left off? Returnees always disrupt the social calm of communities to which they return after many years.

People's Democratic Republic

The collapse of the pro-Western governments in Vietnam and Cambodia in April 1975 had an immediate impact on the situation in Laos. The confidence of royalist members of the Coalition Government was severely shaken. In contrast, the Pathet Lao began to feel that they were lagging behind their Vietnamese comrades and that they could govern the country on their own, without the need for a coalition with their former enemies.

The communist take-over took place without a shot being fired, between April and December 1975. Students were encouraged to demonstrate in Vientiane; individual royalist ministers left on visits to Paris, and did not return. In August, the King was deposed and taken, as a private citizen, into detention in Sam Neua in the Pathet Lao heartland. The Lao People's Democratic Republic (LPDR) came into existence on 2 December 1975, with no royalists in the cabinet. Many of the leading officials of the former government who had not left the country, were taken away for 're-education'.

The established order had been overturned. Many of the new leaders were not only from the countryside, but were members of the ethnic minorities. The Lao of the Mekong valley had for centuries treated these minorities as inferior, as 'younger brothers' at best, or as 'slaves' at worst. Now the younger brothers had taken over from their elders; the slaves had become the masters.

The system of patronage, under which ordinary Lao families tied their fortunes to those of a high-ranking official or military officer of the royalist government, through jobs, either in his ministry, military unit or household, broke down. The exodus began.

Exodus

With the exception of Luang Prabang and Pakse, all the major Lao towns lie on the Mekong River, directly opposite Thai territory. Families began to hire boats to cross the river and to present themselves at the nearest Thai police station.

For many families the decision whether to go or to stay was an agonising one. Those who had existing ties in a Western country, through education or the presence of close relatives, found the decision easier. Those who had been active politically in opposition to the Pathet Lao left as soon as they could. Others who had relatives in the Pathet Lao, or had quietly kept their contacts open, hoped that they might be looked after, or at least allowed to retire quietly. But for the many townspeople who did not have ties abroad, but who were worried about the arrival of communism, it was a time of traumatic and often permanent separations. Daily life in Vientiane changed dramatically. Loudspeakers were set up in every community. At six every morning, the daily dose of propaganda would start blaring out of them.

As I sat in my office planning the next round of the return to villages programme, from time to time there would be a furtive knock on the door and a Lao friend, or a friend of a friend, would come in and explain that he had decided to leave. I would play dumb (and politically cautious) and ask where he was going. Invariably, the answer was France, the US or Australia. Playing even dumber, I would ask if I could come and see him off at the airport. Oh no, he would say, I am going across the river. So you are going to Thailand, I would say. No, no, he was going to France, but he would cross the river first.

Once we had got past this formality, I would ask my friend if he would still be leaving if he knew for certain that there was no chance of reaching France or the US. In other words, would he go if the only choice was to remain in Thailand? Of the more than a dozen people to whom I posed this question, mostly young and well educated, not one said 'yes'. For them, the choice was not between staying in Laos and crossing into Thailand; it was between staying in a country newly taken over by communists and emigrating to the capitalist West.

The realisation that this was the reality for many, though assuredly not all, of the Lao who took boats clandestinely across the Mekong, called into question, in my mind, the appropriateness of the response developed by my own organisation, UNHCR. As I discuss in the next chapter, I believe it constitutes one of the great humanitarian dilemmas of the second half of the twentieth century. Was it right to apply universally the principles of refugee law laid down for Europe in the immediate aftermath of World War II? Hundreds of thousands of Cambodian, Lao and Vietnamese families left their countries in the years after 1975 and made new lives not in Thailand, Malaysia or the Philippines, but in Europe, North America and Australia. Was that really a good idea?

Most of those who crossed the Mekong from Laos to Thailand did so clandestinely at night in small boats or in car tyres. Some swam. Most of them made it, but some did not. Some were turned back by Lao government patrol boats. Most of those would try again. Some were shot by those same government patrols and drowned. Some appeared to make it across into Thailand, but were never heard of again. They may have resisted the efforts of Thai bandits to separate them from their valuables, or to take away the women, before they could reach a Thai police post. As far as I know, nobody has made any serious effort to estimate the number of people who died trying to escape, but it was clearly a significant number.

Prince Sadruddin in town

A feature of life with a UN humanitarian organisation in the field is the visit by senior officials from headquarters. The higher the political profile of a particular operation, the more senior and numerous the visitors. It was no surprise, therefore, when we heard, in September 1975, that the UN High Commissioner for Refugees, Prince Sadruddin Aga Khan, would be visiting us, accompanied by his wife, Princess Catherine.

Some of the best advice that I ever received from Jacques Cuénod surrounded this visit. 'Take nothing for granted, double-check all the arrangements, make sure you have a Plan B', were his constantly repeated instructions.

The visit plan called for the prince and princess to arrive from Bangkok. After meetings in Vientiane, they would travel to the Plain of Jars and to Luang Prabang to see progress in the return to villages programme. They would then return to Vientiane and from there fly to Hanoi. From Hanoi they wanted to fly directly to Bangkok. However, at the time there was no flight link between Hanoi and Bangkok.

Cuénod explained to me some of the unusual features of the prince's tenure as High Commissioner. Firstly, he took a salary of $1 per year and met all his own travel costs. Expense was no barrier. Secondly, his wife was extremely strict in her dietary requirements. She drank only Contrexeville water from France and she took no salt whatsoever in her food. At all the places where she would eat, the chefs would need to be informed of this requirement. I was put in charge of logistics. With Cuénod's instructions ringing in my ears, I felt prepared for anything – well almost.

In Luang Prabang, we were the only guests at the recently opened Phou Vao Hotel. After an early meeting with the provincial governor, we were driven out to a village to which some displaced people had recently returned. They had received some basic assistance from UNHCR towards their resettlement. The village headman made a suitable speech, which I translated, and then said that it was their honour to invite the prince and princess and their party for lunch. When I thanked the headman for his invitation, but told him that the prince was invited for lunch in Luang Prabang, a scrawny cooked chicken was produced, which they insisted the prince and princess should consume on the spot.

The princess looked at me with such horror, that I quickly informed the headman that unfortunately the prince's religious principles did not allow him or his wife to eat anything before midday. If they insisted, we would take the chicken with us and I would ensure that it was included as part of their lunch, when the time came. This conclusion seemed satisfactory to everybody.

Since the scheduled flights between Vientiane and Hanoi were extremely few, we decided to charter aircraft from Lao Aviation, which had taken over Royal Air Lao's fleet. For the flight from Vientiane to Hanoi, we had booked one of the DC4s. These were very old aircraft, even in 1975, and I had asked Mr Faiz, a wonderful Iranian who had stayed on with the airline, to make sure we had a back-up aircraft, just in case. So, when the DC4's captain started the port engine and flames shot out, forcing him to shut it down immediately and announce that the aircraft was not fit to fly, we were able to move to Plan B. An even older, but thankfully more reliable, DC3 was wheeled out and was ready to go just 45 minutes later. Prince Sadruddin, who had emerged somewhat shaken from the DC4, was suitably impressed.

For the flight from Hanoi to Bangkok, we had offered the prince a variety of options, involving scheduled flights or charters, with a range of different aircraft. The top of the range was to charter the airline's only jet, a DC9, both from Hanoi to Vientiane and from Vientiane to Bangkok. Naturally, the prince chose this option. I spent most of that day in Mr Faiz's office at the airport. The DC9 left Vientiane empty, on time, picked up the VIPs in Hanoi and started back towards Vientiane. Then Mr Faiz persuaded the control tower at Vientiane to 'land' and 'take off' the plane at Vientiane, while in fact it flew straight overhead and continued on to Bangkok. It was the first aircraft to fly non-stop from Hanoi to Bangkok for a very long time, possibly the first ever.

At first sight, VIP visitors may not appear to achieve much. But they bring the work of the agency to the attention of the most senior people in the government of the affected country. They also attract media coverage. The main beneficiaries of such visits are often the national officials acting as counterparts to the UN agency. It gives them face-time with their most senior leadership and allows them to advertise the programme's achievements in the press. Handled well, such visits can have a very positive impact on the relations between the UN agency and its national counterparts.

It was no doubt partly thanks to the success of his visit to Laos, that High Commissioner Sadruddin agreed to give me a year's 'leave without pay' after my two-year assignment in Vientiane, to allow me to write up my doctoral thesis. This meant that there would be a job waiting for me at UNHCR, and that I would not have to apply all over again.

In February 1977, I said goodbye to Laos for the third time. During the six years that I had lived there, in spite of the constant backdrop of conflict, this beautiful country and its people had worked their magic and whetted my appetite for more.

Thailand:
UNHCR assisted Laotian, Cambodian and Vietnamese refugee camps in Thailand, 1980s and 1990s

Figure 2 Map of Thailand.

2

ACROSS THE MEKONG
With Indo-Chinese refugees in Thailand

In January 1978, Poul Hartling, a former prime minister of Denmark, took over as UN High Commissioner for Refugees from Sadruddin Aga Khan. Within a year, he would be confronted by three major new crises, in Indo-China, Afghanistan and the Horn of Africa. New staff were recruited, governments poured in money and UNHCR quickly became one of the most high-profile components of the UN system. In June 1978, at the end of my 'leave without pay', I was assigned to the UNHCR Regional Office in Bangkok, Thailand.

My association with this office had begun three years earlier. Until the events in Vietnam and Cambodia in April 1975, the office had been a rather sleepy outfit – a small suite of rooms on the seventh floor of an office block on Sukhumvit Road. The team dealt with a wide range but relatively small number of individual refugees, including Burmese dissidents and stranded White Russians.

In August 1975, while working with the UNHCR office in Laos, I was asked to help the Bangkok office with several groups of newly arrived refugees from Laos. Arriving in Bangkok from Vientiane, I made my way to the office building and found several hundred Vietnamese refugees milling around noisily outside. I threaded my way through the crowd to the entrance and then pushed past people all the way up the stairs and into the UNHCR office. There the outer open-plan area of the office was completely full of Vietnamese families. In the middle I could just make out Norma Fraser sitting at the only desk in the room. She was painstakingly recording the details of one family at a time, in order to register them for assistance.

When I finally got through the crowd into the inner offices, I found the Deputy Representative, Angelo Rasanayagam, in his office. Angelo told me what they knew about three groups of recent arrivals from Laos, all of whom had been detained by the Thai authorities in temporary camps, one in northern Nan province and the others in the north-east, in Loei and Roi Et provinces. We would be travelling together to visit the three camps. My job would be to see if I could persuade any of them to go back home to Laos.

The groups were very different in their ethnic origins and social background, but similar in their determination not to return home. For the most part, they were the families of people who had chosen the losing side in the war and did not expect a generous reception from the new communist leadership. Those in Nan were mainly ethnic Lao from the north of Laos, but also some from minority Tai groups and other hill tribes who had worked for the royalists and the CIA-supported militias.

In Ban Vinai in Loei province, the refugees were almost all Hmong, supporters of General Vang Pao, the CIA's main man. In Roi Et, housed in an old military base, was a group of Lao mostly with close links to the American military effort. While the Hmong in Loei were keen to start farming the land in the sparsely populated area where they were being accommodated, the Lao in Roi Et were already thinking of their move to the United States or France.

The living conditions of the group in Roi Et were adequate, but conditions in Nan and Loei were awful. In Nan it had been raining, the whole place was a sea of mud and the camp needed everything. In Loei, things were not much better.

That was in 1975. Now, almost three years later, I was back in Thailand and was immediately dispatched to work as a UNHCR field officer in the north-east. There were three main camps there, the Hmong camp in Loei that I had visited three years earlier, and two new camps for the ethnic Lao, one near Nong Khai, opposite Vientiane, and the other just outside Ubon, 135 kilometres west of Pakse, in southern Laos. The camp at Roi Et had closed.

Thais feel conflicting emotions when confronted with this kind of situation. They want to protect the country from invasion or unwanted new burdens, but they feel a duty of hospitality towards people in distress. And in the back of almost every Thai's mind is the unspoken question, what does His Majesty the King expect us to do?

As a result of these conflicting influences and shifts in public opinion, the Thai government's policy towards Indo-Chinese refugees changed frequently. At some moments they tried to shut the door and prevent people from coming into the country at all; at others their policy was almost 'open doors', but one thing remained constant: they would not allow any of the newcomers to stay permanently.

The response of the Thai people varied even more dramatically. At one end, there were many acts of kindness and generosity towards the newcomers; but, at the other there were unimaginable acts of cruelty and greed.

In the period after 1975, the Thais had to cope with five quite distinct refugee influxes: the Hmong from Laos; the ethnic Lao and other minorities from Laos; the Khmer from Cambodia; the Vietnamese boat people; and the Karen minority from Burma. UNHCR quickly became involved in assisting them all, except those from Burma.

The Hmong

In the previous chapter I described the role of the Hmong in the long civil war in Laos. General Vang Pao was the only Hmong general in the Royal Lao Army. He headed the Hmong forces that fought alongside the CIA in the 'Secret War' against the Pathet Lao and North Vietnamese. Once the Coalition Government was formed in 1974 and the Americans began to withdraw from Laos, Vang Pao moved to the United States and the families of his closest military colleagues joined him there. But the number of Hmong who crossed into Thailand in the first wave of refugees far exceeded the number that the US was initially prepared to take. Those who were unable or unwilling to follow Vang Pao to the US were accommodated at the Ban Vinai camp.

When I went back to Ban Vinai in 1978, it had been transformed. UNHCR, with the support of several international NGOs, had built schools, a clinic and installed sanitation. In 1978, the population began to grow fast. The 'first wave' of Hmong refugees to cross into Thailand had been mainly military families, who feared reprisals from the Pathet Lao. Now, a second wave began. Drought and the collectivisation policies of the new Lao government had their effect. Every time I visited the camp, there would be new arrivals, and news of others awaiting registration by the Thai authorities at local police stations.

Although Vang Pao had left for the US, he had not given up hope of returning to Laos in triumph. He, along with American and Thai supporters, continued to encourage resistance to the communist government in Laos. Ban Vinai was not far from the border. It was easy for young men to bring their families to the safety of the camp and then return for periods of resistance in Laos.

This insurgency activity in turn led to suspicion and repression of the Hmong in Laos by the new government, which of course made it harder for those Hmong who wanted to stay and were ready to make an accommodation with the authorities. All the pieces were in place for what was to be, inevitably, a desperately sad story.

The Hmong had fled oppression in China in the late nineteenth century, and had found space and a familiar mountain landscape in Laos. Now they were crowded together in a refugee camp in the lowlands of Thailand, with no land to farm, dependent on international aid, and confronted with only bad options. These options were to apply for resettlement in the United States, to return to Laos, or to stick it out in the camp, in the hope that conditions in Laos would improve, or that the Thai government would relent and allow them to stay and settle in Thailand.

While some among the younger generation of Hmong had received some education and were more open to the idea of moving to the US, their parents were for the most part adamantly opposed. For them, the purpose of life was to perform the rituals their parents and ancestors had taught them. Already in Ban Vinai they felt too far away from their shrines. But at least they had walked there. Eventually they might be able to walk back. But if they flew thousands of miles across the ocean, how would they be able to honour the spirits of their ancestors?

So determined were some of them to avoid resettlement in the US that they would smoke opium just before their interview with the American medical team, so that when they were tested for drugs, they would fail and be returned to the camp.

Once they had arrived in Ban Vinai, Hmong families could not in practice return to Laos, even if they had wished to. The pressure of community opinion was too great. I never heard any Hmong say that he wanted to take his family back to Laos, and perhaps none of them seriously contemplated it. So, they were obliged to take part in a cat-and-mouse game with the Thai, Lao and American governments and UNHCR, which began in the mid-1970s and continued until December 2009, when the Thai government deported 4,000 Hmong refugees back to Laos, under an agreement signed between the two governments in 2007.

In this game, the Thai government periodically restricted the freedoms of the Hmong in Ban Vinai and threatened to repatriate the remaining Hmong refugees, by force if necessary. When these threats became too insistent, the US government would announce another quota for Hmong to move to the US. Enough families would be persuaded to come forward for processing and were transported to America for the Thai government to moderate its threats and ease its restrictions. Meanwhile, UNHCR had difficulty raising the money required to feed the Hmong and encouraged the Lao government to welcome the Hmong back and to give guarantees for their safety if they returned.

And Hmong society was torn apart.

Although we could not have imagined that this game would still be playing out 30 years later, the elements of the stalemate were obvious to us in 1978.

Among the basic principles of refugee protection that Jacques Cuénod had drummed into me, there are two that should have been relevant in the Hmong case. One is that refugee camps should be situated sufficiently far from the border of the country from which the refugees have come to prevent the refugees from attempting to destabilise the government of the country they have just left. The second is that if any refugee does take part in activities against the government of his original country, he forfeits any right to protection and assistance.

So, should UNHCR have insisted that the Hmong refugees at Ban Vinai be moved to a site further from the border? And should UNHCR have sought to identify people who were using the camp as a base for resistance activities in Laos and had them excluded from the camp? Of course, we should have.

But, if UNHCR wants to put pressure on a government to change its policy, it needs allies among the governments of other countries. In order to persuade the Thai government to move the camps further from the border, UNHCR needed support from the United States and other Western governments. But, in this Cold War theatre, the US was quite happy to turn a blind eye to resistance efforts in Laos by the Hmong and others; and so the support for UNHCR to insist on compliance with principles was not forthcoming.

For idealistic young staff of UNHCR in Thailand, this was an early lesson in *realpolitik* and in the toothless nature of our organisation. We would be taught several more such lessons in relation to the three other groups of refugees that we were assisting.

For the Hmong, the extent of their upheaval has been astonishing. Many young Hmong, born in the refugee camps or in the US, have had opportunities for education and a monetary standard of living that would have been impossible in Laos, but, like so many migrants before them, they have paid for those advantages with the loss of their cultural identity and social cohesion. Unlike many of their fellow migrants in the US, they really had no choice.

And some of them even went to French Guiana. 'La Guyane' is a sparsely inhabited tropical territory on the north-east coast of South America. It has the status of an Overseas Department of France. Its population was estimated in 2013 at less than 250,000.

In 1977, a French Catholic priest, who had worked with the Hmong in Laos, persuaded the French government to offer 500 places for Hmong refugees in French Guiana. His argument was that they would find a life there much more akin to what they had left behind than would be possible in the United States or France itself.

This offer led to heated debate within the UNHCR office. Some colleagues felt that the Hmong would be too isolated and open to exploitation in French Guiana and that UNHCR should discourage the French from making the offer, or discourage the Hmong from accepting it, or even refuse to process the cases.

In the end, the French accepted two groups of about 500 Hmong each, and settled them in separate villages, a considerable distance apart. A recent study by Patrick Clarkin shows that the Hmong in French Guiana, who by 2005 numbered 2,100, seem to be doing relatively well in comparison with the Hmong settled in the US. Those in French Guiana exhibited fewer signs of stress, less dissatisfaction with their lives, and less desire to return to Laos than a sample of Hmong in the US. The incidence of hypertension in the sample studied in French Guiana was almost half (at 12.9 per cent) that found in a similar study of Hmong in the US (24.4 per cent). Only 3.4 per cent of the Guiana sample expressed dissatisfaction with their lives, as opposed to 16 per cent of those in the US, and only 12.9 per cent expressed the wish to return to Laos at some time in the future, while the figure among the US sample was 44.8 per cent.

One reason why the Hmong are doing better in French Guiana is probably because they are involved in farming, the traditional Hmong way of life. They produce at least 60 percent of the fresh fruit sold in the markets of French Guiana. In contrast, 43 per cent of Hmong in the US are employed in 'manufacturing', which in most cases is on the shop floor of a factory. In his study, Clarkin cites a book by Anne Fadiman, in which she recalls that General Vang Pao had asked the US government, when it accepted the Hmong refugees, 'to be left alone to be Hmong, clustered in ethnically homogenous villages, protected from government interference, self-sufficient and agrarian'. It is a cruel irony that the only group of Hmong who were treated by their hosts in approximately the way Vang Pao had requested would turn out to be those who considered themselves as 'non-Vang Pao Hmong', while so many 'Vang Pao Hmong' ended up in the cities of the American Mid-West.

One of the saddest sights of working with refugees from Indo-China in Thailand was to watch elderly Hmong attending cultural orientation programmes at the transit camp in central Bangkok, before being put on their flights to America. Rarely can people have been more comprehensively uprooted.

In total, over 100,000 Hmong have been accepted by the United States. That number had increased, thanks to a high birth rate, to over 260,000 people of Hmong ethnicity, recorded in the 2010 census.

Of all the groups of refugees from Indo-China after 1975, the Hmong were the least well prepared for resettlement in the West. It was a tragedy that their leaders could not bring themselves to make more of an accommodation with the new Lao government, or at the very least desist from armed resistance. Even as recently as 2009, it was being reported that there remained a small group of Hmong families, perhaps no more than 50, who continued to live, in terrible poverty, in the remote jungles of Laos, refusing to give up the armed struggle.

Perhaps none of this should surprise us. It was a time when the slogan, 'Better dead than red', or better to die than live under communist rule, was a statement of conviction for many.

In 2004, the cat-and-mouse game finally ended. A first group of Hmong were forcibly sent back to Laos by the Thai authorities. And in 2007, more than 30 years after fleeing Laos for the United States, former general Vang Pao and nine others were arrested in California with a cache of arms and indicted for activities intended to overthrow the government of Laos.

The Lao

Just as the flow of Hmong refugees from Laos picked up in 1978, so the numbers of ethnic Lao crossing into Thailand increased at the same time. The reasons for the Lao exodus were more complex. In the UNHCR office, we talked about 'push' and 'pull' factors. The factors 'pushing' the Lao out of their country were similar to those pushing the Hmong. They included the loss of jobs and income, the loss of opportunity for families associated with the former regime and an oppressive atmosphere of enforced political participation, and for some the threat or reality of 're-education' in a remote part of the country. The main factor 'pulling' them towards Thailand was the prospect of resettlement in France, the United States or other countries in the West.

Would the 'push' factors have been enough to persuade people to leave, if there had been no 'pull'? My informal survey of people leaving Vientiane in 1976 and 1977 suggested not. My interviews with individual families in the refugee camps in Thailand tended to confirm the sense that most of those crossing the river knew where they wanted to go before they left home, and would not have set out if they had known that they would have to stay in Thailand.

Did this make them any less qualified to be considered as 'refugees'? In theory they needed to demonstrate that they had a 'well-founded fear of persecution' in Laos. In practice, the question was never posed, because the Western governments that would accept the refugees for resettlement considered anybody leaving a communist country to have a 'well-founded fear'. For these governments, communism was a form of persecution. Anybody sensible enough to seek to escape was justified in doing so, and should be accepted as a refugee. Once again, UNHCR was expected by Western governments to 'do the right thing', to organise the assistance, process the case files for resettlement and not worry too much whether every individual met the criteria for refugee status.

This did not mean, however, that these Western governments were ready to accept everybody under their quotas. While all those leaving Laos were considered to be refugees, those seeking admission to Australia, France, the US or any other resettlement country had to satisfy criteria established by each government which, typically, had absolutely nothing to do with the level of persecution that the individual and family might expect to meet if forced to return home. Most criteria prioritised those with existing family, work or study connections with the country. Many of those who went to the UK, for example, had lived there before as students of radio technology or hotel management.

The policy of focussing on people with family, work or study ties inevitably gave added encouragement to people who fulfilled those criteria to leave Laos and try to reach one of the camps in Thailand. It has been estimated that Laos lost 10 per cent of its population to this process, but it wasn't just a random 10 per cent; it was heavily biased in favour of the best educated and qualified. It was a terrible loss of talent for a poor country with so few educated people.

As I watched this process by which the best brains were leeched out of a poor country and taken away by countries which were already at the top of the development ladder, I felt seriously conflicted. On the one hand, I could not blame my Lao friends for wanting to escape a thoroughly unpleasant situation at home, with what appeared to be bleak prospects for the future, but I could see that UNHCR's programme would make the recovery of Laos from war longer and more difficult than it would have been if my friends had stayed at home.

The camp for ethnic Lao refugees in Roi Et that I had visited in 1975 had been well over 100 kilometres from the Lao border, as refugee camps should be. It had been replaced by a camp in Nong Khai, almost directly on the Mekong River, and therefore less than 5 kilometres from Laos. As far as we could ascertain, the camp, unlike the Hmong camp at Ban Vinai, was not used as a base for insurgency activities against the Lao government; but its proximity to the border facilitated a continuous movement of news, information and people. As one group of family members became settled with their own hut and facilities, they would send word to the next group of relatives to follow.

I was one of two UNHCR field officers covering the camps in North-East Thailand in the second half of 1978. This involved regular road trips between Ban Vinai, Nong Khai and Ubon. At the camps we would discuss the provision of assistance with the Thai camp staff, and then ask our colleagues in Bangkok to take up any problems with the Ministry of Interior. Then we would talk to the refugee representatives in the camp. They would complain that new arrivals were being held in police stations until they could pay bribes, or that the food rations were inadequate or that camp security, health care and education programmes were unsatisfactory, but what all the refugees wanted to know was the progress of their applications for resettlement.

The Americans and the French had their own teams who came to the camps and interviewed applicants. But some of the countries taking fewer refugees would ask UNHCR to contact the refugees, transmit application forms and even, occasionally, conduct interviews. This sometimes posed difficulties of conscience. It was understandable that when a family had identified a link with the resettlement country, they would try and squeeze in as many relatives as possible. But they knew that nephews, nieces and girlfriends were unlikely to be accepted, while sons and daughters would be. So, families would appear for interview, with brothers and sisters suspiciously close to each other in age, and an understandable lack of supporting documentation.

Over the past 30 years a whole society has dispersed across the globe. There are now 22,000 Lao in San Diego, California. Many of them have close relatives in France and others still in Laos. Family visits involve journeys over thousands of miles, for those who can afford them.

At the end of 1978, I was transferred from North-East Thailand to Bangkok as a programme officer drawing up plans and budgets for operations to help all the groups of refugees arriving in Thailand. My focus would soon turn to those arriving from Cambodia.

The Khmer

The Khmer Rouge ruled Cambodia from April 1975 to January 1979, when Vietnamese troops, responding to attacks on Vietnamese villages near the border, entered the country and, with the help of opposition Khmer forces, pushed the Khmer Rouge out of Phnom Penh and steadily westward, until they were confined to an enclave on the Thai border near Poipet. During the Khmer Rouge rule, up to 1.7 million people, or a quarter of the population, were killed or died of starvation or abuse. It was by far the worst crime against humanity since the Holocaust. It had stretched out over four long years.

During Khmer Rouge rule, only a few Khmer refugees managed to cross the border into Thailand. The numbers in the camp at Aranyaprathet, which had opened in September 1976, never climbed much above 15,000. As some departed for resettlement in the West, a trickle of new arrivals, mainly from the provinces neighbouring the border, would arrive. They told stories of horrors and atrocities that we found hard to believe.

The military push by the Vietnamese unleashed a huge movement of people. As they were released from Khmer Rouge control in the early months of 1979, people moved back into Phnom Penh or other towns and tried to find traces of their families and property. Once the routes were open, many people headed for the Thai border, at several different points. At first, the Thai military prevented them from crossing into Thailand. As the numbers steadily grew, and the desperation of the people increased, the Thai military tried to persuade the Red Cross and the UN agencies to provide help to the people massed just inside Cambodia. Eventually, they invited UNHCR to go and see the situation. It was heart-breaking. People were huddled together under the trees, many with nothing. While some help was provided by the Red Cross and NGOs, UNHCR argued that the encampments were vulnerable to attack from inside Cambodia, and that the refugees could not be properly assisted and protected there and must be allowed into Thailand. We could not help them where they were.

In the end, I believe it was public opinion in Thailand that persuaded the Thai government to change its mind. Reports coming from inside Cambodia and from the border spoke of the pitiful situation of the people. Thai commentators began to call on the government to demonstrate respect for the kingdom's humanitarian principles.

I remember as if it was yesterday the moment on 22 October 1979 in UNHCR's Bangkok office when one of the assistants told me that there was a call from the Thai Supreme Command. I was standing up when I took the call. Colonel Sanan Kajornklam told me that the government had decided to let the Khmer refugees cross the border and wanted UNHCR to organise the assistance for them. It is hard to explain why that was such an emotional moment. In an irrational panic, I called out to colleagues to come and listen while I repeated word for word the content of the message, so that if I dropped dead, somebody else would know what had happened.

In 1978, the head of the UNHCR office in Thailand was Leslie Goodyear, a kindly British gentleman. As the numbers of new refugees arriving from all sides surged, and the anxiety of the Thai authorities increased, Goodyear's innate caution became a problem. As each new crisis hit the office, he retreated further. Since his response to any suggestion was almost invariably 'No', my colleagues and I would sit together to see if we could formulate our requests in ways such that the answer we wanted was negative. This was neither easy nor satisfactory and soon people in headquarters realised the need for a change.

When Poul Hartling took over as High Commissioner for Refugees in January 1978, he quickly dispensed with the services of Zia Rizvi, Sadruddin Aga Khan's chef de cabinet, and sent him to Rome as the UNHCR representative. There, Rizvi had the misfortune to be stabbed in the stomach by a deranged refugee, who had burst into his office. He had made a good recovery and now, with the situation deteriorating in Thailand and the numbers leaving Laos, Cambodia and Vietnam rising rapidly, Hartling sent Rizvi to Bangkok as regional representative for Southeast Asia.

Although still frequently in pain from the aftermath of his knife wound, Rizvi drove himself mercilessly. He travelled frequently from Bangkok to Hanoi and Vientiane, to Kuala Lumpur, Manila and Hong Kong, and back and forth to Geneva, and sometimes New York. He gathered a team of bright young people around him, with whom he enjoyed discussing the policy options facing us. He particularly enjoyed defending his decisions, when some colleagues felt that he was planning to abandon an important principle of refugee protection. Sometimes these discussions would continue late into the night in the coffee shop of the President Hotel in Bangkok. On one occasion, after he had put me in charge of the programme for Khmer refugees, I had been trying for days to see him alone to get his endorsement for a list of decisions we needed to make. I knew he was leaving at seven the next morning for Hanoi. I tracked him down late in the evening at the President Hotel, sat through another heated discussion with members of our team, and finally, at midnight, followed him back to his apartment where he needed to pack. When we got there, he had to make phone calls to Geneva, and I eventually left with the answers to my questions at 3 a.m.

Rizvi could easily come across as arrogant. He could infuriate older officials by arriving late for meetings, puffing away at his Cuban cigar and casting doubt on their sanity and intelligence with the acerbity of his put-downs, but for the most part the younger professionals admired him for his intelligence and his willingness to entrust them with responsibility and to support them in their decisions.

In October 1979, Rizvi gave me the glorious title of chief of the Regional Office Kampuchea Unit (ROKU) and found me a suite of offices away from the main UNHCR office. I persuaded Glen Dunkley, who had just joined UNHCR as an adviser on education to forget about that for the moment and join me as my deputy, and we set about putting together a team to respond to the imminent influx of refugees from Cambodia.

Rizvi also told me that I would need a mentor, somebody to help me confront the huge management challenge he had just dropped in my lap. He found Everett Ressler, who was then a young lecturer and trainer at the Asian Institute of Technology in Bangkok. Everett spent a week with us at the outset, helping us to think about planning and work through scenarios. Once we got going, Everett and I would meet for three to four hours every Saturday morning, so that I could tell him what I had done during the previous week and discuss what the priorities should be for the next.

Everett's help was invaluable. There is no doubt in my mind that UNHCR would have done a less good job receiving the Khmer refugees in Thailand without him. I cannot understand why the humanitarian and peacekeeping worlds have not recognised the value of mentors for humanitarian coordinators and special representatives, when they are confronted with the enormous challenges of a crisis in Darfur or Somalia, or by a tsunami. Most people appointed to these tasks are unprepared to face at least one of the many elements of these complex jobs. To have an experienced mentor, as a confidential sounding-board, can be a big help.

The Thai government insisted that the first UNHCR camp should be for Khmer stuck on the border south of the town of Aranyaprathet. This was where the Khmer Rouge remnants, with their families and civilian hostages, were holed up, having been progressively beaten back by the Vietnamese. A camp for them was to be established in Sa Kaeo district, about 20 kilometres west of Aranyaprathet. As soon as we were shown the site, the Thai military started to move people from the border onto it. It was a disaster. We were completely unprepared. We had nothing. The site was a large rice field, especially designed to flood when it rained. It was not supposed to rain in October. Perversely, it did, often. The condition of many of the refugees was absolutely desperate. To start with, many died every day. Gradually, as we delivered shelter materials, food and water, and the Red Cross and NGOs established feeding centres and clinics, the number of deaths dropped and the situation stabilised.

Sa Kaeo gave us two major policy tests. We received some heavy criticism on both. The camp had been set up to receive refugees from the Khmer Rouge (KR) enclave south of Aranyaprathet. Some families had got on the buses because they hoped to escape the KR. Others, who were KR supporters, were so ill and so desperate, that they thought it would be the only way to survive. Other KR supporters had joined the exodus, because they did not realise that the KR remnants, with Thai support, would be able to resist the final Vietnamese push and would in fact retain control of their enclave for many years to come. So, when the sick had recovered and the KR cadres realised that their enclave had not fallen, they started to leave the camp in the middle of the night and return to the border. Undoubtedly, the hard core KR cadres 'persuaded' some Khmer who wanted to escape from their clutches, to join them back on the border.

After a great deal of debate, and protracted negotiations with the Thai military, we were able to organise a 'voluntary repatriation' process, under which families came forward and, in the privacy of a tent, with an international UNHCR staff member and an interpreter from outside the camp, were asked to confirm that they wished to go back to the KR enclave. In order to allow for families who had been pressured by the KR cadres into 'volunteering', but were in fact unwilling to go, we gave these families the option of going instead to the new camp at Khao I Dang, north of Aranyaprathet, so that they did not have to go back into the Sa Kaeo camp and explain their change of heart.

Some colleagues felt that we should not have undertaken the 'voluntary repatriation' exercise, on the basis that some of the people were clearly going back to fight, and that others were being coerced into going, and were effectively being taken hostage. In the end, Rizvi and I felt that this arrangement was the only way to stop the uncontrolled midnight departures, and that it was preferable to having everybody shipped back to the border by the Thai military. We also felt that the atmosphere in the camp might improve once most of the KR cadres had gone. In the end only a minority of the camp population took up the offer of return to the border, and the departure of the KR cadres did indeed improve the situation in the camp for those who remained.

Unaccompanied minors

The other contentious issue was what to do with the many children who arrived in Sa Kaeo, and later in the other camps, without an adult family member. Among those, the most immediate concern was for some of the youngest children. Some NGOs wanted to take them for adoption in the West.

When Sa Kaeo first opened in October 1979, some parents, unable to provide food for their children, had taken them to the 'orphan centres' that were set up by NGOs, telling the staff that the child's parents had died. This included a number of infants whose mothers were too weak to provide any milk. The plight of these 'orphans', displayed for fundraising purposes by the NGOs, attracted worldwide media attention. Before we realised what was happening, Mme Giscard d'Estaing, the wife of the French president, had announced that Cambodian orphans would be coming to France for Christmas. Twenty-six children were whisked out of Sa Kaeo by Terre des Hommes and flown to France for adoption by French families. There was uproar.

Investigations in Sa Kaeo showed that nearly all these infants had at least one parent in the camp. The parents had no idea their children had been taken. The incident was the trigger for an extended debate between the UN agencies, notably UNICEF, the donor governments and the NGOs about appropriate arrangements for looking after the children who became known as 'unaccompanied minors'. We held several meetings on the topic which attracted over a hundred people. Discussion was immensely heated. In the end, the conclusion was that infants should, if at all possible, be brought up in their own cultural milieu and not offered for adoption abroad. Those children who were in fact orphans, or whose surviving parent was unable to look after them, were handed over to Khmer foster parents, who had often watched their own children die, and were delighted to be able to bring up another child.

Reading the reports of the international response to the Haiti earthquake in 2010 and the attempts to remove 'orphan' children for adoption abroad, was another reminder of the importance of capturing and passing on the lessons of earlier operations.

Of course, most 'unaccompanied minors' from Cambodia were no longer infants and the situation of the older children was even more complex. Some were certainly orphans, but others had become separated from their parents, and had simply assumed them to be dead. Everett Ressler, my mentor, did a detailed study for a group of NGOs of 2,000 unaccompanied minors and concluded that more than half of the children had been separated from their parents by circumstances, not death. Tragically, the long political stalemate that would prevent the recognition of the new Cambodian government would also prevent the return of these children to their parents in Cambodia. Many of them were eventually accepted for resettlement and went to foster families in the West.

Khao-i-Dang

In mid-November 1979 Colonel Sanan indicated that the Thai government was ready to open a new camp north of Aranyaprathet. This was the news we had been waiting for. Tens of thousands of people had been surviving on the border, some for several months, with minimal help and in totally unsatisfactory conditions. I drove down to the border with a young colleague, Mark Malloch-Brown, who had cut his teeth in the Sa Kaeo camp and seemed to have just the kind of drive that would be needed to run the new mega-camp. (Subsequently, Mark would become Deputy Secretary-General of the United Nations and, as Lord Malloch-Brown, minister of state in the British Foreign Office.) Colonel Sanan stopped the car on the main road north from Aranyaprathet and pointed to a site on the east side of the road. 'We will put the refugees here,' he said. I could see immediately that the site would suffer from the same drainage problems as we had encountered at Sa Kaeo. I could also see that it would be difficult to secure the site from encroachment from the border only a few kilometres away. On the other side of the road, to the west, barren land rose gently to a low hill. 'This side the land will drain much better,' I said. At that moment, a villager rode up on a bicycle. The colonel stopped him and asked what the hill was called. 'Khao-I-Dang.' The colonel agreed that we could build the camp there.

In Sa Kaeo, Mark had already teamed up with a bright young Thai, Kasidis Rochanakorn (who would become a director in UNHCR headquarters). So, once back in Bangkok, we loaded them up with large denomination dollar bills, and sent them off to build the camp. They performed miracles.

Four days later, on 21 November 1979, the first buses unloaded the first Khmer refugees at the front of the new site. There were, as yet, no buildings, but the camp design had been laid out, the blocks where the first refugees would live had been identified and the first pit latrines dug. Thai merchants were beginning to arrive with the thatch and other building materials that Mark and Kasidis had ordered. Over the next four days, over 80,000 people arrived. Although conditions were extremely hard in the early weeks, several key decisions ensured that they remained bearable and that the camp became a reasonable place to live over several years. First, Mark immediately asked the refugees who had settled in a given block to elect representatives, with whom he would discuss the management of the camp. Initially, he met with them every day. They would argue and disagree among themselves and sometimes accuse each other of all manner of trickery, but Mark kept the meetings going and relied on the leaders to maintain discipline and good order.

The maintenance of good order was immensely aided by the design of the camp. Wide straight avenues went up and across the hill, creating squares or blocks in which a group of huts could be constructed by their occupants, using the materials provided. Each block was not only a physical, but also an administrative entity. When, much later, accusations were made that the block leaders were inflating the numbers and stealing the extra rations, we were able to lock down the camp and do a house-by-house census in a single day. We discovered that the real numbers were extremely close to what was being claimed. If there was fraud, it was on a very small scale.

The first thing that the refugees' representatives decided when they met with Mark was that they would use the thatch being delivered to the camp for school roofs and not for family housing. Families had been living in the open or under plastic sheets for months already. They could survive a bit longer. But children had been deprived of schooling by the Khmer Rouge for almost four years. Books and libraries had been burned, and teachers murdered. There was no time to lose. Education must start at once.

Modern-day camp managers will understand the difficulty we had in authorising the use of materials procured for refugee shelter for the purpose of education, which has often not been considered a priority in emergency relief operations. There are times when you have to just do it, and explain to the auditors later.

The education programme would quickly become the jewel of Khao-I-Dang. The joy and enthusiasm of the former teachers and of their pupils of all ages was extremely moving. Textbooks were found in libraries in Europe and rushed out to be reproduced; classical dance groups were formed. The work done in Khao-I-Dang would kick-start the revival of Cambodian society and culture after the genocide.

At its peak, Khao-I-Dang housed over 120,000 people. We claimed that at the time it was the most highly populated Khmer city, outstripping even Phnom Penh, which was only beginning to recover from the exodus under the KR. Khao-I-Dang would remain the largest and most important camp, but refugees were arriving at other border points and more camps were needed. UNHCR built camps at Kamput, near Chantaburi, at Mai Rut, near Trat, and at Kap Cherng, near Surin. The camp at Sa Kaeo, which was constantly flooding, was moved to a new site. It was a period of frantic activity.

The arrival of the Khmer refugees was front-page news throughout the world. Aid and potential aid workers poured in. They exhibited the best and the worst that such situations throw up. Lactating mothers arrived from the United States and breast-fed starving babies alongside their own. Doctors showed up in such numbers that we had no work for the late-comers. On the down side, we heard of representatives of Christian charities who spent a day touring a camp and went back home claiming to be the only organisation bringing relief to the starving refugees. One demented visitor drove around one of the camps throwing sweets out of his car window, causing a stampede of children, in which several were injured. And we had the greatest difficulty persuading any of the many NGOs to provide us with sanitation engineers. The president of one of the very best of the American refugee NGOs came to my office in Bangkok to tell me that his NGO would be able to provide three fully equipped medical teams. I told him that that was great news, but I would be grateful if he could swap two of them for sanitation teams. He didn't think he could do that, but he would try for one. A few days later, he called from the US to say that he had tried his best, but that he could not persuade the donors of any of the medical teams to spend the money on sanitation instead. It was just not sexy. But he had found a first-class sanitation team. The only problem was that his NGO could not find the money to pay for it. They would have to charge us $250,000 for a year.

I asked him why it was that donors wanted to pay for things of which we already had too many, and refused to pay for something which would save far more lives than any number of doctors. He understood, he sympathised, but he had been unable to persuade. We paid for the sanitation team. It was the best investment we made.

Commercial companies offered donations that were not always welcome. One company wanted to donate a ship full of orange juice. Because of shipping delays, it would be past its use-by date by the time they could get it to Japan, its intended destination. So, they offered to give it to UNHCR for distribution to Khmer refugees. After consulting our doctors, we politely suggested to the company that they should pour it into the sea. The risk of an outbreak of diarrhoea was too great, and the cost and logistics of distribution would have been prohibitive.

I was given unprecedented, and I believe never repeated, powers to hire staff for the operation. Dale de Haan, the Deputy High Commissioner, authorised me to recruit international professional staff on one-month contracts, without reference to headquarters, enabling me to recruit people and put them to work immediately. Once on board, the paperwork was done, and, provided they fulfilled the basic criteria for recruitment, they were given another three-month contract.

My experience in UNHCR up to and including the Cambodian operation led me to the conclusion that staff employed on emergency operations should be young. I had watched more senior colleagues 'freeze' when confronted by a crisis. They seemed unable to process the information about the situation, and convert it into possible solutions, in the same way that Mark and other younger colleagues did. Military forces around the world apply this principle. It is the lieutenants and captains who come face to face with the enemy or with the population being protected. These officers are invariably under 30. The difficulty for the United Nations can be that responsibility for a large field operation would seem to require a senior-level person, and senior grades can only be reached by people with many years of experience. In some situations, too much experience can be a hindrance. It helps you to know all the reasons why the problem cannot be addressed in what appears to be the best way.

Human resources management is a vital component of the management of emergency humanitarian operations. For people in distress, the calibre of the aid workers and the speed with which they are deployed can make a major difference to the quality of the help they receive and the timeliness of its arrival. UNHCR was extremely fortunate to have found Mark and Kasidis to run one of the largest and most high-profile camp operations in its history. The search for people who could deliver that sort of result was one that preoccupied me throughout my career.

Getting people from different organisations and backgrounds to work together effectively and efficiently has been the most prominent concern of my professional life. My early immersion in Lao culture and study of social anthropology showed me how easy it is for misunderstandings to turn into disputes, and for good intentions to lead to bad results. My work in Laos with displaced persons and in Thailand with Hmong and Lao refugees had given me a taste of the challenges of coordination: bringing together refugees, governments, UN bodies, NGOs and well-meaning private individuals to work in harmony towards a common objective. The Khmer refugees in Thailand raised these challenges to a new level.

The Khmer refugee crisis in Thailand attracted an unprecedented number of NGOs from the Western world. These were of every conceivable type and size. Some, like CARE, the International Rescue Committee (IRC) and Save the Children were already well established and had good reputations. Others were brand new. Their motivations and levels of competence were extremely varied.

Fortunately, by 1979 a group of major NGOs had established a body called the Coordinating Committee for Services to Displaced Persons in Thailand (CCSDPT). This offered a forum for information-sharing and a resource for new organisations. UNHCR made full use of it. As soon as I was put in charge of the Cambodian refugee operation, I started to attend the regular CCSDPT meetings and give briefings on what we were doing, what we saw as the most important needs and then answer questions. At times there were several hundred people in the room. After a time, the Thai government also began to attend and use the meetings as a way of getting official messages to the NGOs.

Since that experience, I have been convinced that the best people to organise information-sharing during a humanitarian crisis are not the government or the UN, but the NGOs. Questions of who gets invited to attend meetings can be fought out among the NGOs themselves. Those elected by the NGOs to chair the meetings have to decide how much 'UN-bashing' goes on. They soon discover that if they let it go too far, the most senior UN people will stop attending, although agencies very rarely boycott meetings altogether.

These big information-sharing meetings could not be the forum for detailed consultations with NGOs about the provision of services in refugee camps. For that, we invited the major NGOs to meet with us and to see if we could persuade them to organise themselves so that there was adequate coverage for each sector of activity in each camp.

We developed a simple matrix (without computers or photocopiers!), with the services (education, health, nutrition, etc.) across the top, and the camps and their main sections down the side. Over a period of weeks we encouraged, cajoled and occasionally bribed the various organisations until we had our matrix full. The identification of a major NGO for a sector in a particular camp did not prevent other NGOs from joining in, but it gave us a certain guarantee that the issue would be addressed and that other contributions could be made in support of the lead NGO.

As the number of NGOs grew, we became aware that some NGO staff were suggesting to the refugees that their problems could be ascribed to the inadequacy of their religion, and that if they would only convert to Christianity, their troubles would be over. Indeed, the NGO concerned would ensure that they got more assistance than their benighted brothers. Remarkably, given the situation in which people found themselves, few refugees fell for this temptation. Indeed, many would have been aware of missionary groups operating in Cambodia before the war. Christian missionaries had very limited success in Theravada Buddhist Cambodia, Laos or Thailand at any time.

Reports of these activities set off alarm bells for UNHCR. On the one hand, it was the Thai government's responsibility to decide which organisations could work in the camps, not ours. On the other, the Thais had asked us to coordinate the international response and UNHCR had a responsibility for the 'protection' of refugees. We could not allow discrimination in the distribution of assistance in the camps, even if the assistance being distributed in this way was not ours.

In consultation with the major NGOs of the CCSDPT we developed a code of conduct on the issue. Its basic point was that the provision of assistance must be based only on need, and never on religious affiliation. This became one of the elements of UNHCR's first emergency handbook.

Political stalemate

While everybody, or almost everybody, had rejoiced at the defeat of the Khmer Rouge, Western governments were not at all happy about the way it had been done. The Vietnamese Army, which only four years earlier had defeated the Americans, had pushed the KR up against the Thai border, but showed no sign of leaving Cambodia itself. The Vietnamese had achieved their victory with the help of Khmer fighters, many of whom were disaffected former supporters of the KR. A group of former royalists was hurriedly encouraged to set up camp on the north-west border with Thailand. The Thais were ready to support anyone who would help them keep Vietnamese troops away from their border.

A political solution, allowing the Vietnamese to withdraw and a new government to take power, might have been reached had it not been for the Chinese government's position. China was alarmed at what it saw as Vietnamese aggression against one of its allies and insisted that the KR should retain Cambodia's seat at the United Nations. The US and UK governments were not unhappy with this. However, public opinion in the West was so outraged by what appeared to be a deliberate attempt to rescue and shore up the most murderous regime since World War II that the credentials of the KR representative at the UN were eventually withdrawn. In order not to 'reward Vietnamese aggression', the Cambodian seat at the UN was left vacant. This Cold War impasse prolonged the conflict in Cambodia for another 14 years and meant that many Cambodians, whose only thought on arriving in Khao-I-Dang in November 1979 was to get back home to their towns and villages in Cambodia, ended up with no choice but to accept resettlement in the West. A deeply traumatised people would be dispersed around the globe.

When the Thai government decided to allow, indeed encourage, groups of Khmer, including families, to install themselves at sites along the border, Thai officials asked UNHCR to extend our assistance programmes to include these sites. We refused. We said that UNHCR could not agree to assist people who were not clearly located on Thai territory, and who were also taking part in armed activity in their own country. To our surprise, the World Food Programme (WFP), which was providing the food in UNHCR's camps, agreed to feed the people in the border sites, against our advice. The WFP had no mandate for such activity and had never done anything like it before. Initially they did it under the flag of the UNDP office in Thailand. Later, a separate office was established called the UN Border Relief Operation (UNBRO), which continued to coordinate the delivery of aid by WFP and NGOs to the people in these sites for many years.

One of the UN's most senior and respected officials, Sir Robert Jackson, who had been a leading figure in the founding of UNDP, came to Thailand as special envoy of Secretary-General Kurt Waldheim and set up UNBRO. I found the politics of this episode bizarre and inexplicable. Why would the UN sacrifice its well-established principles for the treatment of refugees to shore up the remnants of the most murderous genocidal regime since Hitler's Reich? The US and UK governments were able to point to the Chinese refusal to recognise the overthrow of the KR regime, but this seemed to suit Western governments quite well. It perpetuated a simmering low-level conflict that simultaneously isolated and punished Cambodia, Laos and Vietnam for embracing communism, while shoring up Thailand as the bulwark against further communist expansion.

Vietnamese 'boat people'

As the emergency phase of the Khmer refugee crisis wound down in 1980, Zia Rizvi decided that the Regional Office Kampuchea Unit (ROKU) should be folded back into the Regional Office in Bangkok. When Rizvi's deputy, Pierre Jambor, left for Geneva, I took over his job. This meant becoming involved again in UNHCR's work with the Hmong, the Lao and with the Vietnamese 'boat people'.

The departure of the US military from South Vietnam in April 1975 and the North Vietnamese entry into Saigon had sparked understandable panic among officers of the South Vietnamese Army, officials of the South Vietnamese government and their families, as well as the many families who had in one way or another served the US presence. People had fled the country, using any means they could.

Once the North Vietnamese arrived in Saigon (and changed its name to Ho Chi Minh City), the flow of departures was initially quite limited. Senior officials in the South Vietnamese regime, who had not managed to escape, were quickly rounded up and taken away for 're-education'. Their families had no way of knowing how long the men would be away, and if they would ever return. People waited to see what life would be like under new rulers.

Nevertheless, a steady trickle of Vietnamese took to boats and set out for Thailand. They had to go around Cambodia. Some arrived on the coast west of the Cambodian border and east of Bangkok. Others aimed further south and arrived close to the border with Malaysia. They were detained by the Thai police and held in detention centres.

In 1978, the numbers of 'boat people' began to increase substantially. Once again there were 'push' and 'pull' factors at work. The new Vietnamese government remained isolated. Aid from the Soviet Union was limited. The government found itself in a new war against China. The economy was in tatters. The war had destroyed the transport network and much other infrastructure. The government's effort to set up New Economic Zones and force families to move into them only exacerbated economic hardship and opposition to the government's policies. As educated Vietnamese families in the south became more and more pessimistic about their future, the United States announced that it would accept more refugees from Indo-China for resettlement. This decision was made after a highly effective lobbying campaign by young, mostly civilian Americans who had worked in South Vietnam, some of whom were already involved in the US government's refugee programme based in the US Embassy in Bangkok.

As the situation in Vietnam got worse, and the readiness of Western governments to receive refugees improved, it transpired that many of the new communist officials in southern Vietnam were open to bribery. Perhaps the leadership recognised the difficulty of dealing with people who were adamantly opposed to their form of government. For whatever reason, it became easier to organise departures. Over the coming years, hundreds of thousands would leave by three main routes. About 250,000 ethnic Chinese went north to China, Hong Kong and Macao. Ethnic Vietnamese either sailed south-east in the hope of getting into the main shipping lanes where they might be picked up by freighters, or of making it to the Philippines, Malaysia or Indonesia; and others aimed south-west for the coast of Thailand and Malaysia. All these routes were fraught with danger. Many boats were unseaworthy; almost all were overcrowded; most had inadequate supplies of fuel, food and water; and there were pirates. While many refugees died of thirst or because boats could not ride out the storms, others died at the hands of Thai pirates who preyed on their boats either on the open sea or once the exhausted Vietnamese had reached one of the islands off the coast of southern Thailand. Although most pirate attacks involved theft of the refugees' belongings, others involved murder, rape and forced abduction. In one year, 1982, UNHCR recorded, on the basis of testimony from refugees reaching Thailand, that 5,900 people had arrived on 218 boats, 65 per cent of all boats had been attacked by pirates, most more than once, and that from the population of those boats, 155 people had been killed, 179 raped and 157 abducted. Nobody was able to say, of course, how many other boats had sunk, or been destroyed, with the loss of all aboard.

This was an utterly shameful situation, and it took its toll on UNHCR staff as well. A young American field officer stationed in Songkhla in the far south of Thailand, where boat people were housed in a camp, showed extraordinary bravery in rescuing refugees from the clutches of the pirates. He cajoled and persuaded reluctant Thai naval officers to take him out on patrol to some of the islands where he had heard that boat people had landed. Sometimes, when he could no longer persuade the navy, he hired a fishing boat and went out on his own. There he witnessed horrific scenes of savagery. His reports to us in Bangkok became increasingly desperate. We urged the Thai government to send out patrols, to arrest the pirates and to support our team. It had little effect. As the weeks went by, we became concerned that our colleague's mental health was suffering. We brought him up to Bangkok and sent him to the doctor. After a brief return to the south, it became clear that he was seriously ill. He went home to the US.

Some months later, we received a message from headquarters saying that the medical insurance company had queried whether the mental illness of our colleague was 'service incurred'. Were we sure that his illness resulted from the performance of his official duties, or had he suffered the breakdown in the normal course of his life? The outcome of this enquiry would determine whether the insurance company would pay for his treatment after he had ceased to be a UN staff member. For us, this was a no-brainer. We had seen the transformation in our friend caused by the terrible things he had witnessed. We drafted a careful and detailed response. Eventually we heard that his claim on the insurance company had been upheld. It was the first case of Post-Traumatic Stress Disorder (PTSD) that I personally came across and sparked an interest in the impact of exposure to traumatic events on the mental health of aid workers that continued all through my career.

By 1980, when I started to look seriously at the phenomenon of 'boat people', I had become convinced that the primary cause of the massive exodus was not the situation in Vietnam, dire though it was, but the offer of resettlement in the West, and particularly in the US, for large numbers of Vietnamese refugees in camps in Thailand, Malaysia, Indonesia, the Philippines and Hong Kong. It seemed to me that Western governments were indirectly encouraging people to risk their lives on the open sea. Nobody has ever worked out how many Vietnamese did not make it, and certainly we had no way of knowing it at the time, but all the evidence was that it was a significant proportion. In addition, many of those who did make it to shore would endure deeply traumatising experiences that would mark them for the rest of their lives. While the resettlement countries never offered more places than the number of refugees who were already in camps, it soon became clear that most of them would announce annual quotas. They were preparing to receive refugees who had not yet left their homes. Could UNHCR justify its support for a process which was enticing such large numbers of people to risk a terrible death?

In 1980, UNHCR organised a meeting in Singapore for its resettlement officers in the Southeast Asia region. I would not attend the meeting, but sent to the head of UNHCR's resettlement section in Geneva a memorandum setting out my views. He thought it would stimulate debate at the meeting and had copies made for all those attending. From there, a copy reached the hands of a journalist on the *Far Eastern Economic Review*. A summary of what I had written appeared in their next edition.

This caused a rumpus within UNHCR, but my note also helped to stir a brief public discussion of the policy of Western governments towards people leaving the three countries of Indo-China. But the countries in which the refugees were arriving – Thailand, Malaysia, Indonesia, Philippines and Singapore – were adamant in insisting that they would not accept the refugees, unless Western governments continued to offer resettlement places. This position, completely contrary to the intent of the 1951 Convention on the Status of Refugees, went unchallenged. The communities of resettled refugees, particularly in the United States, had vociferous political support. Once these attitudes became entrenched, there was little chance of changing the pattern. People would continue to leave their homes, the countries in which they first arrived would continue to put them in temporary transit centres, and Western governments would announce new quotas every year.

Moving on

I hope that this account of three extraordinary years, when we confronted four distinct refugee crises at once in a single country, has given some sense of the feeling we had of being part of history. Many of the dilemmas that we had grappled with in Thailand would appear again in my next assignments.

By early 1981, the situation of all four groups of refugees had settled into a pattern that would last for several years. The West had no interest in a political accommodation with the pro-communist countries of Indo-China, and there was still plenty of domestic support for the refugees in Australia, Canada, France and the United States. The newcomers were proving for the most part intelligent and industrious, and were welcome. So, when I received a letter from my father about a post being advertised in London for director of a new British NGO for refugees, being created by merging two existing organisations, I applied and, to my surprise, was offered the job. When I discussed the move with senior colleagues at UNHCR in Geneva, they were pleased at the idea that a UNHCR insider would be heading the new British NGO, and suggested that I should see some of the other major refugee problems in the world, before taking up the job. So, in June 1981, exactly three years after arriving, I left Bangkok and travelled to London via Hong Kong, China, Pakistan and Somalia.

Hong Kong and China

Hong Kong was coping with an influx of Vietnamese 'boat people' similar to those affecting Thailand and the other countries of Southeast Asia. But Guangdong province in mainland China revealed a very different story. Over 250,000 ethnic Chinese refugees from Vietnam had arrived in China and been accepted for permanent settlement by the Chinese government. In a village near Guangzhou (Canton), 500 refugees from Vietnam were living alongside a similar number of resident Chinese.

Although both groups were Cantonese speakers, their experiences of life up to that point could hardly have been more different, and they faced one overwhelming practical problem: the Chinese economic system had been designed as an incentive for the one-child policy. All village families received a basic living allowance for each person. Earnings from work went first towards covering the cost of that allowance. Anything earned above that could be kept by the worker and boosted the family's income. If a family had more than two children, they could never earn more than the state allowance for their family. Everything they earned would be taken by the state as a contribution to the family's allowances. So, the families from Vietnam, who had six or seven children, had no incentive to work, since however hard they tried they could never earn more than the total in allowances that the state paid them anyway.

This may seem like a relatively unimportant historical detail, but it is actually a brilliant example of why, when dealing with the movement of large numbers of people, you can never take anything for granted. Planners in Geneva may have thought that Chinese going to China would be an easy win; but they should not have been surprised when many of these families tried to move again – this time to the United States.

Perhaps this urge to move on was also fuelled by the phenomenon of the 'refugee family photo' taken outside a nice house in California, with a Mercedes parked out front. Refugees in the US would take such photos and send them to friends and relatives in China or in the camps in Southeast Asia. They usually neglected to point out that neither the house nor the Mercedes belonged to them.

Pakistan

When President Daoud of Afghanistan, who had overthrown King Zahir Shah in 1973, was himself assassinated by radical communist army officers in 1978, a wave of infighting between two communist factions prompted the Soviet Union to intervene militarily. On 24 December 1979, Soviet troops entered Afghanistan, killed President Hafizullah Amin and installed Najibullah as president. As the new government sought to extend its control over the rural population, it encountered resistance from a new popular force, the *mujahideen.*

As resistance intensified, and the government's response became more brutal, so the numbers of Afghans fleeing to Pakistan and Iran steadily mounted. By the time of my visit in May 1981, there were well over 1 million Afghans living in camps in Pakistan. By the end of that year there would be 2 million.

UNHCR had opened its office in Pakistan in November 1979 and expanded its operations extremely rapidly. I visited camps in the North-West Frontier Province (NWFP) and Baluchistan with UNHCR field officers. Long lines of tents covered the barren ground on sites outside Peshawar and in the tribal agencies of Bajaur and Mohmand in NWFP. As soon as the UNHCR field officers got me away from their offices, they began to unburden themselves of their worries and frustrations. My guide in NWFP was Joachim Bilger, a brilliant young man who would perish in the Swissair crash off Nova Scotia in September 1998. Joachim felt that his efforts to apply UNHCR's basic principles were not being supported by his bosses. He had two main concerns: Afghan tribal leaders were being allowed to register long lists of refugees for assistance, without UNHCR being able to verify that the names were of real people, or that these people were actually receiving the aid; and the Pakistani government was siting some of the camps very close to the Afghan border.

In Baluchistan, I was taken to a camp near the border town of Chaman that had been set up within just 500 metres of the Afghan border. This kind of camp site would make an ideal base for *mujahideen* resistance activities in Afghanistan.

Back in Islamabad, UNHCR's senior staff in the country told me the same story I knew so well from Thailand; their efforts to insist on the essential principles of UNHCR's mandate were not being supported by diplomats of major donor countries or by UNHCR headquarters. Ronald Reagan had been in the White House for five months. The Afghan Holy War against the Soviet presence in Afghanistan was just getting under way. Principles were not a priority.

Geneva

After a brief visit to Somalia to see UNHCR's programme for ethnic Somalis fleeing from Ethiopia, I arrived back at UNHCR headquarters in Geneva and handed in a short report on my trip. I was asked to give a briefing to relevant staff. To my surprise the room was packed. Word had got out that my report on the situation in Pakistan was critical of UNHCR's approach there. I tried to describe the situation factually and unemotionally. Camps were on the border; refugee leaders were distributing the food without oversight; and, camps were being used by the *mujahideen* resistance groups as bases for activities against the government in Afghanistan. There was a lively discussion. Some colleagues asked how UNHCR could allow this to happen, but I think most realised that there was only so much that UNHCR could do without the support of the US and European countries. The most flagrant abuses of food aid could be addressed, and eventually were, but the huge Afghan refugee population in Pakistan would be the reserve base for the *mujahideen* cause throughout the 1980s, extending beyond the departure of Soviet troops in February 1989 until the fall of Najibiullah in 1992, when the *mujahideen* leaders finally went home to Kabul.

After my experience in Thailand, this was another sobering reminder that the United Nations always operates in a political context. However universal its principles, the UN's ability to insist on their implementation is constrained by the larger political context of each situation.

3

REFUGEES, ASYLUM-SEEKERS AND THE INTERNALLY DISPLACED

The view from Europe in the 1980s

My father's letter, telling me that two British NGOs working with refugees had decided to merge and were advertising for a director, had come at exactly the right time. My parents were getting old and I had been away a long time. Many UN staff regret that, unlike diplomats, there are no home postings. With this new assignment I would be able to spend time at home.

The new job would give me a chance to see the refugee problem from the perspective of European countries receiving people seeking asylum as well as refugees accepted for resettlement.

I started in July 1981. It was the beginning of a seven-year period of momentous changes in my personal life. In 1982, Keolila and I were married; in 1984 and 1986 our sons, William and Tom, were born; and in 1987 and 1988 my parents died. These dramatic changes in my personal life took place against a backdrop of continually shifting professional challenges. I was fortunate to have great support teams, both at home and in the office.

A turbulent decade

While Vietnamese, Lao and Cambodians were pouring into countries in Southeast Asia, Afghans were arriving in huge numbers in Iran and Pakistan, and Ethiopians were fleeing their country in all directions. At the same time, three other major political crises were generating new flows of refugees in other parts of the world.

In February 1979, the Iranian Revolution had deposed the shah and brought Ayatollah Khomeini back from exile as supreme leader. In

September 1980, one of the bloodiest and most pointless wars ever fought started between Iran and Iraq. It would last eight years and cost millions of lives. The early 1980s saw a steady stream of refugees arriving in Europe from Iran and Iraq.

On 11 September 1973, President Salvador Allende of Chile was assassinated, his democratic government overthrown and General Augusto Pinochet seized power; he would not relinquish it until 1990. Many opponents of his regime and victims of his oppression arrived in Europe in the early 1980s.

In Sri Lanka, rioting and violence against the Tamil minority had begun in 1977 after the Tamil United Liberation Front (TULF) began to call for a separate Tamil state. This convinced many Sri Lankan Tamils that there would be little future for them at home, and they began to take any opportunity to leave.

The British NGOs

Since World War II Britain had received considerable numbers of refugees from Europe, particularly Poland. Now there were Vietnamese, Cambodians, Lao, Chileans, Iranians, Iraqis, Ethiopians and Tamils from Sri Lanka to welcome. Understandably, the British government and NGOs were not well prepared.

The British Council for Aid to Refugees (BCAR) had been set up in the aftermath of World War II to help refugees from Europe arriving in Britain. It offered advice and counselling and ran homes for elderly refugees.

The Standing Conference on Refugees (SCOR) had been set up by the major British overseas charities to provide a forum for the discussion of refugee issues and to develop policy positions, which could be presented to the government and to UNHCR.

My job was to take over as director of both organisations, arrange the merger, and then set up and run the new body. From a technical point of view, the merger was not difficult, although at the human level it was much less easy. The two long-serving general secretaries, Nora Morley-Fletcher of BCAR and Nancy Rice-Jones of SCOR, were eventually persuaded to retire.

The most important debate was over the governance structure of the new organisation. We wanted to commit the major British NGOs like Oxfam and Save the Children to the new organisation. We also wanted to encourage refugee community groups and smaller NGOs to feel that it was their organisation too. Full membership, with voting rights, was open only to NGOs, and not individuals. While final authority was vested in the Annual General Meeting of members, the real power rested with the Executive Committee. This had six seats for the big NGOs, which could be re-elected, and four for the smaller NGOs and community groups, elected for two-year terms. We were looking for a manageable size, continuity among the major NGOs and regular injections of new blood.

While the members of the Executive Committee were institutions, the officers were elected individuals. Who should we invite to be the first chair? The choice of Sir Arthur Peterson, recently retired from the Home Office, caused some surprise. But the conservative veterans of BCAR were afraid that the radical campaigning NGOs would set the new body on a collision course with the government and jeopardise government funding. The appointment of Sir Arthur allayed those fears. In the event, Sir Arthur, liberated from the constraints of the civil service, but with an insider's knowledge, fulfilled his role admirably, leading delegations to tell ministers and former colleagues in the civil service that they were not doing their job.

There was much debate over the choice of a name for the new body. We chose 'British Refugee Council' (BRC). Some worried that people might think we were working for British refugees. But Denmark and Norway already had the Danish and Norwegian Refugee Councils. In 1992, my successor dropped the 'British', and it is now the 'Refugee Council'.

I was extremely fortunate to find Alan Phillips to be my deputy. He had come from a well-regarded British NGO, the World University Service (WUS), and proved to be a great colleague as well as a tough and effective negotiator and fundraiser.

Receiving refugees from outside Europe

The extraordinary flows of refugees generated by conflicts around the world in the late 1970s and 1980s were a severe shock to European countries. Since World War II, Western Europe had had to cope with only two major refugee crises in the 1950s and 1960s: the Hungarians arriving after the events of 1956 and Czechoslovaks after 1968. Limited and manageable numbers had continued to arrive from other Eastern European countries. These new flows from outside Europe presented completely new challenges to European governments, UNHCR and NGOs.

European governments faced two distinct problems: who should be allowed in, and how should those allowed in be assisted? UNHCR and the NGOs faced a related problem: what could they reasonably advocate for? What was the appropriate response to this extraordinary development?

For the refugees from Vietnam and Afghanistan, who were living in camps in Thailand or Pakistan, this question 'who shall we allow in?' meant 'how many shall we agree to accept, and how shall we select them?' Most of those coming from other countries were not waiting to be invited. They were arriving at ports and airports and seeking asylum, or they were people already in Western Europe, who, seeing what was happening at home, were unwilling to go back when their student or tourist visas expired. So the questions in relation to them were, 'who should be allowed to stay, and who should be sent back?'

Britain was never one of the preferred destinations for refugees from Indo-China, but UNHCR and the United States government had developed the concept of 'burden-sharing'. The 'burden' of receiving refugees from the camps for resettlement should be shared by all countries that believed in the cause. This meant all non-communist developed countries – Europe, Australia, New Zealand, Canada, the US and Japan. These were the same countries that contributed almost all the funds used by UNHCR to run its programmes. While the US, Australia, Canada and France would offer thousands of places every year, Iceland might offer 15. Every European country would take some. Between 1975 and 1995, Britain received 250 refugees from Cambodia, 300 from Laos and over 19,000 from Vietnam.

There was not the same pressure from Pakistan and Iran for Western countries to receive Afghan refugees for resettlement, and the number of places offered was therefore much lower. Many Afghans were, of course, desperate to get out of the huge, hot and densely packed refugee camps. Those with ties of family or education in the US or European countries soon started to apply. Their contacts in the West and the advocacy groups that had been set up in support of the Afghan cause, put pressure on governments to be as generous with Afghan refugees as they were being with Indo-Chinese.

Asylum-seekers

Many people from Iran, Iraq, Ethiopia, Sri Lanka and Chile were already living in Western Europe when the situation in their home countries changed. When they applied for asylum, it was on the grounds that they feared persecution if they were forced to return home. They came into the category known by the French term of refugees '*sur place*'. Other applicants travelled to Europe either directly from their home countries, or from other countries where they had been living temporarily. The number applying for asylum in European countries was rising quickly.

As soon as I arrived in London, I was plunged into the debates about how Britain should respond to this situation. I met regularly with Irene Khan, then at the London office of UNHCR (who later became Secretary-General of Amnesty International) and the representatives of the British NGOs giving advice to asylum-seekers. We mapped out our strategy towards the British government and prepared for regular meetings with the Home Office.

On the surface, the issue was straightforward. Individuals applying for asylum had to persuade British officials that they had 'a well-founded fear of persecution' under the terms of the 1951 Convention on the Status of Refugees, and that consequently they should not be forced to return home. In reality, it was much less simple.

The most common problem arose when individuals were unable to demonstrate that they would be personally targeted for persecution if they went home, but were nevertheless afraid to go because of a general climate of violence, unrest and economic misery. Was it reasonable to expect young Iranian students to return to Iran, when they would inevitably be enrolled in the armed forces and sent to fight in a war with Iraq in which millions were dying? Was it reasonable to send a Tamil back to Sri Lanka, when Tamils were being attacked in the streets?

A second problem arose when British officials were reluctant to believe the accounts given by asylum-seekers of the mistreatment they claimed to have suffered at the hands of their own governments, particularly when those governments were allies of Britain. Applications were being rejected even from people who could show evidence of torture.

A third problem occurred when the British authorities tried to retrace the movements of asylum-seekers. They found that some had spent time in several other countries before reaching the UK, and told them that they should have applied for asylum in those countries.

Each of these problems highlighted a difficulty with international refugee law, founded, as it is, on a Convention adopted in 1951, which related only to events in Europe before that date. The Protocol of 1967 had removed the restrictions of date and geography, without really considering whether a treaty designed to deal with a known past episode in a specific geographic area could simply be universalised in both time and space, without throwing up serious difficulties. I once asked Gilbert Jaeger, UNHCR's Director of Protection, whether a national of Papua New Guinea who feared persecution in that country, could leave his home there and travel to Venezuela, or any other country in the world that was a state party to the 1951 Convention and 1967 Protocol, and submit an application for refugee status there without having any ties to that country, and expect to have his application considered on its merits. Gilbert answered that the Venezuelans were obliged to consider his application, provided that the man had travelled there 'with deliberate haste'; that is, that he had not spent an extended period (undefined) in any of the countries he had passed through on the way.

While this might constitute the letter of the refugee law that states had signed up to, it was not a commitment that many European states recognised, particularly when they were suddenly confronted by large numbers of people seeking asylum from distant continents.

In practice, the British government eventually accepted that there were certain countries to which they could not forcibly return anybody, because of the levels of conflict or violence there, and the degree of public support for people escaping from those places. In the early 1980s, this applied on the whole to Afghanistan, Chile, Ethiopia and Iran, and also, of course, to the countries of Indo-China.

People from other countries were assessed on the merits of their individual cases, and it became increasingly clear that the British government on the one side, and the NGOs and UNHCR on the other, had diametrically opposed interpretations of the meaning of the Convention. Indeed, I became so exasperated at some of the decisions being made by Home Office officials in relation to people from countries which were off the public radar, but where the individuals concerned had clearly been persecuted in the past and would inevitably be at risk again if they returned, that I advocated with my colleagues that we should encourage the British government to denounce the 1951 Convention, rather than remain a state party, if it was determined to disregard so blatantly the Convention's basic provisions.

Most of my colleagues felt that to encourage states to denounce the Convention would be a recipe for chaos, and that whatever was negotiated to replace it would inevitably be worse. While that might well have been true, it did not seem to me that anybody was served by a

Convention to which states paid lip-service, but did not in fact apply. They did not apply it when considering those fleeing from communist states, since they simply determined that anybody fleeing from such a state qualified as a refugee under the Convention; and they did not apply it to individuals fleeing non-communist countries with oppressive regimes, since they were unwilling to accept hard evidence of brutal repression being carried out by governments with which they had friendly relations. I have been unable to find many allies for my view on this, but have seen nothing since to make me change my mind.

The Tamils

One group that caused us endless difficulties was the Tamils from Sri Lanka. In the early 1980s, it was not clear to me that a Sri Lankan Tamil family without any political involvement would face persecution, or an unreasonable level of personal risk, if forced to return to Sri Lanka. Were the NGOs supporting the Tamil cause justified in urging the British government to allow all Tamils to stay in the UK, regardless of their personal situation? Then some Tamil political leaders based in London became involved in the campaign to allow Tamils to stay; they encouraged some young Tamil men who were being held in detention on a ship in the port of Harwich to go on hunger strike, to protest their detention. At BRC we were campaigning vigorously for all those being held on the ship to be let off it, but our efforts became mixed up in the debate over the fate of the Tamils on hunger strike.

So, having visited the Tamils on the ship at Harwich, I went to the home of one of the Tamil leaders and asked him to call off the hunger strike. He made a brief effort to persuade me that the boys were on strike of their own volition, but when I told him that, if the strike did not end quickly, I would have to make it more widely known how the young asylum-seekers had been manipulated by him and his political colleagues, he agreed to see what he could do. The hunger strike was abandoned a few days later.

A few days after my visit and the end of the hunger strike, the east coast of England was hit by a violent storm and the ship holding the asylum-seekers was blown off its mooring in the middle of the night. Fortunately, it ran aground on the other side of the port, without hitting anything. The Home Office minister immediately ordered the removal of the detainees from the ship to a facility on land. Soon after that, the Tamils were released.

European consultations

Governments and NGOs all across Europe were facing similar problems. Government officials dealing with these issues met regularly with their counterparts from other European countries. The NGOs needed to do the same. Denmark and Norway had Refugee Councils like ours, but every European country had one or more NGOs working on these issues.

In 1974, a group of five European NGOs had set up the European Consultation on Refuges and Exiles (ECRE), an informal group with a part-time secretary based at one of the Dutch NGOs. The group met once a year. By 1984, many European NGOs had recognised the need for more regular meetings and a more permanent secretariat with full-time staff. The ECRE Secretariat moved into the BRC's offices in London and my good friend, Philip Rudge, agreed to run it. Among his many accomplishments, Philip speaks fluent French, German and Spanish. ECRE became a privileged interlocutor with UNHCR and the European institutions, and Philip was able to provide valuable support to NGOs in many European countries who were faced with the same problems. ECRE is now called the European Council on Refugees and Exiles, is based in Brussels, and has 69 member organisations in 30 countries.

ECRE played an invaluable role in helping NGOs in different European countries both to improve their services for people seeking asylum and to stand up to their governments. ECRE is another example, after the CCSDPT in Thailand described in the previous chapter, of the importance of associations of NGOs in international humanitarian work.

Links with home

One of the dilemmas of working with refugees is that the focus on their plight can distract attention from the situation of the people still living in the countries from which the refugees are fleeing. The BRC intervened and made representations on behalf of a few hundred asylum-seekers from Iraq and Iran, but we did little to uncover or denounce what now appears to have been a cynical indifference by European and American governments to a war that would leave millions dead. We agonised over the plight of Tamils coming from Sri Lanka, but we did little to push for serious international initiatives to prevent the communal violence between Sinhalese and Tamils from growing and sowing the kind of death and destruction that ravaged Sri Lanka for more than 20 years.

There are many more such examples. Perhaps the refugee lobbies were too successful. For governments, gestures made towards refugees were easy and cost little. Diplomatic or, heaven forbid, military interventions to address the situation in the country producing the refugees were far more difficult, particularly in a Cold War environment, which had effectively frozen the mechanism for dispute resolution foreseen in the UN Charter for the Security Council.

Often, the refugees themselves understood this dilemma better than we did. They were constantly confronted by the difference between what was happening to them and what was happening to those who had remained behind. Many of them were deeply frustrated by the difficulty of persuading people in Britain to focus on what was happening in their home countries. Chileans wondered how we could allow General Pinochet to carry on his murderous oppression; Ethiopians wondered the same about Mengistu. One of the symptoms of Post-Traumatic Stress Disorder (PTSD) is 'survivor's guilt'. Many refugees in Britain felt that, in a sense, they had left their compatriots to die, and that they, and their compatriots in other asylum countries, were the only survivors.

As an anthropologist, and with my personal connections to the refugee community from Laos, I felt this dilemma powerfully. How can one best help refugees to draw public attention to the situation back home? I never found a complete answer, but one thing that certainly helped were the community groups that refugees were able to set up, often with our help.

Helping refugees settle

Unlike most other European countries, British services for refugees and asylum-seekers are primarily the responsibility of local authorities. The appropriate entitlements of people seeking asylum were, and still are, a matter for constant debate with central government. Should asylum-seekers be entitled to housing provided by the local authority, if that would deprive local people in need? What should be the limits, if any, to the entitlement of asylum-seekers to education and health provision? And should asylum-seekers have the right to work, while awaiting the result of their applications? We argued that the dignity of the individual was paramount. If asylum-seekers were decently housed, able to work and take courses, they would be better prepared for the future, whether they were allowed to stay in Britain or had to return home. It would also cost the government less if asylum-seekers worked, than if they were locked up in detention centres at tax-payers' expense.

In spite of the Conservative government's suspicion of the motives and intentions of many asylum-seekers, and in spite of its concern that a liberal policy would encourage others to come to Britain to try their luck, we were broadly successful in persuading the government to allow asylum-seekers to work, attend courses and have access to health care. The government recognised, however reluctantly, that a liberal policy would reduce the problems that they and local authorities had to face, and improve the circumstances of the families concerned. During this period at least, this policy stood up against the cries of those who feared it would encourage more to come. The popular press liked the watery images; we were in danger, they told us, of being 'deluged' by 'floods' of asylum-seekers.

In the 1990s, under a Labour government, when the number of new asylum applications rose sharply, many of these hard-won advantages were rolled back.

In 1951, three school teachers, one of whom was Joyce Pearce, brought three Latvian refugee children from a camp in Germany to the Ockenden house near Woking in Surrey for education. Inspired by the success of this first project, they founded the Ockenden Venture in 1955. By 1981, Ockenden had become one of the main NGOs receiving the Vietnamese boat people accepted by the British government from the camps in Southeast Asia. Joyce was a formidable advocate for the rights of refugees, and particularly refugee children. The Ockenden Venture had been built on private charitable donations, but, like many other successful NGOs, it grew into a powerful voice for the uprooted thanks to government funding for its resettlement work.

Alongside Ockenden, the Save the Children Fund (SCF) also ran a reception programme for Vietnamese boat people. In 1981 two SCF staff members, Colin Hodgetts and Julia Meiklejohn, founded Refugee Action, which took over SCF's programme and promoted the idea that refugee communities should lead the efforts to support their own resettlement. This approach was given a huge boost from an unlikely source, the European Commission (EC).

Alan Phillips, BRC's deputy director, was able to negotiate a major series of grants from the EC, beginning in 1982, under which BRC acted as a managing agent for the Community Programme. Under this scheme, refugee community groups and other NGOs supporting refugees in the UK were allotted places; these places allowed unemployed people to be recruited and paid an allowance for working on the programme. The organisation employing the people received a small fee to cover administrative costs.

Before BRC agreed to take part in the programme, there were heated internal debates over the ethics of the scheme. Could we justify employing people to whom we were paying an allowance rather than a salary? Was this an acceptable substitute for 'real' jobs? The problem with the arguments against the scheme was that there were no 'real' jobs available for the kind of people who joined the programme. If there had been other jobs available, the scheme would have had no takers. Those who objected were eventually over-ruled. There was no shortage of candidates for the places.

The Community Programme played an enormously important role in enabling civil society groups, based in the refugee communities, to get started. Once the funding ceased, some of the groups folded, but others had acquired enough momentum to keep going with funding from local authorities and other sources. The scheme allowed community groups supporting refugees of all the major nationalities to offer advice and help to new arrivals or those who were still struggling to cope with life in a new country.

It is hard for many of us to appreciate the loneliness of a middle-aged man or woman, used to a lively family life in a tropical country, living most of the day alone in a cold council flat, half a world away from family, friends and familiar surroundings, and unable to speak English. The community groups were able to bring some comfort to such people, while giving those employed on the scheme an invaluable introduction to work in Britain.

Of the 19,000 refugees from Vietnam who came to Britain between 1975 and 1995, most came from camps for boat people in Southeast Asia; but, from the early 1980s onwards increasing numbers began to arrive under the so-called Orderly Departure Programme (ODP), designed by UNHCR, the government of Vietnam and the countries of resettlement to discourage Vietnamese who wanted to leave the country from doing so illegally and dangerously by boat, and to enable them to leave legally and directly from Vietnam. It was a groundbreaking initiative, but it did not stop the flow of boat people.

As the first families reached the UK under the new programme, it became clear what a terrible toll the refugee experience had taken on the boat people. I visited a centre being run by Refugee Action for Vietnamese refugees in the north of England. The manager told me how those arriving directly from Vietnam could not wait to get out and explore the town, to go shopping, study English and look for work. Their reactions were those of most people arriving in a new country to start a new life.

But the boat people were apathetic and lethargic, expecting everything to be organised for them, and seemingly lacking in initiative. Their experience as refugees on the seas and in the camps of Southeast Asia had knocked the stuffing out of them. They had been profoundly traumatised. I was greatly affected by this evidence of the damage that prolonged detention in camps can do to the human spirit and have tried to advocate since then for the maximum involvement of those receiving emergency aid in the administration of that aid. It is always better to allow families to cook their meals rather than eat from a communal kitchen, and it is never too soon to introduce education opportunities for children in camp settings.

Advocacy

BRC serviced four Regional Committees – for Africa, Asia, Europe and Latin America. These were forums where NGOs working with refugees in those regions met to share information and develop policy positions. The biggest NGOs – Christian Aid, Oxfam and Save the Children – were major players in the British voluntary sector and could get the attention of ministers when required.

Almost as soon as BRC came into existence, I received a call from the Overseas Development Administration (ODA), the government department dealing with international aid (now the Department for International Development, DfID). Would I come to a meeting with a number of the major NGOs to discuss the ODA's programme of small grants to NGOs for projects benefiting refugees around the world?

At the meeting I found the big three NGOs represented at senior level. After welcoming the establishment of the BRC, and me as its director, the ODA representative said that he would like BRC to advise the government on the distribution of the small grant fund. The government received a large number of applications and did not have the expertise to decide between them. What did the director of the BRC think of this proposal?

I glanced quickly round. Looks of horror had appeared on the faces of my NGO colleagues. With as light a tone as possible, I asked the ODA official if he wanted to kill off the BRC before it had even got started. Member NGOs had surely not set up the BRC with the idea that it would act as a filter for their grant applications. Another quick look around confirmed that I had passed my first test; the NGO representatives were smiling with relief.

While the NGOs did not expect the BRC to come between them and the British government's money, they did expect us to help them formulate common positions on refugee issues and communicate these positions to the government, as well as in international NGO forums and to the United Nations. To do that effectively, we would need to work closely with the chairs of our four regional committees.

Before my arrival, most chairs of the regional committees had been former British diplomats with an interest and past involvement in the region concerned, but one chair was David Ennals, a Labour Member of Parliament and government minister. During my first year, I attended all regional committee meetings and observed that David was a much more effective chair than his diplomatic colleagues on other committees. I developed the view, based admittedly on limited evidence, that politicians were likely to be more effective as chairs of such committees than retired diplomats. The diplomats were used to giving advice, but rarely took decisions on issues of policy. The politicians, on the other hand, were constantly required to make decisions on the basis of advice from civil servants, and then had to justify them to the electorate.

As chairs of our committees, politicians were more in tune with the political context in which we had to formulate and present our recommendations; if they were personally committed to an issue, they could often rally support from other members of their party. I made sure that the chairmanship of all committees was reviewed regularly, and when a vacancy occurred, encouraged my colleagues to identify parliamentarians of all major parties who could be persuaded to join us. Identifying the best people for important jobs is often the key to success in humanitarian operations. This issue is a major theme of this book.

International Council of Voluntary Agencies

Many of the issues that concerned BRC's regional committees related to the work of the UN system, and particularly UNHCR, so it was important that we acquired allies among NGOs which shared our concerns. The main way we did this was through our membership of the International Council of Voluntary Agencies (ICVA), based in Geneva. In 1981, ICVA also had a new director, a dynamic young American, Anthony (Tony) Koslowski.

ICVA had been founded in 1962 as a network of international NGOs working with refugees and on other humanitarian issues. It is governed by a general assembly of its member organisations, held once every three years. Its largest and most important members were a mix of secular organisations working with refugees, like the Danish and Norwegian Refugee Councils, and international faith-based humanitarian groups, like Catholic Relief Services, the Lutheran World Federation and the World Council of Churches.

The first ICVA General Assembly after Koslowski's appointment was held in Colombo in November 1982. The meeting has remained vividly in my memory, not only for the location, but for the sharp lesson in organisational dynamics that it provided.

Koslowski arrived in Colombo with six important new initiatives which he wanted the General Assembly to endorse. However, as each idea was presented, objections were raised, most often from the large faith-based organisations. Koslowski had not made sure that his key members were on board. On several issues, the refugee councils tried to rescue something for him, but each time one or other of the 'big boys' would stand up and apologetically re-affirm that their organisation did not feel that the idea was sufficiently thought through to be approved.

This experience taught me a lesson which has remained with me: when managing a council of member organisations, the best ideas are those that come from the members. Ideas can be planted; and success is more important than pride of ownership. Koslowski learned his lesson and came back strongly, but those who were there would not forget that day.

Internally Displaced Persons

As the number of refugee-generating conflicts grew during the 1980s, so did the number of conflicts causing displacement of people within countries' borders. The long Cold War saw a reduction in wars between states, but a rise in the number of wars within states. But while international law codified the rights of refugees who had fled their country, there was no legal framework to deal with 'internally displaced persons', or IDPs.

As described in Chapter 1, in Laos UNHCR had assisted IDPs to return home at the end of the conflict, using its 'good offices' at the request of the UN General Assembly and the Lao government. But UNHCR had no mandate to assist IDPs, nor did any other agency of the UN system. Of course, IDPs were by definition within the borders of their own state and so fell under the jurisdiction and protection of their national government. But there were many situations in which national governments were not in control of all their territory, or in which national governments were actively persecuting members of a particular political, social or ethnic group. BRC and other NGOs argued that in those situations IDPs were in no position to receive protection from their national authorities, and that UNHCR, or some other UN agency, should be given a mandate to advocate for their rights and to provide them with help.

Countries in which conflicts generated large numbers of IDPs during the 1980s included Afghanistan, Ethiopia, Mozambique, Nicaragua, Sri Lanka and Sudan. In each country, the UN adopted a different approach to planning and delivering humanitarian aid. In some cases, like Sudan, clearly defined arrangements were eventually agreed, and Operation Lifeline Sudan, led by UNICEF, with strong support from WFP, was set up in April 1989, to provide a framework for assistance to IDPs in the south who could not be assisted from Khartoum. In other situations, no specific arrangements were made, and UN country teams and NGOs did their best, which was often not enough to prevent much avoidable suffering.

Efforts to persuade UNHCR to move into this area of work were met with the response that they had no mandate, that they could only act where requested to use their good offices by the UN General Assembly or Secretary-General, and that countries rarely liked having UNHCR helping their own nationals. To invite UNHCR in was seen as an admission of a country's inability to control events on its own territory. Other solutions would have to be found.

This did not seem at all satisfactory. Eventually, BRC wrote to Viru Dayal, the chief of staff of Secretary-General Perez de Cuellar. He was a former UNHCR official and we thought that if anybody would be sympathetic to our idea, he would be. But we were naive. The General Assembly was never going to accept the idea of giving UNHCR a general mandate for IDPs. Another approach would be needed. That would emerge slowly over the following ten years. I would be able to watch it happen, first in Afghanistan and then in New York.

New International Humanitarian Order

In 1981, the UN General Assembly adopted its first resolution on the New International Humanitarian Order (NIHO). This was an attempt, promoted by the government of Jordan, to translate the ideas behind the concept of the New International Economic Order for the benefit of the humanitarian sector. In 1983, the Independent Commission on International Humanitarian Issues (ICIHI) was established, with Prince Sadruddin Aga Khan and Prince El Hassan bin Talal of Jordan as co-chairs and Zia Rizvi as secretary-general. They assembled a remarkable group of commissioners, including Robert McNamara, Sadako Ogata, David Owen, Salim A. Salim, Desmond Tutu, Simone Veil and Gough Whitlam. This reflected the seriousness with which people viewed the humanitarian emergencies of the time, and their frustration at their inability to respond adequately.

The Commission produced an overall report in 1985 called *Winning the Human Race?* It also published a number of thematic reports and books on issues from hunger to the environment. Perhaps the most widely read and praised was *Famine*, published in 1985. The BRC took the lead in writing the book on refugees and internal displacement, entitled *Refugees: the Dynamics of Displacement*. Jeff Crisp and a colleague wrote most of the chapters. I wrote one and edited the rest, and Zia Rizvi provided the finishing touches. The book addressed the issues facing IDPs alongside those facing refugees who had left their country, and pointed out how this difference in status was leading to a vast disparity in the quality of protection and assistance reaching the two groups.

The Princes Sadruddin and Talal and the other commissioners provided the big names behind the Commission, but Zia Rizvi and a small staff in Geneva did the work. My own feeling has long been that the Commission's work was considerably more influential than people gave it credit for at the time, or indeed since. It captured the key new ideas of its time on a range of issues and presented them to both general and specialist audiences. All its publications were translated and issued in all the official UN languages.

In 1991, the UN General Assembly adopted resolution 46/182 on the coordination of humanitarian assistance. This resolution created the post of Emergency Relief Coordinator and the Inter-Agency Standing Committee. The Independent Commission on International Humanitarian Issues could have claimed credit for having laid the groundwork for this landmark resolution. It was a chance to conclude the General Assembly's debate on the New International Humanitarian Order and declare victory. Sadly, Rizvi did not see it this way and insisted that the debate on the New International Humanitarian Order should continue. Jordan supported this and the item remained on the General Assembly's agenda for several more years, with little relevance and few participants.

Coordinator and operator

As the BRC settled down, I began to hear the complaint that we had created a built-in conflict of interest for ourselves. We were the coordinators, but we were also one of the operators providing services to refugees in the UK. For instance, we were administering the Community Programme, but we were also benefiting from it by allocating places to ourselves. I would reply that we had assigned these two tasks to different parts of the organisation and that if the other NGOs had a problem with any of our decisions, they could raise the issue in the relevant BRC committees of which they were members. I would point out that this form of redress was not available to the BRC itself when it was unhappy with a decision taken by one of its partners.

These discussions raised the difficult, and always contentious, question of the extent to which a coordinating body can also be legitimately involved in operations. This was a question which I would have to confront repeatedly during my next assignments.

Turning point

In June 1988, Sadruddin Aga Khan came to London and, while we were in the British Red Cross Society for a meeting at which he described his new job as coordinator of UN assistance to Afghanistan, he asked me to join his team, initially in Islamabad in Pakistan.

It was immediately clear that this was a turning point, for both personal life and career. Keolila and I had to decide whether we would take our young family out to Pakistan and, almost inevitably, more moves after that, or politely decline Sadruddin's offer and decide to look for other opportunities in Britain. Sadruddin was persuasive, I was ready to move on from the BRC, my parents had both recently died, and Keolila would be a bit closer to her family in Laos, so we said yes.

Afghanistan

Printing date: April 2014

Sources: UNHCR - UNJLC - UNSDI-T

Feedback: mapping@unhcr.org

Filename: AFG_InsetMap_Publication.wor

The boundaries and names shown and the designations used on this map do not imply official endorsement or acceptance by the United Nations.

⊛ Capital
• Towns of Interest
——— International boundary
     Administrative boundaries
– – Provincial Border
········ Line of control as promulgated in the 1972 SIMLA agreement

Figure 3 Map of Afghanistan.

4

AFGHANISTAN
The missed opportunities

On 15 February 1989, the last Soviet soldier left Afghanistan, crossing the bridge over the Amu Darya River back into what is now Uzbekistan, but was then still the USSR.

The international effort for Afghanistan in the 1980s and 1990s was characterised by a passionate intensity. Afghans had been subjected to the most horrendous suffering, because the leaders of great powers, thousands of miles away, had allowed their Cold War disputes to be played out in a hot war across Afghanistan's stark landscape. Many UN and NGO representatives brought to the country a kind of manic determination to do something, anything, to help alleviate the Afghans' pain.

Afghanistan, like Laos, is a mountainous, land-locked country, whose population is made up of several ethnic groups, most of which are present in greater numbers in the country's neighbours. Of the six largest groups, only the Hazara in the central mountains around Bamyan are the product of an earlier and longer migration from China. The Pushtoon are more numerous in Pakistan, the Tajik in Tajikistan, the Uzbeks in Uzbekistan and the Turkmen in Turkmenistan.

The foundation of modern Afghanistan can be credited to Ahmed Shah Durrani, who took power in 1747 and brought the territory of the modern-day nation under his rule. Since then, Afghan nationalism has been kept alive, with varying success, by kings and their advisers, through a mixture of consensus, coercion, bribery and forced migration. For the elite, the symbol of the Afghan nation was Kabul, the great capital, the one place where individuals could lose their provincial and tribal identity and become urban Afghan citizens.

The turning point for Afghanistan came in the years after World War II when the government of King Zahir Shah (r. 1933–73) opened

75

up the country to embassies and teachers from around the world and encouraged young Afghans to take up the offers of scholarships being made by the US, Europe, the USSR and the Islamic schools of the Middle East.

With hindsight, it seems tragically inevitable that, with the departure of the king who had held the country together for 40 years, the three different worldviews, represented by the capitalist West, the communist Soviet Union and the Islamic Middle East, would compete for dominance. Afghanistan's strategic location ensured that each group of returning scholars found willing sponsors for their political ambitions in the various embassies in Kabul and in the capitals of neighbouring countries.

After the overthrow of King Zahir by his cousin Daoud in 1973, and Daoud's five years of presidential rule (1973–78), the first opportunity to impose its distinct political vision on the country fell to the communists, supported by the USSR. When the communists split into two factions, the Soviet Union sent troops to Kabul in December 1979 to support their protégés. The communists' ill-considered efforts to forcibly impose modern ideas about education for girls on the tribal villages sparked the first resistance movements. These *mujahideen* groups grew during the 1980s from spontaneous uprisings to defend tribal values into increasingly organised operations. The Islamist ideology of President Zia Ul Haq of Pakistan ensured that the bulk of the US funds and weaponry, channelled by the CIA through Pakistan's Inter-Services Intelligence (ISI), went to Afghan leaders espousing an Islamist political ideology.

Afghans who supported a more moderate 'Western' vision found themselves under threat from the Islamist groups in Peshawar, in Pakistan's North-West Frontier (now Khyber Pukhtoonkwa) province, where hundreds of thousands of Afghans had fled to escape war and communist rule. Some moderate leaders were murdered, others went into exile and some buried their political ambitions for the time being by joining the international NGOs set up in Peshawar to send aid to villages in the *mujahideen*-controlled areas of the countryside.

By 1988, the Soviet Union had had enough. The delivery to *mujahideen* commanders of American hand-held Stinger missiles capable of bringing down aircraft as they came in to land demoralised the whole Soviet effort. The impending collapse of the Soviet Union, itself accelerated by the Afghan debacle, pushed the Soviets to seek a way out. The Geneva Accords of April 1988 were the result.

The Geneva Accords provided an exit route for the USSR, but did nothing to resolve the fundamental disagreement among Afghans, their neighbours and their neighbours' sponsors over what kind of country Afghanistan should become. When the Soviet Union collapsed and the Berlin Wall came down, many countries took advantage of the new friendly relations between Washington and Moscow to sort out their conflicts. Perhaps because Afghans were fighting over three worldviews rather than two, their country did not benefit from the thaw between Washington and Moscow. The problem was handed over to the United Nations to provide humanitarian relief, while Kabul fell first in 1992 to the *mujahideen* and then in 1996 to the Taliban. On 11 September 2001, Osama Bin Laden catapulted the country back into the international spotlight, from which, in 2014, it has still not escaped.

Humanitarian coordination

In the 1980s, UN humanitarian operations were routinely coordinated by a 'lead UN agency', usually UNHCR or UNICEF. Otherwise, UN efforts in countries emerging from conflict were coordinated by the UN resident coordinator. In 1988, the establishment of the post of Emergency Relief Coordinator, and today's UN architecture for co-ordination of humanitarian assistance, was still three years in the future.

Afghanistan in 1988 posed unique challenges. The withdrawal of Soviet forces left the Kabul government of President Najibullah without external military support. Most international observers thought that, after the departure of Soviet forces, it would only be a matter of weeks before Najibullah's government would fall and the *mujahideen* would take over. A massive international effort would be needed to provide humanitarian aid, help the refugees in neighbouring countries return and start the reconstruction of destroyed infrastructure. UN Secretary-General Perez de Cuellar decided that, in these circumstances, neither the 'lead agency' nor the resident coordinator formula would be adequate and invited Sadruddin to head up a self-contained office within the UN Secretariat, reporting directly to him.

Sadruddin decided that if he was to maintain his impartiality towards the parties to the conflict and their international sponsors, he could not establish his headquarters in the region, so he set up shop in Geneva. The charming Villa La Pelouse in the grounds of the Palais des Nations became the headquarters of the United Nations Office for the Coordination of Assistance Programmes relating to Afghanistan (UNOCA). Sadruddin assembled a team of staff, invited the major UN agencies to second senior people to the team and set out on a first trip to the region to negotiate agreements with each of Afghanistan's neighbours – Iran, Pakistan and the Soviet Union – for UNOCA to set up offices. It was on his return from that trip that he asked me to leave for Pakistan as soon as possible and to be his chief of mission there.

As the UNOCA team discussed how we should operate in and around Afghanistan, two central ideas kept surfacing. First, if we were to deliver aid to all parts of the country, we would have to persuade all the fighting factions to agree to the passage of aid through the areas they controlled to people in need in other parts of the country, even if they were at war with those people. In other words, we would need to introduce the humanitarian principles of humanity, impartiality and neutrality. This approach, which we called 'humanitarian consensus', was extremely ambitious.

Up until that point, the whole approach to aid to the people of Afghanistan had been overtly partisan. Aid to people in the areas controlled by the Afghan government came from the Soviet bloc, while aid to people living in areas controlled by the *mujahideen* groups came from the US and its European allies. Several of the NGOs based in Peshawar that delivered aid across the border had included the word 'solidarity' in their names, indicating that the motivation for their work was political as well as humanitarian. The idea that aid might be delivered impartially, on the basis of need, was new.

The second idea, closely linked to the first, was dictated both by politics and geography. The UN operation should be able to deliver assistance from all of the neighbouring countries, Iran, Pakistan and the Soviet Union. This concept was known as 'humanitarian encirclement'. It meant that aid should be able to enter Afghanistan across all the country's borders.

In mid-August 1988, Sadruddin came to Pakistan for formal meetings with the government. He needed the government's approval for us to operate across the border from Peshawar and Quetta into eastern and southern Afghanistan. The highlight of the visit was to be a meeting with President Zia Ul Haq in Islamabad. His word to the military and particularly to the Inter-Services Intelligence (ISI), which ran the clandestine CIA-funded operations in support of the *mujahideen*, would be critical.

The meeting was a success. After a discussion lasting over an hour, the President agreed to set up the links we needed with the military and the provincial authorities. After the meeting we were invited to lunch. The atmosphere was relaxed.

The next day we were having lunch at the hotel and going over plans for a visit to Quetta the following day, when we received the first reports that there had been a plane crash. It was soon confirmed that President Zia, many of his top military officers and the US Ambassador had all died in the crash. We had been the last foreign visitors to see the President alive.

Zia Ul Haq's death ushered in the return of democracy in Pakistan and the first election victory of Benazir Bhutto. Benazir, however, would have little influence over the government's policy towards Afghanistan. That remained firmly in the hands of the military establishment, with the backing of the United States.

For the Afghan operation, Sadruddin brought back Zia Rizvi, the brilliant Pakistani who had been his chief of staff at UNHCR and my boss in Thailand (Chapter 2). He and Rizvi had an unusual relationship. Rizvi is a man of quite extraordinary intellectual capacity, driven by ambition and a contempt for sloppy thinking; this could make him appear arrogant and impolite. Sadruddin and Rizvi could be contemptuous of the other in private, but each needed the other to do what he could not do on his own. In Sadruddin's case, he needed Rizvi to provide the intellectual substance to his diplomatic and political initiatives. In Rizvi's case, he needed Sadruddin to provide the top cover for his brilliant ideas.

Rizvi was behind most of the ideas that drove the UNOCA operation in its first three years. Sadruddin opened all the doors to power. It would be my job to put together a team to carry through UNOCA's programme, across the border, from the Pakistan side.

As I settled into the first UNOCA office in Islamabad, I began to identify the individuals and institutions with whom we would need to cooperate and who would need to be convinced of the merits of the 'humanitarian consensus' and 'humanitarian encirclement' approach. There were a lot of them.

Within the government of Pakistan, responsibility for Afghan questions was divided between three ministries, Foreign Affairs, States and Frontier Regions (SAFRON) and Defence. The Foreign Ministry was part of all discussions, but was not influential. SAFRON was the home of the commissioners for Afghan refugees in Peshawar and Quetta. They were the key interlocutors for UNHCR on everything to do with the Afghan refugees in Pakistan. Within the military, by far the most significant actor was the Inter-Services Intelligence (ISI). It was this outfit which President Zia had put in charge of support for the Afghan resistance to the Soviet military intervention. They were the vehicle for distributing funds and weapons from the CIA and other donors to the *mujahideen* groups. We would need to build up good relations with all these Pakistani players, but particularly the ISI.

President Zia had authorised seven Afghan political groups to set up offices in Peshawar. Four of these were Pushtoon groups with strong Islamist leanings, but cleverly the President had also allowed a Tajik party, a Hazara Shi'i group and a Royalist group to set up offices in Peshawar, where he could keep an eye on them.

President Zia deliberately divided the money and weapons among a number of competing leaders and prevented the formation of a unified opposition to the communist government in Kabul. The largest share of the resources went to the most unsavoury, least popular and most ruthless of all, Gulbuddin Hekmatyar, leader of the Hezbi Islami (G) party. Impeccably dressed and icily polite, Hekmatyar espoused a radical Islamist version of Pushtoon nationalism. He eliminated his opponents, particularly the unarmed liberal intellectuals, without compunction. But he was savvy enough not to bite the hand that fed him. He would take instructions from the ISI.

The favourite *mujahideen* leader among the foreign NGOs, and particularly with the French, was the charismatic Ahmed Shah Masood, the Lion of Panshir, the top field commander of the Jamiat Islami party, led by Burhannudin Rabbani, an Islamist professor of Islamic theology. The Jamiat was a predominantly Tajik party representing the dominant ethnic group in the north-east of the country. The ISI tolerated Rabbani and his party's offices in Peshawar, but kept them constantly short of resources. Rabbani and Hekmatyar had been radical Islamist student leaders at Kabul University and were bitter rivals. Where Hekmatyar was scheming and duplicitous, Rabbani often seemed bemused by what was going on around him, and was inevitably overshadowed by the glamour and mystique surrounding his top field commander, Ahmed Shah Masood.

Among the remaining five leaders, Pir Gailani, Abdul Rasool Sayyaf and Sibghatullah Mojaddedi had all been minor personalities in Afghan society, distinguished by their place in Sunni religious circles. A dapper, articulate young Hamid Karzai was a member of Mojaddedi's group, popular with the foreigners on account of his personal charm and excellent English. Maulvi Younus Khales led a Pushtoon Islamist group in the south of the country, and Ayatollah Mohseni led the Harakat Islami, a group representing the Shi'i Hazara population of the mountainous central region.

While President Zia authorised these seven to operate from offices in Peshawar and Quetta, the Iranian government, in a rather obvious attempt at one-upmanship, hosted eight Afghan opposition groups. In truth, several of the Iran-based groups existed only in name, and all were significantly less well-resourced than their counterparts in Pakistan.

The chief function of the seven groups in Peshawar was to channel weapons and other resources to the 'commanders' in Afghanistan who professed loyalty to their party. With few exceptions, this loyalty was based on immediate self-interest. Commanders were constantly negotiating for a larger share of the cake, and the most adventurous and ambitious switched parties whenever they were able to negotiate a better deal with another leader. We would have to get to know this complex network of parties and commanders.

The United Nations development agencies had kept their offices open in Kabul throughout the 1980s. UNDP, FAO, WHO and others had continued to run programmes, mainly in Kabul, but also in the main cities under government control (Herat, Kandahar, Jalalabad and Mazar-i-Sharif). In Pakistan, UNHCR had opened its offices in 1979, to respond to the arrival of the first Afghan refugees. Until the establishment of UNOCA in 1988, no UN agency had been involved in working in the areas of rural Afghanistan outside the control of the government in Kabul. That had been the role of the NGOs.

Alongside the heavily guarded compounds of the *mujahideen* leaders in Peshawar stood the offices of a remarkable range of international NGOs. Very few of them bore the familiar names of the organisations normally encountered in humanitarian emergencies around the world. Many bore the name of the country of their foundation, like the Norwegian and Swedish Committees for Afghanistan. Most were openly committed to the *mujahideen* cause of defeating the pro-communist government in Kabul. They had been founded by activists shocked by news reports of Soviet military action in the country and inspired by tales of heroic resistance by Afghan fighters. They had relied for years on secrecy and disguise, and the tacit approval of the Pakistan government, to make their deliveries across the border to the communities in the areas controlled by the *mujahideen* commanders.

When I went to Peshawar to address a meeting of over 100 representatives of these NGOs, my suggestion that we could all be open and public about what we were doing was met with incredulity. How could we believe that the Kabul government would not target our aid convoys if we told them where we were going?

In spite of the scepticism of the NGOs, over the following two years the whole nature of the international aid effort in Afghanistan changed. In place of heavily armed Soviet deliveries down the Salang highway to Kabul and secretive NGO cross-border missions from Pakistan, there gradually emerged a more or less integrated effort that transported supplies in from all neighbouring countries and crossed internal lines between various warring factions.

While UNOCA developed its relations with the governments of Afghanistan and its neighbours, as well as with the *mujahideen* parties and the international NGOs in Peshawar, its principal partners were of course the agencies of the United Nations system. The arrival of UNOCA allowed these agencies to develop programmes in the rural areas of Afghanistan and to run them from offices in Islamabad or Peshawar. In several cases, this set off internal competition between the offices responsible for the agencies' work in Kabul and the emergency divisions at agency headquarters which managed the new cross-border programmes. WHO's programme in Kabul, for example, was managed from the WHO Regional Office in Egypt, but the WHO programme in eastern Afghanistan was run from the WHO headquarters in Geneva.

Alongside the government and *mujahideen* parties in Afghanistan, the governments of neighbouring countries, the NGOs and the agencies of the UN system, UNOCA also needed to develop good relations with the embassies of donor countries and with the media, both local and international. This task was similar to that faced by all UN humanitarian coordinators, but the complexity of the *mujahideen* parties and the number and variety of international and Afghan NGOs gave us an unusually large list of players who needed to be kept happy.

While the international NGOs operated out of Peshawar and Quetta, the UNOCA office in Pakistan was in the capital, Islamabad, with sub-offices in Peshawar and Quetta. In Iran, UNOCA opened up in Teheran; but in the Soviet Union, UNOCA's team worked from Termez, the border town on the Amu Darya River, in what is now Uzbekistan. The fourth UNOCA field office was, of course, in Kabul.

Sadruddin convened several meetings of participating UN agencies at the Villa La Pelouse in Geneva. At these meetings we tried to divide up the responsibility for each of the major sectors of activity, such as health, education and agriculture, among our UN partners. At an early meeting, UNOCA tried to persuade UNDP and FAO that one or other should take overall responsibility for irrigation, an important sub-sector of the agriculture programme. But both agencies insisted that that was unnecessary, and that they would coordinate among themselves. We reluctantly conceded. By 1996, irrigation projects were being carried out not only by FAO and UNDP, but by UNCHS (Habitat), UNDCP (Drug Control Programme), UNHCR, UNICEF and WFP as well. In practice, agencies would do anything for which they could raise funds, whether or not they had expertise in that sector. Each agency would approach its preferred donors to fund these activities and we were powerless to prevent it. This kind of fragmentation of effort in specific sectors of activity was a major reason for the introduction of the 'cluster' system as part of the humanitarian reforms of 2005.

Sadruddin resigned as UN coordinator in December 1990 after two and a half years in the job. The Secretary-General used this as an opportunity to make the first of several changes to the way in which responsibility for political, humanitarian and development operations was divided up. UNOCA became the UN Office for the Coordination of Humanitarian Assistance to Afghanistan (UNOCHA) and was placed under the Personal Representative of the Secretary-General (PRSG), who was also responsible for the UN's political office. The table below shows how five different arrangements for the management of the UN's political, humanitarian and development operations were tried out between 1988 and 2001. It would not be until 2000, and Kofi Annan's reforms described in Chapter 6, that these arrangements would become predictable.

Coordination of UN operations in Afghanistan, 1988–2001.

	Political	Humanitarian	Development
1988–90	PRSG	UNOCA	UNOCA
1990–92	PRSG	PRSG	UNDP
1992–94	PRSG	PRSG	UNDP
1995–96	PRSG	UNOCHA	UNDP
1996–2001	PRSG	UNRC/HC	UNRC/HC

When, in 1991, UNOCHA was placed under the supervision of Benon Sevan, the Personal Representative of the Secretary-General, some people expressed concern that aid might be manipulated to promote the UN's political agenda. But by that time, the *modus operandi* of UNOCHA was so well established that it would have been extremely difficult to manipulate. We did not need to remind Sevan, or his successor Sotirios Mousouris, what the consequences would be for the overall UN effort if the humanitarian operation lost its reputation for impartiality.

In any crisis situation, much depends on how people work together. In Afghanistan, it was my good fortune to work from 1991 to 1996 alongside David Lockwood. While fulfilling the role of resident coordinator with great skill, and taking every opportunity to prepare the UN system and the Afghan government for the time when development and reconstruction would be possible, he always accepted that the humanitarian operation was the UN's priority and supported UNOCHA's role in coordinating it.

Chapter 9 looks in more detail at the systemic issues surrounding the coordination of humanitarian assistance programmes. Chapter 6 looks at the debates in New York over the appropriate arrangements in the field to govern relations between the political, humanitarian and development parts of the UN system.

De-mining

Nothing in my career has given me more pleasure and excitement than my association with the efforts to rid poor countries of the anti-personnel landmines that lie in wait, ready to rip a leg from a passing child. Chapter 7 is devoted to this topic, but the story begins here in Afghanistan.

In the report that I submitted to Sadruddin on 31 August 1988, two weeks after his visit to Pakistan and the death of President Zia, the first and longest section was devoted to the topic of 'de-mining'. Meetings had been held with senior Pakistani military officers to plan a training programme for volunteers among the Afghan refugees, so that they could be taught how to clear their own villages of landmines, once they returned home.

The hospitals run by the Red Cross in Peshawar and Quetta were stark testimony to the horrors being inflicted on Afghan villagers by anti-personnel landmines. In village after village in the Afghan provinces bordering Pakistan, Soviet and Afghan government forces had driven the civilian populations either into the cities or across the border into Pakistan, so that they could not provide bases and support for the *mujahideen* fighters. Then, to prevent the villagers from returning, they had laid thousands of anti-personnel landmines.

These landmines were mainly of three types, all made in the Soviet Union – the POM-Z, an explosive charge which propels fragments off a stake planted in the ground and is activated by a trip-wire; the PMN, a mine buried just under the surface that detonates when stepped on, and the 'butterfly' mines, scattered from large tubes, either fired from mortars or dropped from aircraft. These were cheap, simple, but not normally deadly. Anti-personnel mines are not designed to kill. They are intended to incapacitate, so that the wounded soldier will be a burden to his comrades and slow the unit down. Used against civilians, they spread terror, confronting families with the awful task of caring for a child who has lost a limb or an eye.

Of course, in spite of the designers' intentions, many AP mine victims did bleed to death before they could reach a hospital. Dilapidated taxis made the excruciatingly bumpy day-long journey as quickly as they could over pot-holed tracks to try to reach a clinic before the patient died. They did not always succeed.

To compound the problem, the *mujahideen* had themselves laid mines, but for the most part these were anti-tank, or anti-vehicle mines, many made in the US or the UK, intended to blow up Soviet or Afghan government military vehicles. They would not detonate if people walked over them, but would blow up under any bus or pick-up truck carrying refugees returning home.

What should the UN do? If the departure of Soviet forces led to a mass movement of refugees back across the border from the camps in Pakistan, there would be carnage. Although the *mujahideen* were aware of the problem, most villagers had left their homes before the anti-personnel mines had been laid there and had not returned since. However many legless refugees there were in the camps, individual Afghans did not seem concerned about the dangers of these hidden killers. A survey of 1,500 refugees in camps in Pakistan undertaken in the summer of 1988 had shown that 100 per cent of those responding intended to return to their own villages, many of which were certainly mined.

On top of this, many of the *mujahideen* commanders who had laid the anti-tank mines on the roads that returning refugees would need to use, had been killed, moved to other areas, or had simply forgotten where they had laid the mines. Roads would need to be closed and by-passed until they were cleared.

We concluded that we should focus on two top priorities: train as many Afghan volunteers as possible to locate and destroy the landmines; and alert as many civilians as possible to the risks that they would face, by training them to recognise and avoid those risks. We would need a mine clearance training programme and a mine awareness programme.

A lively debate ensued among military experts from Britain, France, Turkey and the US over what was required to train somebody to be a de-miner. The professional military engineers from Europe said they would need three to six months. The American Special Forces team said it could be done in two weeks. We went with the Americans.

On 11 February 1989, four days before the departure of the last Soviet soldier from Afghanistan, we opened the first training camp at Risalpur, near Peshawar. A few weeks later, a second camp opened at Baleli, near Quetta in Baluchistan. The basic mine clearance training programme was given over a period of two weeks by teams of military officers seconded to the UN by governments of interested countries, assisted by interpreters, many of them Pushto speakers from Pakistan's military. Over the following years, military trainers would be provided by Australia, Canada, Denmark, France, Italy, New Zealand, Norway, Turkey, the UK and the US. Some of these countries also provided teams of mine awareness trainers, who offered classes in the refugee camps to families planning to return home. Canada sent teams of women officers, so that they could offer training to groups of women in the camps, who could not be taught by men.

When the de-miners graduated at the end of their two-week course, they received a simple kit, put together by the US Special Forces team that had devised the course. They insisted that a simple treasure hunter's metal detector from Radio Shack costing less than $50 was as effective as a sophisticated $1,000 detector. They may have been right from a technical point of view, but what they did not explain to us before the detectors arrived was that the Radio Shack detector was half the length of a normal detector, so that the operator had to be on hands and knees, and, crucially, that it came in a lurid pink colour that did not exactly chime with the macho image of a serious, bearded ex-*mujahideen* fighter leading his family back to their ancestral village. The detectors began to appear on the stalls of the Peshawar bazaar.

Over 11,000 Afghan men went through the basic de-mining course. While I have no doubt that some of these men used the training in Afghanistan – indeed, there was immediate anecdotal evidence that casualties from landmines among the *mujahideen* operating around government-controlled cities like Jalalabad and Herat decreased as the fighters became more skilled at dealing with the mines without blowing themselves up – the programme's key failure was that it did not offer an organisational framework in which the trainees could operate after completing the course. Although we certainly harboured unrealistic expectations about what the Afghans could do on their own with their basic kits, we soon began to recognise that we needed an organisational structure of some sort.

The United Nations could not fund and support mine clearance operations undertaken by Afghan military forces, whether those forces were from the government in Kabul or aligned with the *mujahideen* parties in Peshawar. There was no UN agency that had ever managed or funded mine clearance operations in other countries. There were no international NGOs doing it either, although an organisation called HALO Trust had just been set up by a retired British colonel, Colin Mitchell, universally referred to in British military circles as 'Mad Mitch', owing to earlier exploits in the deserts of Yemen. He had set up an office in Kabul. Another retired British soldier, Rae McGrath, had persuaded the NGO, World Vision, to fund a small operation in Paktia province from a base in Peshawar.

Neither World Vision nor HALO Trust would be able to provide an institutional home for the scale of programme that we had to contemplate. We needed a way of organising and supporting teams of de-miners that would be efficient, effective and acceptable to both the Afghan government in Kabul and the *mujahideen* parties, as well as neighbouring countries and international donors. The idea that Rizvi came up with was to support the establishment of Afghan NGOs.

There were many sceptics. How would we identify the Afghans to manage these NGOs? How would we prevent them from stealing the money, employing only their relatives and de-mining only the areas where they had identified business opportunities? We started slowly. We invited prominent Afghans in Peshawar to nominate possible candidates. The first to be identified was Kefayatullah Eblagh. He was the son of a well-known and highly respected Afghan lawyer, who had never been affiliated with a political faction. Kefayatullah himself had the rank of colonel, had links to Professor Rabbani's Jamiat Islami, but was also respected amongst Afghan Pushtoons in Peshawar. We sat down to negotiate.

The deal, as it developed over the months after our first meeting, was simple. UNOCA would fund the de-mining activities of Kefayatullah's NGO, provided that he accepted our conditions. Kefayatullah, and the other NGO directors who came after him, agreed to have all their senior staff appointments approved by UNOCA; to adopt a common salary scale for all their staff, including themselves; to appoint as their finance officer somebody (initially of Pakistani nationality) identified by UNOCA; to employ only de-miners who had been through the UN's basic training and the additional pre-deployment courses that were soon introduced; to send their de-mining teams to sites identified by the UN after reviewing surveys carried out by another Afghan NGO; to appoint executive committees of prominent Afghan personalities, to whom they would report regularly; and to make public announcements only with UNOCA's agreement.

Kefayatullah's Afghan Technical Consultants (ATC) began with just two teams of 30 men each clearing a road in Kunar province, one of two provinces totally under *mujahideen* control. We waited for Kabul to protest that the UN was supporting military operations; we waited for the objections from donor governments that this was military work unsuited to a humanitarian office like UNOCA. Instead, to our genuine astonishment, we were subjected to press releases from the Red Cross and Rae McGrath complaining that our programme was pathetically small and that if we continued at this speed, it would take 1,200 years to finish de-mining the country. We were not being criticised for going beyond our mandate; we were being lambasted for doing too little. We waited for the opposing arguments. They didn't come. We suddenly realised that the only things holding the operation back were money and our own technical and managerial capacity. It was a sharp reminder that sometimes the best thing that can happen to an aid programme is for it to be criticised as slow and inadequate.

Initially, money was a serious problem. We had two start-up grants, one from the United States and one from Japan. Neither government was keen to repeat the exercise until others had joined in. But all the governments we approached gave us essentially the same response: de-mining is a military activity; we have no provision for funding it from humanitarian budgets, please talk to our ministry of defence. When we talked to the ministries of defence, they told us they would be delighted to send us some technical experts to advise us (provided we didn't ask them to go to Afghanistan), but they had no money. We would have to talk to the ministry for development assistance. This circular argument continued for several months, going nowhere, until all at once, a group of governments – primarily those who had sent us military trainers, plus Japan – agreed that de-mining could be considered a humanitarian activity after all, and could be funded from humanitarian budgets.

That solved the funding problem; developing the capacity would take longer.

Kefayatullah's ATC was the first NGO to be set up. They would do mine clearance in the eastern provinces. Three more NGOs followed quickly, one for clearance operations in the south-west around Kandahar, a second for operations in the west as well as mine awareness, and a third for national survey and planning work. These NGOs all received 100 per cent of their funding from UNOCA and were not allowed to accept other funds, so that there would be no risk of double-counting. A few months later, USAID brought 14 dogs from Thailand that were trained to detect mines. The Mine Dog Centre was set up as an NGO to house them.

USAID funded the mine dog programme through a US-based commercial company, but then, in 1993, they came to us to explain that the US government, as part of its general retreat from involvement in Afghanistan, would not be able to continue to fund the programme. Could we take it over? We would be delighted, if we could find somebody to pay for it. By one of those happy chances that make this kind of work so rewarding, Mr Right came along just when he was needed. Gunter Mulack was the official in the German Foreign Ministry in charge of the funds that could be used for de-mining. He fell for the dogs. The German government was for several years the sole funder of the mine dog programme, through UNOCA, and the Mine Dog Centre became one of the principal Afghan NGOs involved in de-mining operations.

All these activities were part of what came to be known as MAPA (pronounced 'mapper'), the Mine Action Programme for Afghanistan. It grew steadily. Whatever new political or military disasters beset the country, the MAPA kept on doing its work, respected and accepted by almost everybody. For a former *mujahideen* foot-soldier to become a de-miner was to acquire some status in society. The pay was reasonable, and although the work was risky, the de-miners knew that the MAPA would look after them in the case of an accident. Two measures that we were able to introduce symbolised that commitment to de-miners who were killed or injured during their work. The first was that we adopted an unshakeable policy that, if a de-miner was injured and the UN aircraft could get him to a hospital in Pakistan more quickly than any other available means, the aircraft was always diverted from whatever else it might be doing. Although senior UN staff sometimes found themselves spending extra days in places they had not planned to be, nobody ever complained. It was simply understood that this was the least we could do.

The second thing we did was to persuade a Pakistani insurance company to give the de-miners life insurance cover. This was really quite remarkable. Of course, the pay-out in case of death was not enormous, but it was significant and extremely important for the families.

A story that began to circulate after the de-mining programme had been going for a few years illustrates how people felt about it. We began

Figure 4 UN aircraft flying humanitarian workers to Afghanistan, 1996.

to hear that Afghan village families were reluctant to give their daughters in marriage to *mujahideen* fighters. After the departure of the Soviet troops the fighting had become less about freedom from oppression and more about greed, and ordinary people knew that. But the same families were happy to give their daughters to marry de-miners. This was an honourable profession, bringing credit and respect to those involved.

Of course, the MAPA had its problems. There were allegations that some of the directors were getting richer more quickly than their salaries, although generous, should have allowed. The books were audited repeatedly, including by the UN's external auditors and by the European Commission. Only minor irregularities were ever found. There were complaints that some directors had employed rather more of their relatives or fellow tribesmen than was appropriate. Complaints were sometimes received about the quality of a team's work, or about the behaviour of some de-miners among the local population. But when such complaints were received, corrective action was usually taken quickly, and the overall level of satisfaction with the de-miners was very high.

The operation was run by a management committee consisting of the UNOCA programme manager, of whom the longest serving and most influential was Ian Mansfield. Ian had first come to Islamabad as a serving lieutenant-colonel in charge of one of the Australian military contingents. He resigned his commission to join the UN and run the MAPA. He chaired the management committee, with the directors of the Afghan NGOs as its members. This committee decided on every detail of the programme's operations. When their decisions would affect UNOCA's relations with other partners, Ian would come and discuss them with me, but the MAPA team developed comprehensive standard operating procedures for everything imaginable. This attention to detail, and the tight discipline that the NGO directors imposed, taking their example from Kefayatullah, helped to minimise the difficulties that the MAPA encountered. By 1995, MAPA was employing over 8,000 people. Kefayatullah's ATC employed some 2,000 of them and had an annual budget of over $5 million. At one time, it was suggested that the MAPA was the biggest single employer in Afghanistan.

As the number of de-miners grew, the results became increasingly spectacular. Large tracts of contaminated land were cleared and handed over to communities; roads were cleared of anti-vehicle mines and opened to traffic; irrigation channels were cleared of mines, repaired and water flowed again; and thousands of returning refugees were given mine risk education courses before they went home.

* * *

In 2002, when the Taliban had been defeated, and all the UN offices for Afghanistan finally left Pakistan and moved back to Afghanistan, UNOCHA was wound up and most of its functions taken over by the new UN Assistance Mission in Afghanistan (UNAMA). What should become of the MAPA? After intense negotiations it was agreed that the UN Mine Action Service (UNMAS), based in New York, and of which I had been the director since December 2000, should take over headquarters responsibility, with the assistance of the UN Office of Project Services as the management agency. After six years away, I found myself once again responsible for the UN's de-mining programme in Afghanistan. On returning to Kabul with this new responsibility, it was with genuine pride and delight that I found the old team, including Kefayatullah of ATC, Fazel Karim Fazel of OMAR, Abdul Sattar of DAFA and Shohab Hakimi of the Mine Dog Centre, finally installed back in Kabul and drawing up plans to deal with thousands of unexploded cluster bombs dropped by the US Air Force in their operations to remove the Taliban. This part of the story is recounted in Chapter 7.

Aircraft, radio and security

In addition to de-mining, UNOCA had operational responsibility for two key logistical support systems, the UN aircraft and the UN radio network. These are now routinely managed by WFP. Efforts by WFP to take over these tasks began in Afghanistan. I was vehemently opposed to the idea of losing these key logistical tools of coordination. As the person responsible for coordination, I decided personally on the aircraft schedule and who got priority when there was competition for seats. Our aircraft provided the only way to reach most parts of Afghanistan. I could not delegate this responsibility and hide behind some bureaucratic explanation for why an aircraft was not available or why a seat could not be found on a particular flight.

The seven years I worked in or on Afghanistan produced their share of shocks and tragedies. There was no more shocking and tragic day than 1 February 1993, when two UN vehicles travelling between Peshawar and Jalalabad were ambushed about 20 kilometres east of Jalalabad. Four people were killed; two Afghans, one British and one Dutch. A Dutch colleague working for UNHCR managed to escape by diving out of the front seat of the car into the ditch beside the road. The gunmen jumped into their pickup and sped south along the road towards Khost in Paktia province. Eyewitnesses suggested that they were not Afghans.

In Islamabad David Lockwood, the UN designated official for security, convened the UN security management team and we tried to come to terms with the fact that, a few days earlier we had sat around the same table and agreed to allow the team to go.

David and a team of security colleagues flew to Jalalabad to ask the Governor of Nangahar province to track down the killers and to explain what had happened. The Governor said he would. Diana Russler, deputy head of UN security in New York, flew out to investigate. Relatives of the dead colleagues came to Islamabad for a moving memorial service.

Although we did not realise it immediately, it now seems clear that this was in fact the first atrocity perpetrated against a Western target by Osama Bin Laden's Al-Qaeda. These men were out practising for their future activities. When they drove away, they were probably returning to the camp that would later be the target of President Clinton's cruise missiles after the bombing of the US embassies in Kenya and Tanzania in August 1998. The Governor of Nangarhar never told us anything, although we asked for a report every time we met him over the following two years, but he certainly had a very good idea of who was involved. Ironically, in 2003, the Governor himself fell victim to assassins in Kabul.

Security had been a constant preoccupation before, but this was the first time we had to confront the fact that we had authorised a mission which had led directly to the deaths of colleagues, not because of a traffic accident, pilot error or mechanical failure, but because of deliberate premeditated action by people who saw us as their mortal enemies, and who had been taught to believe, in defiance of centuries of contrary teaching by Islamic leaders and scholars, that their religion justified such action.

During the remaining three years that I worked on the programme, security was a constant concern, but it did not become the overwhelming constraint on UN operations that it is at the time of writing. We continued to work on the basis that we let all the relevant people who controlled territory know where we were proposing to travel, and sought the agreement in advance of all the commanders whose territory we intended to go through. But we realised there were now people out there who did not control territory, but could pose a deadly threat.

For most UN operations in the eastern and southern provinces of Afghanistan, obtaining security clearances had, from the outset, involved several steps. We would go to the ISI in Islamabad and ask them to let 'their people', by which we meant their agents in Peshawar or Quetta, know what we intended and ask them to set it up with the relevant *mujahideen* leaders. At the same time, the UNOCA field officer in Peshawar or Quetta would go and see the relevant Afghan party leadership and ask them for the same. In many parts of the country this would involve a relay system of escort vehicles containing armed men loyal to the commander whose territory we were passing through. When we reached the limits of his domain, we were handed over to the next. Up until the fall of the government of President Najibullah in 1992, there was an additional step; the UNOCA office in Kabul would inform the government military liaison team of the routing and dates, with a request to ensure that the Afghan Air Force did not select our vehicles for some bombing practice. After an early scare, in which a UN mission in the western province of Herat, which had crossed the border from Iran, came under attack from the air, fortunately without sustaining casualties, the system worked quite well.

The system relied heavily on radio communications. At UNOCA, it was our view that, if we were to coordinate a humanitarian operation in such a large, complex and often forbidding landscape, we had to manage the radio network. Although the individual UN agencies maintained their own base stations, the UNOCA office in Islamabad became the acknowledged hub. We maintained seven-days-a-week coverage, and eventually provided 24-hours-a-day presence. The operators, all Pakistani nationals, became, for many nervous travellers in remote areas of Afghanistan, a source of comfort and reassurance, although frustration and anger could be part of the mix too.

First, short-wave radio communication remains an imperfect science, susceptible to disruption by weather and mountainous landscape. How many times, sitting alongside the driver in a white UN Landcruiser, did UN field officers attempt to call in to 'Sierra Base' from 'Sierra Mobile', to find silence, static or crackle was the only response? What was wrong? Was the operator talking to somebody else? Perhaps he had left his post for a bathroom break. Perhaps he couldn't hear. Perhaps the car radio had died. Let's try calling another station. Same result.

As is well known to everybody in the business of humanitarian aid, crises only ever break out at weekends, usually very early in the morning, when you are trying to catch up with some long overdue sleep.

One of UNOCA's first initiatives was to establish an operational base for the UN agencies in the province of Paktika, which, together with Kunar, was one of only two provinces in Afghanistan where the Kabul government had no presence. We had recruited a remarkable Frenchman of American origin called Michael Barry. Michael is a writer, philosopher, linguist and expert on Afghanistan. He had agreed to lead a Salam Mobile Unit, or SMU – pronounced 'smoo' – in Paktika, to help the UN agencies identify projects for rural rehabilitation. He had established the UN base in a rather imposing traditional compound in the town of Urgun, recently abandoned by the Kabul forces. The compound was surrounded by a high wall and the entry gates were overlooked by a large watchtower.

One Saturday morning at seven, I received an apologetic phone call from our radio operator at the UNOCA office to say that Michael needed to speak to me immediately. I would have to go to the office. Driving myself along the deserted roads, I wondered what on earth could have happened.

Michael's radio call sign was Mike Uniform Papa. As soon as I arrived, the unmistakeable rapid-fire voice came on, 'Mike Uniform Papa, Mike Uniform Papa, Mike Uniform Papa, calling Sierra Base, there has been a murder, I repeat murder, at the United Nations compound in Papa location'. Of course, I was shocked. Was the deceased part of the UN team? No, he was a local. Was the murder related to the UN presence? No, Michael did not think so. How could I help in the matter? Michael suggested that the Secretary-General of the United Nations must immediately deliver a protest. The sanctity of the UN compound had been violated. How could the mission continue if this kind of thing was to be allowed? After many minutes, Michael accepted that, in practice, there was not a lot that could be done anywhere except where he was. He should protest in the strongest terms, on behalf of the United Nations, to the local commander and seek assurances that this kind of thing would not happen in the future. We would deliver a similar message to the appropriate *mujahideen* leader in Peshawar, but there was not much point in intervening with the government of Afghanistan in Kabul, since they had relinquished all control of the province.

A very different situation that began in the same way, with the early morning call from the radio room, involved a team of three UN international staff who were on mission to Bamyan in the central mountains. Some people had come to them from a village some way down the road to the north-east, claiming that they were in desperate need of UN assistance and asking for help. The team decided to go to check out the situation. A local commander in a village on their route, who had not been consulted about their trip, had detained them and was refusing to let them go without the payment of a substantial ransom. The team had helpfully provided him with my name and suggested that he talk to me on the radio.

We began a series of conversations over several days, during which we discussed many aspects of the current situation in Afghanistan, and he never wavered from his position that he required a ransom of 4 million Pakistani rupees (about $100,000), if the team were to be allowed to return to Bamyan. I played for time. The UN would be happy to survey the needs of the villages under his control – indeed that was what the team had been trying to do – if he would let them go. We regretted that we had not sought his permission before entering his area. That would not happen again. But we would not be able to provide assistance to the people of Afghanistan if we had to pay millions of rupees every time we went through a commander's territory.

While this was going on, our colleagues in Peshawar were trying to persuade his *mujahideen* party leader to instruct him to let the UN team go. The problem was that the commander seemed to be a fickle follower. He had frequently switched parties and his current party leader had little influence over him.

Then, by a stroke of good fortune, the solution presented itself. Kefayatullah, the director of ATC, was on his way to Bamyan to inspect the operations of his de-miners in the area. I called him on the radio and told him of the situation. He persuaded some leading figures in Bamyan to convene a meeting of the *shura* (council). He explained to them how devastating it would be for the whole region if anything untoward happened to this team. The food aid from WFP, on which this mountainous area depended for its survival through harsh winters, would be jeopardised. They agreed to organise a delegation of senior commanders to pay a visit to the kidnapper and bring the team back. The potential firepower represented by this delegation was enough to persuade the hostage-taking commander that the team should be released without payment of ransom.

This incident provided an important lesson. Firstly, all our field staff, especially those entrusted with the leadership of a field mission, needed to understand what constituted a guarantee of safe passage and what did not. Secondly, what came naturally to Kefayatullah, but perhaps not always to us, was to seek out those who wielded effective power, meet them in a forum where they risked losing face, and confront them with the consequences of doing nothing to defend the principles of humanitarian action.

Afghan NGOs

It was one of the enormous benefits of the way the de-mining programme was designed that we had on our side senior Afghan personalities who were running their own operations, who had a respected status in Afghan society and who were always available to help us navigate through difficult situations. Of course, the UN employed many highly competent and experienced Afghan staff, but, almost by definition, in subordinate positions. A young international field officer, with little experience and knowledge of the country might have as his assistant a grizzled world-weary Afghan 20 years his senior. However intelligently and sensitively the young international managed that relationship, it did not change the fact that the Afghan was subordinate to the foreigner. Kefayatullah and his fellow NGO directors were not my subordinates or Ian Mansfield's. We channelled resources to them, but they were our partners. If the UN chooses international NGOs as its partners in preference to national organisations, it forfeits the opportunity to support national initiatives and to promote national ownership. Some UN colleagues felt that all Afghan NGOs were politically biased and that international NGOs were more likely to be impartial partners. That was not my experience. International NGOs were just as likely to be dominated in their Afghan personnel by people affiliated with one political group. But since the senior Afghans in the international NGO were not ultimately responsible for the NGO's reputation or results, they did not feel the same sense of accountability.

I feel a great regret that this approach of encouraging the emergence of large, competent and viable national NGOs has not been followed in other sectors of activity, and that it did not even take hold in the field of mine action outside Afghanistan.

One other UN programme in Afghanistan sought specifically to promote the activities of Afghan NGOs – in the field of rehabilitation of rural infrastructure. UNDP funded a programme managed by my friend Bob Eaton that supported projects of irrigation and road repair proposed by Afghan NGOs. In spite of their efforts, relatively few of these NGOs were able to sustain a substantial level of operations for any length of time. In the sectors of agriculture, education and health, the largest organisations working in rural Afghanistan were all international NGOs, of which the largest was the Swedish Committee for Afghanistan.

I have often wondered why so few national NGOs have been able to flourish in countries emerging from conflict. The advantages for the United Nations and international donors in promoting these organisations as partners seem so obvious. I explore this further in the final chapter of this book.

Kabul 1994

By the end of 1993, the fragile agreement among the *mujahideen* parties that had allowed first Sibghatullah Mojaddedi and then Burhanuddin Rabbani to follow the pro-communist Najibullah as presidents of Afghanistan had broken down. In early January 1994, Gulbuddin Hekmatyar's Hezbi Islami and the Shi'i parties of the Hazara tribes left the Rabbani government. There then began a year of unrelenting long-range warfare between Rabbani's forces, led by Ahmed Shah Masood in north and central Kabul on one side, and the Hazara in the south-west of the city with Hekmatyar to the south-east, on the other.

On 8 January 1994, it was decided that the small group of UN international staff remaining in Kabul should be evacuated to Pakistan. David Lockwood, the UN resident coordinator and designated official for security, picks up the story:

Hamid Karzai had been Deputy Foreign Minister under President Mojaddedi. When President Rabbani took over, Karzai was arrested by Ahmed Shah Masood, because of a cheque for $10 million, given to Mojaddedi when he became President by the Government of Pakistan, which was unaccounted for.

Karzai was being held in a house in Kabul and being interrogated by Masood's people. As the fighting between pro-Masood, pro-Hekmatyar and the Shia forces intensified, a rocket exploded in the courtyard of the house, blowing a hole in the wall of the room where Karzai was being held.

When he came around from the shock, Karzai climbed out through the hole and made his way to Hekmatyar's camp. There he was given a vehicle in which to drive to Pakistan. However, he had not gone far when he was stopped by armed men, the vehicle stolen and he was left beside the road. As he was standing there, a convoy of UN vehicles carrying the group of UN staff being evacuated to Pakistan, drove up. The convoy was being led by Denis Lazarus, the UNDP deputy representative, who radioed to the UN HQ in Islamabad to say that they had come across this rather well-dressed hitch-hiker. I told Denis to pick him up and bring him along.

Personal communication from David Lockwood

During that terrible year, Masood flattened with rockets much of the Hazara-dominated south-west of the city, while Hekmatyar did the same to its southern and eastern districts. It was utterly pointless. The international community was too pre-occupied with Rwanda, South Africa and Bosnia to do anything about it.

As winter closed in, Hekmatyar sought to tighten the pressure on Rabbani and Masood, by imposing a blockade on the flow of food supplies from Pakistan into Kabul. For the thousands of poor in Kabul without money for food or fuel, the situation became increasingly desperate. Sitting comfortably in our offices in Pakistan, we sent faxes to New York, we briefed the ambassadors of donor countries, but still nothing happened. We had to do something to draw the world's attention to the situation, and at the very least persuade Hekmatyar to stop his blockade. So we called John Burns, the *New York Times* correspondent in New Delhi. Burns came to Islamabad, we flew him to Kabul and his report on the desperate plight of the civilian population in the city appeared on the front page of the *New York Times*, above the fold.

Finally, our phones began to ring. The Secretary-General wanted to see a report. We re-sent the ones we had already sent. And finally, the ISI let us know that Hekmatyar might be amenable to allowing an aid convoy into Kabul, if we asked nicely. Great, when could we see him? If we could get ourselves to Charasyab, Hekmatyar's base south-east of Kabul, he would probably see us. It was to the great credit of David Lockwood and the UN security team in New York that they agreed to allow me, together with a UNOCHA field officer, Mohammed Mao, and a WFP colleague, to make the trip by road with our Afghan assistants and drivers from Jalalabad by the southerly Gandamak route to Charasyab.

It was a cold December evening when we arrived in Charasyab, a small town tucked in behind the first mountain on the south-east corner of the Kabul plain. Truck-mounted rocket launchers pointed over the mountain towards Kabul. We were received by one of Hekmatyar's deputies. The leader might see us in the morning. We were served dinner and shown to our guest rooms. After breakfast, we were shown into a long room, with chairs set at one end. We waited. Then Hekmatyar walked in, smart, icily polite. When we had listened to him denouncing the outrageous behaviour of everybody else, including the United Nations, we made our appeal for him to respect the agreement he had made all those years before, to allow humanitarian aid to reach those who needed it. Of course, these were formalities. The deal had been agreed in advance; but the formalities still had to be played out.

Hekmatyar gave the instructions for the WFP convoy to be allowed to leave Sorobi, where it had been stopped by one of his commanders on the way from Jalalabad. We waited until we had confirmation from the convoy leader that the whole convoy had left Sorobi behind, and then we drove across a totally deserted Kabul plain, past the abandoned jail of Pul-i-Charki, into the city.

That evening the trucks rolled into the city and we were able to watch them begin to unload. The city seemed to emit a sigh of relief. The blockade had been lifted. There would be bread in WFP's bakeries in the morning.

Politics, governance and the future

I left Afghanistan in June 1996 to become Deputy Special Representative of the UN Secretary-General in Bosnia and Herzegovina. In September, the Taliban entered Kabul, dragged former President Najibullah out of the UN office where he had been living since being ousted from power by the *mujahideen* in 1992, and hanged him from a lamp-post. They ran the country, apart from an increasingly small pocket of territory in the north-east, unrecognised by the international community, until the murder of Ahmed Shah Masood in Taloqan on 9 September 2001, and the attacks on New York and Washington two days later, provoked the United States to evict them.

In December 2001, after US forces, with the support of a revitalised Northern Alliance, had cleared the Taliban out of Kabul and the other main Afghan cities, the UN organised a meeting of Afghan political groups, excluding the Taliban, in Bonn and identified Hamid Karzai as a suitable interim president.

While this was happening, there were indications that the US and other major powers were likely to approve a role for the United Nations in helping to stabilise the country. By this time, I was heading the UN's Mine Action Service, a division of the Department of Peacekeeping Operations (DPKO) in New York. Jean-Marie Guéhenno, DPKO's head, knew of my earlier association with the country and asked me to lead the department's technical assessment mission.

The events since that apparently golden opportunity to rebuild the country, with the goodwill of the entire world, have been a tragic tale of missed opportunities, blindness to history and the triumph of personal ambition, corruption and vested interests over common sense, leaving lovers of Afghanistan deeply sad and frustrated.

To understand exactly how this has happened, the reader can do no better than refer to Ahmed Rashid's masterly account in his book, *Descent into Chaos*. In this final segment of this chapter, I will only identify a few of the decisions which, in my view, contributed to prolonging the conflict, and suggest a few simple insights which might contribute to its resolution.

Much has been written about how, after removing the Taliban, George Bush's White House took its eye off the ball and became obsessed with Iraq. While this certainly had an impact, the decision which, in my view, has contributed most to the failure of the international intervention in Afghanistan is contained in the Afghan constitution adopted in 2003.

It had been obvious to many of us in the UN operation in the 1990s that the seed of the Afghan disaster had been sown as early as 1963, when a steady process of centralisation of power into the hands of an educated and de-tribalised elite in Kabul had begun. The original seven provinces were subdivided and re-subdivided, and that process would continue, until there are now 34 provinces. Ministers in Kabul, with little understanding of the political dynamics of the rural areas, developed centralised programmes and sent teams of national and foreign experts to implement them. The historic consensus about the relationship between the national government in Kabul and the tribes was lost.

The drafting of a new constitution in 2003 presented a historic opportunity to reverse the destructive process of centralisation. Tragically, not only was the opportunity lost, but the centralising trend was extended to its ultimate extreme, the election on the basis of universal suffrage of a president with the power to appoint all national and provincial officials. To compound the insult, the interim president, Hamid Karzai, was not disbarred, as he obviously should have been, from contesting the first presidential elections under the new constitution.

To get an idea of how absurd this situation was, remember that Karzai was not the leader of a political party. Before being plucked from obscurity by the Bonn Conference, he had served as an aide to one of the seven Peshawar-based *mujahideen* party leaders, and then briefly as a deputy foreign minister in Kabul. Not only did he not have a base of organised political support, he was basically unknown when he became interim president. The two years he spent in that position meant that people knew his face, but the average Afghan voter had no basis on which to judge whether he was likely to be a better choice than any of the other candidates.

While Hamid Karzai was a reasonable choice as an interim president, he was disastrous as an elected one. As Ahmed Rashid points out, Karzai has never been an acceptable choice to Pakistan. If 9/11 had not happened, he would have been expelled from Pakistan by the end of the month (September 2001). In Islamabad, he is seen as far too close to India, which has been aggressively building up its presence in Afghanistan, further provoking Pakistan to side with Karzai's Taliban opponents.

Seth Kaplan has written an excellent book, *Fixing Failed States*, which points out how democracy in countries like Afghanistan can only be built from the bottom up and not, as the Afghan constitution tries to do, from the top down. Read that book alongside Paul Collier's *Wars, Guns and Votes*, and it is hard to understand how the international experts assisting the Afghans to draft their constitution could have allowed them to head down this destructive road. Ahmed Rashid recounts in devastating detail how the international advisers assisted Hamid Karzai to push through the highly centralised 'French' model that he saw as being in his interest and the interests of the Pushtoons, against the advice of the leaders of the Northern Alliance who favoured a more decentralised 'Swiss' model. Ironically, the Pushtoons in the south of the country have suffered more than any other ethnic group from Karzai's misguided approach.

Mistakes in the drafting of the constitution were compounded by the design of the international support package.

When drafting my report for the DPKO technical assessment mission, I advocated for as few international personnel as possible, with Afghans doing the technical support jobs, as they did for the UN agencies already in the country. I also argued for small, low-profile saloon cars for routine use within the Kabul city boundaries. This provoked furious reactions from DPKO administrators: clearly I did not understand how peacekeeping missions were organised, and I was told that 'DPKO doesn't do saloon cars; we only have contracts for 4x4s'.

In the overall scheme of things, these were perhaps small matters, but they rendered dead-in-the-water the vision of a 'light footprint', which Lakhdar Brahimi, the UN's first Special Representative of the Secretary-General, rightly saw as essential to a successful UN presence.

Having decided that its administrative support system should be large and heavy, the UN mission then decided that the key support functions for the new Afghan government should be divided up among the contributing donor nations. Critically, it was decided that, unlike in Bosnia, where, as is described in the next chapter, the UN played a major role in re-establishing the police force, this role should be delegated to a single nation – Germany. With hindsight, I should perhaps have done more to contest this decision. In Bosnia, the UN had a civilian police mission of over 2,000 people; the DPKO technical assessment mission's initial modest proposal for some 200 trainers for Afghanistan was reduced to just one liaison officer. The fact that the police support function was slow to get going and that valuable time was lost, which would not have been the case if the UN had done the job itself, was not really Germany's fault. The Germans were persuaded to take on a task which no doubt they did not initially understand and for which they were completely unprepared.

The weakness in the international support for the Afghan police stands in stark contrast to the support for Afghanistan's military forces.

But the country faces no credible military threat from its neighbours, so why does it need such an enormous army? The answer can only be that the army is filling the gap left by the lack of a serious political strategy of reconciliation, engaging both the Taliban and Pakistan. But, of course, for such a strategy to work, a decentralised national political framework is required where the eight natural regions of the country can rediscover their historic identity and work together to build a Swiss-style confederation, in which an ambitious Afghan would rather be a provincial governor than a minister in Kabul.

* * *

Living and working in Islamabad with a young family had been very different from the relative routine of running an NGO in London. Responding to an emergency often meant changing family plans at very short notice. My next assignment, in Sarajevo, would be an even greater disruption to family life.

The 1995 Agreement for Peace in Bosnia and Herzegovina

Figure 5 Map of Bosnia and Herzegovina.

5

CRISIS IN EUROPE'S BACKYARD

Coordinating international efforts in
Bosnia and Herzegovina

Bosnia and Herzegovina, just like Laos and Afghanistan, is a country in-between. It is mountainous, virtually land-locked and is populated by people belonging to the three major religious communities of Eastern Europe: Catholics, Orthodox and Muslims. It suffered regular bouts of brutal conflict throughout the twentieth century.

Also like Laos and Afghanistan, community leaders in Bosnia and Herzegovina, or Bosnia, as I shall refer to it, offered themselves as conduits for external aid to 'resist aggression' or 'protect their identity' against the real or perceived threats mounted by other communities. Bosnia was another ideal territory for proxy wars.

In November 1995, at a series of extraordinary meetings in a US military base in Dayton, Ohio, the most recent of these wars, which had begun in 1992, was brought to a close by the Dayton Peace Accords, orchestrated by US Ambassador Richard Holbrooke.

The Dayton Accords identified eight main tasks for the international community in support of peacebuilding in Bosnia: disarmament and demobilisation; elections; mentoring the new political leaders; refugee return; police training and reform; protection of human rights; reconstruction of infrastructure; and economic development. The responsibility for each of these tasks was assigned, seemingly at random, to a different lead international body. Indeed the coordination of the whole effort was entrusted to a brand new body, the Office of the High Representative, set up especially for this purpose. In most sectors of activity, other bilateral and multilateral organisations soon joined in, creating a dizzying array of partners for Bosnian officials to work with. This would pose unprecedented challenges of internal coordination among international organisations. I would be in my element.

I arrived in Sarajevo, in June 1996, as Deputy Special Representative of the UN Secretary-General. The opportunity to join a peacekeeping mission in Europe had come at just the right time. Our sons had finished primary school in Islamabad and needed a new environment. But peacekeeping meant separation from the family. It was a big wrench, but it was a situation that so many UN colleagues routinely accepted, that it did not seem too dramatic at the time.

My job was to be deputy head of the UN Mission in Bosnia and Herzegovina (UNMIBH). UNMIBH had succeeded UNPROFOR (United Nations Protection Force), which, with inadequate mandates and resources, had tried to ensure the safe delivery of humanitarian aid during the conflict. UNMIBH, had been given a very different mandate.

Many of my new colleagues had served with UNPROFOR and had been marked by the horrors they had lived through, most particularly the massacre, just a year earlier, of 7,000 Muslim men and boys at Srebrenica, a town designated a 'safe area' by UN Security Council resolution 819 of 16 April 1993.

The dominant sensations of my time in Bosnia were dismay at the futility and waste of the war; disgust at the arrogance, mendacity and intolerance of ethnic nationalists; incredulity that modern Europe could have allowed the war to continue for three years without intervening to stop it; and a wry amazement at the architecture of the international effort that had been put in place to impose the peace settlement.

Six months after the end of the war, Sarajevo was still a ghost town. There was very little traffic, apart from the vehicles of the international organisations. There were no functioning traffic lights between the UN office and my apartment, a route which would require me to negotiate 15 sets of lights only 18 months later. The rubble of fallen buildings was everywhere. Most of those that still stood were pockmarked with bullet holes. A few new cafes had opened to accommodate the international workers. Occasionally one would see a Mercedes with German licence plates, cruising the streets. My driver, who had remained in Sarajevo throughout the war, would say, with heavy sarcasm, 'Oh, look at the poor refugees coming back for a visit!'

I took an apartment on the north side of the town, on the hill behind the Catholic Cathedral. On Sundays I would take walks in the streets of the old town and in the suburbs on the north side. Everywhere there seemed to be cemeteries, with the fresh gravestones of teenagers and young adults, the victims of this futile war.

As in Laos and Afghanistan, the multi-ethnic composition of the country, for so long an asset, was ruthlessly exploited by neighbours and external powers, promoting ethnic nationalism. These divisions had been exploited before; they reflected the country's geography and history that had placed it uncomfortably on the fault-lines between Muslim Turkey, Orthodox Serbia and Catholic Croatia.

Three armies had fought for control of territory for three years. Once in control of an area, the Serb Army had terrorised populations belonging to the two other ethnic groups in a campaign that became known as 'ethnic cleansing'. In the towns, apartments belonging to members of the other nationalities had been taken over by Serbs. In the countryside, the houses of members of the other communities had generally been blown up using anti-tank landmines. On the drive north from Doboj to the Croatian border, every house along the roadside had been destroyed in this way.

These tactics were the hallmark of the army of Karadzic and Mladic, but similar tactics had been adopted by the Muslim Bosniacs and the Catholic Croats, particularly in the south-west of the country, where the Croats were in the majority and sought to remove the minority villages of Bosniacs and Serbs. While the Dayton Accords spoke loftily about the right to return to places of origin, in practice, with a few symbolic exceptions, the peace settlement recognised the facts on the ground.

On 5 October 1996, I represented the UN at the formal swearing-in ceremony at the National Theatre in Sarajevo of the newly elected presidents, ministers and members of the national assembly. The ceremony began three hours late, as the High Representative, Carl Bildt, tried, unsuccessfully, to persuade the Serb members to come to the ceremony from their base in the nearby mountain village of Pale. The wait gave me the opportunity to listen to my neighbour in the theatre, the Mufti of Sarajevo, the senior Muslim cleric in the country. This is his account of the recent history of his country, as I recorded it immediately after the event.

The West has abandoned spiritual values. Its civilisation has no spiritual goal. Its goals are in process and method, but not in spiritual or religious values. The West teaches material goals, which encourage jealousy and greed. You have stopped teaching the values which promote tolerance and compassion. You have developed the technology of communication, but do not communicate with each other. You have developed such power, that all other societies and civilisations are in some senses subject. The West could have prevented the war in Yugoslavia, and could have stopped it at any time. The fact that it did not do so encouraged those who were making the war to continue. They knew they could have been stopped, and saw the fact that they were not as an invitation to continue. The seeds of the decline of the West's great empire and civilisation are already visible. As with other empires, its leaders of course will not see the dangers until it is too late. Islam and Judaism are religions of the Law. The Law is a spiritual guide against which the individual can measure himself. It is timeless. It is immune to the changes in circumstances of different generations. It keeps people together in a society in which the relationships between members are understood. Western civilisation is all about questioning and overturning the Laws and spiritual values of its great religions. Homosexual 'marriage' is an example. The West emphasises the 'rights' of the individual to a point at which the individual can trample on the rights of his neighbours without fear of punishment. The West has abandoned the pursuit of justice as a goal of its civilisation. It allows injustice to flourish if it assists the West's material goals. For this, the West will surely be punished, for God must punish injustice. God will forgive individual weakness. Everybody is weak in one way or another. But God will not forgive injustice.

This was one of many long and passionate narratives that I would listen to during my time in Bosnia. What they all had in common was fatalism, a sense that events were shaped by forces beyond the control of the speaker or the group to which he belonged, forces that he had understood and analysed, but could not influence or control. These narratives were often used, although not in the Mufti's case, to justify violent acts by the speaker's group, which were presented as legitimate responses to threats to the group's identity.

Institutional architecture

Dayton provided for a three-headed national presidency, one president for each ethnic community and two 'entity' governments, the Serb Republic and the Federation of Muslims and Croats. The Federation was divided into 12 cantons, each of which also had a president. And finally, the whole country was divided into 153 municipalities, the lowest level administrative units.

Interacting with this dysfunctional political structure were the international organisations. The political leadership of the effort was in the hands of the High Representative, appointed by a 'Peace Implementation Council', an *ad hoc* body of 55 states, whose activities were sanctioned by the UN Security Council and managed by the European Commission in Brussels.

Military matters were in the hands of NATO, and under the command of the Supreme Allied Commander Europe, an American general based in Mons, Belgium. The Implementation Force (IFOR), later SFOR (Stabilisation Force), consisted initially of some 40,000 soldiers. Command of this operation in land-locked Bosnia was given in the first instance, for reasons which escaped me, to an American admiral. The force was divided into three divisions, commanded by major-generals from France (Mostar – Croat), the UK (Banja Luka – Serb) and the US (Tuzla – Bosniac) respectively. Sarajevo was in the French zone.

The mandate for organising elections to the new Bosnian legislatures was given to the Organisation for Security and Cooperation in Europe (OSCE), an organisation based in Vienna with no prior experience of running elections.

Coordination of humanitarian relief operations was left in the hands of the Office of the UN High Commissioner for Refugees (UNHCR), which had fulfilled the task throughout the war.

The European Commission and the World Bank were asked to coordinate the reconstruction effort together. The UNDP resident representative was left to coordinate the rather limited development programmes of the UN agencies.

And then there was our mission, UNMIBH, responsible for the International Police Task Force (IPTF) set up under Annex 11 of the Dayton Agreements. The IPTF employed 2,400 police men and women from 42 countries to monitor the activities of the three Bosnian police forces and to train them in 'democratic policing'.

In addition to the civilian personnel needed to administer the IPTF, UNMIBH also employed a team of civil affairs officers, who worked alongside the international police in the canton and municipal centres, advising and assisting the police in their interactions with the local political leadership, as well as promoting confidence-building measures to bring the communities together where they could.

Three special representatives

The official in overall charge of the UN effort in Bosnia was the Special Representative of the UN Secretary-General (SRSG). The first of these to be appointed after the conflict, and therefore my first boss, was Iqbal Riza, a delightful, urbane and skilful diplomat from Pakistan. He had made his name in peacekeeping operations in Central America, and had been Kofi Annan's deputy in the UN Department of Peacekeeping Operations, until his appointment to Sarajevo in January 1996. He was a man of such evident integrity, sharp intellect, human decency and compassion, that he immediately inspired confidence.

He wanted a deputy who would help to link UNMIBH to other parts of the UN system and to the numerous NGOs operating in Bosnia. He had approached Martin Griffiths, but Martin had just been appointed director of the Geneva office of the Department of Humanitarian Affairs, and had recommended me in his place.

Riza served as SRSG from January to October 1996, when he left on leave. While he was away, Kofi Annan announced that he was a candidate for the post of Secretary-General. Riza decided to join the campaign team and did not return to Sarajevo. I was therefore acting SRSG until February 1997, when Ambassador Kai Eide of Norway came to take over.

Eide had spent most of his career working on issues of security in Europe, and in January 1998 he would leave Bosnia to become Norway's ambassador to the OSCE in Vienna. Eide came across as bright, energetic and ambitious, but he could be abrasive and our relationship was not always an easy one. He knew everything there was to know about European security issues and was most interested in Bosnia by the issues that were really within the mandate of the High Representative and not the UN. Eide's interest in political matters was matched by a lack of interest in the activities of the rest of the UN family in Bosnia.

Eide arrived on 11 February 1997. I met him at the airport and took him to his new office. When we sat down, he got out his appointment letter from the Secretary-General and read from it. 'Look,' he said, 'I am Special Representative of the Secretary-General and Coordinator of UN Operations in Bosnia and Herzegovina. What does that mean?'

I explained that in addition to UNMIBH, with its International Police Task Force, civil affairs officers and human rights team, there were also a number of UN agencies involved in humanitarian work, which were being coordinated by UNHCR, and a growing number of UN development agencies, being coordinated by the UNDP representative,

1a Teams representing local Buddhist temples compete in the annual boat races in Luang Prabang, Laos, 1969.

1b Luang Prabang celebrates Lao New Year, April 1970.

1c A temple in Luang Prabang, 1970.

1d Luang Prabang airport, 1970.

2 Camp for Cambodian refugees in Thailand – aerial view of Khao-I-Dang camp, 1983.

3 Boat people from Vietnam being rescued in South China Sea, September 1987.

4 Hmong refugees from Laos resettled in California, USA, 1984.

5 Afghan refugee returning home from Pakistan, 2002.

6 New Afghan refugees at Roghani camp near Chaman in Pakistan, December 2001 (Also cover photo).

7 UN High Commissioner for Refugees Sadruddin Aga Khan and his wife Princess Catherine visit Lao people displaced by the war being resettled in the Plain of Jars, September 1975.

8 UN Coordinator Sadruddin Aga Khan leads high-level delegation to Afghanistan and Pakistan – Islamabad, October 1990. (l–r: author; Benon Sevan, Personal Representative of the Secretary-General; James Ingram, Executive Director, WFP; Thorvald Stoltenberg, UN High Commissioner for Refugees; Sadruddin; President of Pakistan, Ghulam Ishaq Khan, and Foreign Minister, Sahabzada Yaqub Ali Khan.)

9 Bosnia and Herzegovina – destruction in Derventa region, 1998.

10 Bomb destroys part of UN headquarters in Baghdad, killing UN Special Representative Sergio Vieira de Mello and 21 others, 19 August 2003.

11 Unexploded ordnance awaiting destruction in Laos.

12 Mine detection dog and handler in Afghanistan.

13 Princess Diana visits UN Mine Action Coordination Centre in Sarajevo, 17 August 1997.

14 A de-miner in Lebanon uses a detector to locate hidden mines or bombs.

15 The author bids farewell to Secretary-General Kofi Annan upon retirement from the UN, 2 August 2005.

who had been appointed UN resident coordinator. On top of that, the World Bank, which is formally a part of the UN system, had been asked by the High Representative to coordinate the reconstruction effort, jointly with the European Commission.

'So, there are already three other UN coordinators,' said Eide. 'As coordinator of UN operations, do I have any authority over them, or am I a sort of coordinator of coordinators?'

'You don't have the authority to tell them what to do,' I replied, 'but you are recognised as the senior UN official in the country, and I think they would welcome a regular opportunity to get briefings and advice from you and discuss their programmes.'

Eide would have none of it. If he had no authority, how could he be expected to coordinate them? Having spent my whole career 'coordinating' people over whom I had no authority, and believing that this was a worthwhile activity, I felt that I should have been able to explain to Eide the benefits of making the effort; but I was not successful, and he took very little interest in the activities of other parts of the UN family, focussing on the political and security agenda.

When Eide left in January 1998 and was replaced by Elisabeth Rehn, the first woman to be defence minister in Finland and a former special rapporteur of the UN's Human Rights Commission, I tried again. Rehn was far more receptive. She made a point of visiting all the UN agency representatives in their offices, and becoming familiar with their work. This produced an immediate change in atmosphere, with agency heads calling up for advice and help when they faced problems.

The differences in attitude of the three SRSGs towards their role as 'coordinator of UN operations' convinced me that it must be possible to develop a system less dependent on the personality and inclinations of individuals and more predictable for participants in the UN effort. The opportunity to take part in an effort to do something about this would come during my next assignment, in New York.

Coordinating the international effort

An inevitable consequence of the complexity of the institutional arrangements was that senior international officials spent an inordinate amount of time 'coordinating' the activities of their agencies with other international bodies.

From the outset, Iqbal Riza tried to persuade the first High Representative, Carl Bildt of Sweden, to hold meetings of the heads of the various international organisations, but his pleas fell on deaf ears initially. Bildt preferred to deal separately with each of his partners. However, in July 1996, with the approach of the elections scheduled for September, Bildt became convinced that a meeting of 'principals' would be required. He identified six principals, himself and the heads of IFOR (military), OSCE (elections), UNMIBH, IPTF (police) and UNHCR (refugee return). All entreaties by the heads of other organisations to join the group were rebuffed. The reason given for this exclusivity was that the meetings were concerned exclusively with security issues and these were the organisations required for that purpose. Once the meetings got under way, Bildt soon acquired a taste for them and they would be convened in his office at six o'clock in the evening up to three times a week.

The early principals' meetings had only two items on the agenda: the arrangements for the return of internally displaced persons (IDPs) to the Zone of Separation between the two entities, and the elections. For most other activities, the High Representative left the lead agencies to set up their own coordination mechanisms. UNHCR had a well-established system for dealing with the delivery of humanitarian aid. The European Commission and the World Bank chaired a group on reconstruction; there was a group on human rights issues; and I co-chaired, with the military adviser to the High Representative, the group dealing with the landmine problem.

Bildt invited the principals to come to his meetings with only one other colleague, so the core membership was 12 senior officials. While this helped to keep the meetings focussed, it could also be a weakness if the two senior representatives were not extremely well briefed by their staff in advance. Generals were not always aware of the arrangements that more junior officers had made in the field.

Shaping international policy

While Eide's disengagement from the UN agencies caused disappointment in the UN family, I had to admit that it had benefits for the overall international effort. He became engaged, on behalf of the international team in Sarajevo, in interpreting the situation in Bosnia to the politicians and diplomats in Brussels, Mons, Vienna, New York and in other national capitals. One of the key institutions in this relationship was the NATO Council.

The institutions outside the country were working on plans with fixed timelines. On this date in the future, a phase of the plan would have been completed, and there would be a corresponding reduction in the numbers of NATO troops. This fixation on pre-determined timelines was alarming the leaders and commanders of the international effort in Bosnia itself. In April 1997, Eide was to make a presentation to NATO Secretary-General Javier Solana and NATO Council ambassadors visiting Sarajevo. He sat with David Harland, UNMIBH's head of civil affairs, and me, and we discussed how he should address this issue. In his speech, Eide told the ambassadors that they must 'focus on the end-state and not on the end-date'. They could not take decisions about troop numbers based on a timeline dreamed up in Brussels, but should do so on the basis of identifiable achievements and benchmarks.

The phrase stuck. We began to hear senior US diplomats talking about 'end-state, not end-date'. It was one of UNMIBH's unsung achievements, and it has passed into the language.

The General's kitchen

With responsibility for policing, UNMIBH and IPTF were constantly working to develop close ties at all levels of the IFOR/SFOR military command. This was immeasurably assisted by the arrival as SFOR commander in June 1997 of a truly remarkable individual, General Eric Shinseki, who would later be sacked as chief of staff of the US Army by President Bush for using his Bosnian experience to estimate the number of troops that the US would require to secure Iraq after the invasion, and who would, in retirement, be appointed secretary of veterans affairs in the Obama administration.

General Shinseki quickly recognised the importance of effective coordination of this complex operation at all levels of command, and got his commanders to focus on this with new and welcome energy. He also understood that he possessed a weapon with which he could quickly improve the atmosphere within the civilian leadership of the international effort – his kitchen. Although a number of restaurants were open in Sarajevo, the fare was generally monotonous and the service grumpy. Invitations to dinner from the General at his headquarters on the outskirts of Sarajevo could not be declined. These principals' meetings with wine and good food were carefully orchestrated to ensure that they achieved the desired operational agreements before they were allowed to move on to team-building and story-telling. In briefings to military officers about to deploy on peacekeeping operations, I always remind them of this precious asset that they have at their disposal.

Support or implement?

Was the international effort designed to run the country, or to support Bosnian institutions in their efforts to do so? In UNMIBH, we certainly started out assuming that our role was to support and assist the work of the Bosnians. The IPTF was there to train, advise and monitor. Of course, the NATO military operation had to keep a lid on hostilities, but within that secure environment, we saw our role and the role of the other civilian agencies as advisory and not executive.

So, when the idea was first discussed that the IPTF might 'certify' individual police officers who had completed a training programme, and even 'de-certify' officers who reverted to their old bullying ways, we were surprised. Perhaps we should not have been; the overall inter-governmental coordinating body to which the High Representative reported had, after all, been called the 'Peace Implementation Council' and not the Peace Support Council. As time went on, it became increasingly clear that Western governments expected us to make things happen, whether Bosnian leaders agreed or not.

UN or not?

If anybody had told a UN official serving in Bosnia in 1997 that, within two years, a UN SRSG would be governing Kosovo under a Security Council mandate, they would not have been believed. After Somalia, Haiti, Rwanda and Srebrenica, there was a sense that the major powers preferred to manage things themselves, rather than entrust delicate peacekeeping tasks to the United Nations. They would use organisations like OSCE, NATO and Offices of High Representatives to do it. UNMIBH's role in charge of policing in Bosnia felt like an after-thought – even possibly a relic.

The major distinction between the United Nations and organisations like the OSCE, NATO or the Office of the High Representative, is that people who work in the UN, with the exception of uniformed military or police officers, are recruited by the organisation in an individual capacity, while those working for the other organisations are generally seconded by their governments. This may seem like a minor bureaucratic distinction; it is not. An organisation that relies on secondments finds it difficult to build up and maintain an institutional memory and identity. In the time I was in Bosnia, less than two years, I worked with up to four different people occupying some of the key posts in the military, the OSCE and the Office of the High Representative. They came, we got to know each other, and they were rotated. Military assignments were typically of six months; civilian secondments were usually longer, but the same principle applied; once the tour was over, the person filling the post would usually return, not to the headquarters of the organisation, but to the service of his or her government.

While we did not envy our colleagues in NATO or the OSCE their institutional structures, we were jealous of what seemed to be their immunity from scrutiny and criticism. Representatives of the Western governments that provided the staff to the High Representative and the OSCE were reluctant to criticise these organisations, while they seemed to feel no such compunction about lambasting the UN in off-the-record briefings to journalists. We could only conclude that they felt less inhibited about criticising an organisation to which they did not provide the personnel than one in which colleagues from their own government's service were employed. After the first elections organised by the OSCE in September 1996, colleagues in UNMIBH remarked that if the UN had run such a shambolic operation, we would have been blasted in the media, rather than offered the flowers of praise that the OSCE received.

Guns and gendarmes

There were two protracted debates in UNMIBH and with our partners relating to the police. The first was: should IPTF officers be armed? And the second was: did Bosnia need formed police units like the French gendarmerie or the Italian carabinieri to deal with civil disturbances?

The first seemed easy; if the international police were supposed to exercise executive powers, the Security Council would have given them the mandate to do so. Since they had not, there could be no reason to arm them. Many experienced police colleagues argued that they would be in more danger if they were armed than if they were not.

In August 1997, while serving as acting SRSG in Kai Eide's absence, I found out that the IPTF could still be asked to play an 'executive' role, even if its officers were not armed. Colonel Werner Schum of Germany, one of two deputy IPTF commissioners, was also acting commissioner in the absence of his boss. The new High Representative, Carlos Westendorp of Spain, convened us to ask for the UN's participation in a raid on the police headquarters in Banja Luka, the major city in the western half of the Serb Republic. It was suspected that the Serb police there were involved in criminal operations and were also actively undermining their own president, Mrs Biljana Plavsic.

It became clear to me fairly quickly that this was one of those situations where you do something first, and ask permission from your headquarters later. If I asked New York for authorisation, I would put senior officials in a most uncomfortable position. Such an operation was clearly outside our formal mandate, but we were expected to support the overall international effort led by the High Representative. It was better simply to put the operation that we managed at the service of the senior representative of the international community and let him do the explaining. Colonel Schum agreed.

We flew up to Banja Luka in a NATO helicopter. The operation went without a hitch. British NATO forces secured the police headquarters and removed the Serb police. UN police took it over and boxed up the evidence. After that, Mrs Plavsic was able to hold discussions with her visitors without the constant oversight of her own police force.

The second issue, on the need for 'formed police units' was less clear-cut. It was probably my British background that put me in the camp of those initially opposed to creating a Bosnian gendarmerie. Since the three communities were still so polarised, there was surely a risk that such a force would be used in the service of community politics. Whatever the merits of the argument, I was clearly on the wrong side of history. Formed police units are a fact of life in most of Europe today.

Staff security

The security of United Nations staff in the field is the responsibility of the UN security coordinator in New York, assisted by a designated official for security (DOS) in each specific country. In countries without peacekeeping missions, the DOS function is almost always assigned to the UN resident coordinator. In countries with peacekeeping missions, the task is usually assigned to the SRSG. The DOS is assisted by one or more security officers, working full-time on keeping people safe. Security management in UN field operations today is considerably more cautious, professional and regulated than was the case in 1996.

Although the SRSG in Bosnia was assigned the role of DOS, each of the three that I worked for regularly asked me to deputise for them and chair meetings of the Security Management Team. We met weekly with representatives of all UN agencies.

UN civilian staff in Bosnia could be divided broadly into three categories: the civilian staff of UNMIBH; the staff of UNHCR and WFP, who had been working throughout the country delivering humanitarian aid during the war; and the staff working for the development agencies, who were coming into the country for the first time, now that the war was over.

Security in a post-conflict environment relies on good communications. In the absence of a functioning telephone network that reached all parts of Bosnia, we had two big problems: Bosnia is a mountainous country in which radio communication is difficult; and the communications systems used by peacekeepers and humanitarian agencies were incompatible, and both were incompatible with the NATO military system. Put simply, the radio in a UNHCR vehicle could not talk to the radio in an IPTF police station, which could not talk to the radio in the local IFOR military base. Communications between civilian agencies, police and military had to be relayed through offices where all three systems were available. Additional links in any communications system lead to mistakes and delays. I spent many hours in meetings trying to get the technicians to come up with ways of making the systems more communicative, and, failing that, to get communications hubs installed in more places.

These efforts were not assisted by the fact that each of the major international players divided the country up in different ways. NATO had three multinational divisions, based in Mostar, Banja Luka and Tuzla. UNMIBH had seven regional offices, UNHCR and OSCE each had five. Each regional office covered a number of cantons or municipality level offices. But each organisation had made different choices about which cantons or municipalities to cover from each regional office.

Surely, something could be done to rationalise this. We persuaded the principals to empower a working group to come up with recommendations. I was designated to represent the UN, in the hope that other organisations would appoint people at an equally senior level. It did not happen. Eventually, the other organisations were persuaded to send somebody to attend a meeting and a time was found when everybody could attend. The enthusiasm of the group members grew. Recommendations were made. But once they got back to their bosses, our mid-level colleagues were told, in no uncertain terms, that there was no way their organisation was going to change its structure just for the sake of better coordination. Perhaps it had been naive to expect otherwise. Organisational structure is one of those things that has to be agreed at the outset. Once the investment had been made, only the UN, of all the international bodies, was willing to go back to its headquarters and tell them that changes were required and would have to be paid for.

Did it matter? In my view it did. If all the international organisations were structured differently, it reinforced in people's minds the idea that the international organisations were more concerned with their internal business than with working together to make a difference in Bosnia. This was yet another serious weakness of the Dayton architecture.

Disaster

On 16 September 1997, a staff member of UNMIBH's transport unit, responsible for internal travel, came to me: the deputy High Representative, Ambassador Gerd Wagner, and a team from his office wanted to travel to Bugojno in central Bosnia on the following day. Could we take them in our helicopter? Wagner had responsibility for relations within the Federation between the Muslims and the Croats. Bugojno town and municipality were on the fault line between Muslim-majority and Croat-majority areas. Relations between the two communities were strained.

It was our practice to accommodate such requests if we could; it promoted inter-agency cooperation. So, we discussed the schedule: the deputy commissioner of the IPTF, David Kriskovich, had booked the helicopter for a trip up to Brcko on the same day. Could we combine the two? It seemed that we could. The flight would go first to Bugojno, drop the Ambassador's party and continue on to Brcko.

The next day I was preparing to fly to Copenhagen with the IPTF commissioner to discuss with the Danish government our programme to train the Bosnian civilian police, when the first call came: the helicopter had not arrived in Bugojno on schedule. Gradually, the facts were pieced together. The flight had left Sarajevo in clear skies; the pilots had plotted a direct course across the mountains. About half way to Bugojno, they encountered dense fog. Trying to climb, they hit trees and crashed into the mountainside. The four Ukrainian crew were all seated in the nose of the helicopter, and were able to escape through the front window. But their efforts to rescue the passengers were in vain, as the reserve fuel tank located inside the passenger cabin, exploded. All 12 passengers died.

It was the most devastating blow imaginable. Everybody working in the international effort knew somebody on the flight. Many of us had felt that Gerd Wagner, who spoke Serbo-Croat, had brought something special to the task of bringing Muslims and Croats together. Both he and David Kriskovich were my direct counterparts at the principals' meetings. David and his friend Al Becaccio had been dynamic, influential characters in the IPTF office. But I also had in the back of my mind the idea that if

I had been less accommodating of Gerd's request to use the helicopter, our relations might have been strained for a while, but at least he and the 11 others would still be alive. And then I wondered what if I had refused the request and they had travelled by car on Bosnia's treacherous roads and been involved in an accident? 'What if?' is a particularly fruitless question in this line of work.

In an effort to banish these thoughts, I threw myself into the organisation of the multi-faith memorial service in Sarajevo's Catholic Cathedral. By coincidence, the great soprano, Barbara Hendricks, was in town as an ambassador for UNHCR. She agreed to postpone her departure and sing the Ave Maria at the service. It was heartbreaking. The names of 12 talented and enthusiastic people had been added to those of the thousands of others whose lives had already been cut short in Bosnia.

De-mining

By the time I arrived in Sarajevo in 1996, it had been decided that the de-mining effort should be coordinated jointly by the High Representative's office and UNMIBH. I found myself co-chairing regular meetings with the military adviser to the High Representative, a two-star officer from the British forces.

Whereas the de-mining effort in Afghanistan had been hard work, but rewarding, the effort in Bosnia was unremittingly frustrating. With an ignorance of the situation on the ground that is breathtaking, the Dayton Accords had required the military forces of the three warring parties to clear all mined areas within 30 days of the signature of the agreement!

Nobody covered themselves in glory during those early days of mine action in Bosnia. The factions were suspicious of our motives, but the people they appointed to work with us saw opportunities for profit. They set up companies to bid for contracts under the World Bank-funded programme. Some mines were cleared, but there was no overall plan. Ian Mansfield arrived from his success in Afghanistan to take over as manager of the Mine Action Centre, and things began to look more promising, but he was quickly tempted away by the offer of a big job with UNDP in New York, and the pace of progress slowed again.

On 9 August 1997, just three weeks before her death in Paris, Princess Diana came to Bosnia to draw attention to the landmine problem. It was a great occasion, but it would be several more years before the people of Bosnia, with international support, would begin to get to grips seriously with their landmine problem.

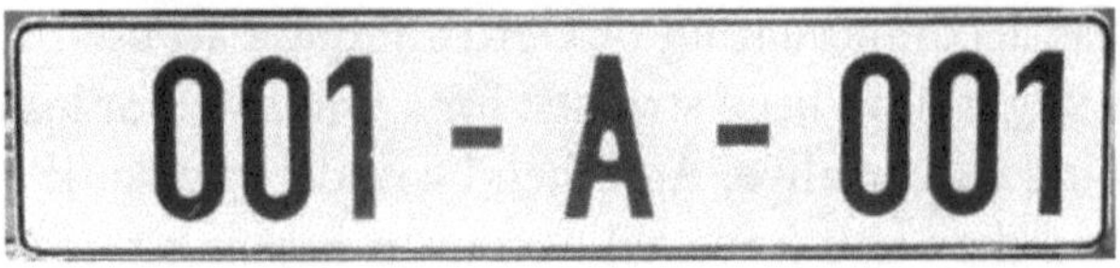

001 - A - 001

Figure 6 Model of new licence plates introduced in Bosnia and Herzegovina in 1998 using nine letters common to the Latin and Cyrillic alphabets.

Licence plates

An effort with a much quicker and happier outcome was our work with vehicle licence plates.

During the conflict, the three communities had each adopted a different design for their plates. The result was that once the peace accords were in place and people began to travel around the country, the local police could identify, from several hundred yards, the ethnicity of a vehicle's driver. This was too much of a temptation. Extortion and harassment, beatings and arrest often awaited drivers of vehicles carrying the 'wrong' plates for the town they were entering.

IPTF police stations reported regularly on these incidents. Finally, in late 1997, SRSG Eide and the High Representative agreed that something should be done. Together they convened representatives of the three sides and we sat down to discuss it. After several meetings we had a reluctant agreement from all that a single style of plate for the whole country was an acceptable idea, but then they gleefully produced the deal-breaker: the Serbs insisted that the letters on the plates should be in Cyrillic script. The Muslims and Croats were united in their outrage at the thought. All sides looked smugly content that an impasse had been reached.

So I asked how many letters the two scripts had in common. It turns out that there are nine. Perfect, we could start with three numbers, randomly selected, that would identify the municipality of registration, then there would be one of the nine common letters, and finally three more numbers, identifying individual vehicles, up to 999.

The system was adopted, implemented with remarkable efficiency and introduced in the spring of 1998, a month after I had left. Colleagues reported that volumes of traffic between the different entities and communities increased by 50 per cent within one month of the full implementation of the new plates. Simple ideas can have a big impact.

Moving on again

Sarajevo was the shortest assignment of my career and last field post. Although the UN Mission in Bosnia and Herzegovina was unique in many ways, it provided rich experience that I would draw on during my time at UN headquarters in New York. Many of the issues that we debated in Sarajevo re-appeared, in a global context, during the discussion of multi-dimensional peace operations and peacebuilding programmes.

6

A SECRETARY GENERAL FROM THE UNITED NATIONS

Kofi Annan's impact on how the UN deals with crises

All new Secretary-Generals (SGs) are challenged by the ambiguities of their job. Are they to be secretaries or generals? The big countries, especially the P5 (five permanent members of the Security Council – China, France, Russia, the UK and the US) expect the SG to be a secretary; smaller countries and the organisation's staff expect him to behave like a general.

Even more challenging than the ambiguities of the office are the constraints placed on the Secretary-General's freedom of action by the General Assembly and its committees. As Simon Chesterman and Thomas Franck point out, 'the Secretary-General frequently lacks sufficient internal authority to be an efficient administrator of the organization, while also lacking the resources to exercise his or her external functions with credibility'. In other words, having over 190 members on your board, intent on micro-managing your organisation, is not a good environment for any CEO.

But a Secretary-General can commission reports, and when he took office in January 1997, Kofi Annan quickly commissioned two, intended to tell the full stories of the UN's actions in Rwanda leading up to the genocide and in Bosnia prior to the massacre at Srebrenica. The commissioning of these reports, and the fact that Annan accepted and published them without seeking to amend a word of the texts – indeed he over-ruled efforts by some of his subordinates to make changes – helped to establish his credibility among staff and diplomats of member states as somebody who could legitimately demand accountability throughout the organisation.

The report on Srebrenica was written by David Harland, a brilliant young UN official, who had worked in Bosnia during the war and with me in UNMIBH after it, while the report on Rwanda was assigned to an external commission headed by the former prime minister of Sweden, Ingvar Carlsson. The authors of the two reports were given unrestricted access to officials and documents. Annan made it clear that he expected all staff members to give the writers their complete cooperation.

The Srebrenica report had a considerable impact on UN staff. People were surprised and encouraged to see that the Secretary-General was ready to issue in his own name a document that contained serious criticisms of the department he had been heading, and by implication of himself. It is rare for an incoming CEO to commission warts-and-all investigations into his previous assignment. Annan's move was both courageous and politically astute. It helped to create the climate in which his proposals for change were more likely to be accepted. Kofi Annan's own account of his time as SG in his memoir, *Interventions: A Life in War and Peace,* gives interesting insights into his thinking at this and other critical points in his journey.

In April 1998, at the invitation of Sergio Vieira de Mello, the new Emergency Relief Coordinator and Under-Secretary-General for humanitarian affairs, I arrived in New York to take charge of the policy development and advocacy branch in his office.

New York! The opportunity to be part of the UN Secretariat's policy-making machinery in the capital of the world was too good to miss. I could not wait to bring my experience from field assignments to bear on policy debates at headquarters.

The move also came at a good time for the family. We would be together, after the separation of Bosnia, and the boys would be able to attend the UN International School, a chance to get on with their secondary education in a stimulating environment.

Internal structural reform

This may look like a really boring topic, but it is all about how people relate to each other, and I found it fascinating.

When Kofi Annan took office, he confronted an organisation of 'stove-pipes' or 'silos'. Each UN Secretariat department (political affairs, peacekeeping operations, humanitarian affairs and so on) had become a world unto itself, in which the heads reported to the Secretary-General, but the staff had little interaction with people in other departments. Even in the humanitarian coordination mechanisms, including the Inter-Agency Standing Committee, introduced in 1991, there was no provision for coordination between humanitarian affairs and the political and peacekeeping departments.

Even within the humanitarian field, there were problems. The Department for Humanitarian Affairs (DHA), designed to coordinate humanitarian operations, did not have the confidence of the UN's main humanitarian agencies such as UNHCR, UNICEF and WFP, who saw the department as an unwelcome and generally incompetent competitor.

In August 1997, Annan presented his first recommendations for structural reform. Two proposals, designed to address the problems described above, were accepted and quickly implemented. They have changed the architecture of the UN's response to crisis and, in my view, led directly to improved performance.

Annan's response to the 'silo' problem was to establish several 'executive committees'. They brought together the heads of departments and agencies to coordinate their activities on particular issues. Two of these committees were to play a particularly important role in relation to countries emerging from conflict, the Executive Committee on Peace and Security, chaired by the head of the political affairs department, and the Executive Committee on Humanitarian Affairs, chaired by the Emergency Relief Coordinator.

These new committees would, for the first time, bring the heads of the political and peacekeeping departments face to face with the often agonising situations confronting their humanitarian and development colleagues, and would also ensure that when they were discussing their field operations, they would have to take account of the humanitarian and development perspectives.

It is hard to exaggerate the significance of this change. Of course, old habits of caution and secrecy die hard, and there were many occasions, particularly in the early days, when heads of departments sent junior colleagues to meetings they were not chairing, and crucial information was not shared. But the committees started to eat away at the silos, and they created forums in which, as we shall see, proposals for new policies could be presented for approval by more or less *ad hoc* coalitions of middle-ranking staff from the political, peacekeeping, humanitarian and development parts of the system.

In response to complaints from UNHCR, UNICEF and WFP that the Department of Humanitarian Affairs was too big, too operational and staffed with desk-bound bureaucrats, Annan removed the department's two main operational components, mine action and Iraq. He moved the UN Mine Action Service into the Department of Peacekeeping Operations and set up the Office for the Iraq Programme as a separate office reporting to him. DHA became the Office for the Coordination of Humanitarian Affairs (OCHA), and as its head and new Emergency Relief Coordinator, Annan brought in one of the humanitarian agencies' most respected professionals, Sergio Vieira de Mello from UNHCR.

After some initial scepticism, OCHA quite quickly became accepted by UN agencies, governments of both donor countries and countries affected by disasters, and even by the Red Cross and many NGOs, as an important facilitator of humanitarian operations.

Key leaders

The United Nations Secretariat is a unique organisation. It can easily appear to the outside world, and perhaps to some insiders, as a vast anonymous bureaucracy, fatally constrained by the infighting among the more than 190 member states in the General Assembly, and by personnel policies which seem to reward mediocrity and stifle initiative. While this depiction may have some validity in some areas of work, it is not relevant to the management of operations in countries affected by crisis. As this chapter tries to demonstrate, the qualities of individual staff members in key positions can have a critical impact on the way the UN performs in the field.

Kofi Annan made three appointments that, in my view, were to be critical to the success of his reform efforts. Sergio Vieira de Mello was a former colleague of Annan's at UNHCR; Mark Malloch-Brown, another former UNHCR colleague, who appeared in Chapter 2, and had been a vice-president at the World Bank, became Administrator of UNDP in 1999; and Jean-Marie Guéhenno, a French diplomat, was appointed head of peacekeeping operations in 2000.

'Sergio'

Sergio Vieira de Mello, a Brazilian, had been Assistant High Commissioner for Refugees before coming to New York. In July 1999, after only 18 months as ERC, he was appointed as the first head of the UN Mission in Kosovo, and then, in November 1999, as head of the UN Mission in East Timor. In both places he acted as de facto head of government, since both territories were under UN interim administration. In

September 2002, having handed over power to the new government of Timor Leste, he was appointed UN High Commissioner for Human Rights, based in Geneva. In May 2003, under strong American pressure, Annan asked Sergio, as he was known to everyone, to leave his post in Geneva and go as his special representative to Baghdad, for four months. On 19 August 2003, a suicide bomber driving a large truck packed with explosives detonated himself and the truck directly outside Sergio's office on the second floor of the UN's Canal Hotel building. Sergio was trapped in the rubble of the building and died about 90 minutes later (see also Chapter 7).

Sergio had radiant charm, great energy, a brilliant mind and a steely determination to get things done. In his brief time as head of OCHA, he oversaw the first stage of its transformation from the slow, bureaucratic and generally unhelpful style of DHA to a lighter 'can-do' OCHA. He launched OCHA as the essential leader of international humanitarian efforts around the world.

Peacekeeping – Guéhenno

Jean-Marie Guéhenno took over as head of peacekeeping operations in October 2000. It is hard to exaggerate the size and complexity of the task that confronted him. He was responsible for the activities of 18 peacekeeping missions, ranging from small missions of military observers to huge multi-dimensional operations, with military, police, political, human rights, mine action and administrative components. Some of these missions, like UNMOGIP (India/Pakistan) and UNTSO (Middle East) had been around for over 50 years. Others, such as the missions in Kosovo (1999), East Timor (1999) and Sierra Leone (2000), had been mounted in quick succession from scratch. By 2007, there were 100,000 people, 80,000 of them in military uniform, taking part in these missions. Guéhenno commanded the largest military force outside its own borders in the world, except for the US Army. But he had to exercise that command with a fraction of the staff available to any national military, and with procedures and constraints that strictly limited his authority.

When he arrived, DPKO was organised at headquarters into functional divisions – Office of Operations, Field and Logistics Division, Military Division, Civilian Police Division and UN Mine Action Service. Each of these divisions had its own sense of identity, ethos and character. In some cases, this identity was associated with the person in charge; in others, such as the military and police, it was more their shared uniform and culture that defined them. But all parts of DPKO shared one characteristic – they were resistant to change.

This was the environment into which Jean-Marie Guéhenno, 'a tall ratiocinative Cartesian', as James Traub described him, walked in October 2000. Over the next few years he set about changing the mindset of DPKO. He introduced some basic modern management principles. He tried to replace the largely unwritten rules of doctrine and procedures with clearly drafted texts. And he encouraged the different parts of the department to talk to each other, work together and even to reach out to staff in other departments.

In these efforts he was hugely assisted by two developments: the Executive Committee on Peace and Security provided a forum in which DPKO could demonstrate its new openness to cooperation with other parts of the UN system; and the Report on United Nations Peace Operations, produced by the panel chaired by Lakhdar Brahimi in August 2000, and described in detail below, provided the blueprint for many of the changes he needed to introduce.

Guéhenno is a manager, thinker, writer and a master of his brief. He has a quick eye for the significant detail. Some felt that he was too often indecisive, that he would rather schedule another round of discussions among his senior staff than come out with a decision and stick by it. But this caution probably came from having been bounced into decisions by one part of his department, whose staff had failed to point out that the decision they were recommending was vehemently opposed by another part of their own department.

While improving performance in New York, Guéhenno devoted equal energy to the quality of the work in the field. He gave particular attention to the large multi-dimensional missions, where mistakes could come to haunt the whole UN. These included the missions in Afghanistan, the Democratic Republic of the Congo (DRC), East Timor, Haiti, Kosovo, Liberia, Sierra Leone and Sudan. He visited, took phone calls from the special representatives, argued their cases in the Security Council and intervened directly with governments. Nowhere was this more critical to the eventual success of a mission than in 2003, when he persuaded the French government to send a military force to stabilise the situation in Bunia in eastern DRC, where UN peacekeepers were unable to cope with the atrocities of rebel groups.

After the disasters of the 1990s, it was by no means clear that the Security Council would have the stomach for a new round of major

UN peacekeeping operations. But by 2007, DPKO would be managing 18 missions with 100,000 personnel, at an annual cost of over $5 billion. It is in large part thanks to the partnership between Kofi Annan as Secretary-General, Jean-Marie Guéhenno as Head of DPKO and Lakhdar Brahimi, as author of his eponymous report, that this remarkable achievement was possible.

But Guéhenno would be the first to admit that he was unable to make enough progress in three key areas: the situations in which the Security Council could not agree on a course of action; the difficulty of managing the transition from peacekeeping to recovery; and the management issues that make the UN Secretariat less effective than it should be, where differences in the General Assembly between the rich Western group of nations and the developing countries have obstructed the modernisation of the UN's administration.

Development – Malloch-Brown

Chapter 2 introduced Mark Malloch-Brown as a young field officer for UNHCR in Thailand. From there, Malloch-Brown went to UNHCR headquarters in Geneva and from there back to journalism. Then, as partner in a US-based public relations firm he advised several people on how to become presidents of their respective countries. Among the successes was Cory Aquino of the Philippines; among the failures Mario Vargas Llosa of Peru.

When, in 1999, his former UNHCR colleague, Kofi Annan, asked him to run the UN Development Programme (UNDP), Malloch-Brown was vice president for external relations at the World Bank. He became the first non-US citizen to head UNDP. He wasted no time in making his presence felt.

At UNDP, he forced an organisation that had taken on an enormous range of different tasks to focus on a few key areas, particularly the issues of governance and poverty reduction. He also worked to improve UNDP's relations with its political and humanitarian UN partners, although he jealously guarded what UNDP insiders saw as their 'turf'. He built up the division responsible for managing UNDP's cooperation with the humanitarian agencies, by upgrading its head to assistant secretary-general and appointing Julia Taft to the post. Ms Taft came from heading an American NGO consortium, Interaction, and had impeccable political connections in Washington. She worked hard to educate her new colleagues in UNDP about the realities of dealing creatively with their political and humanitarian colleagues, and also to explain UNDP to the other parts of the system.

Malloch-Brown's appointments of key personnel in UNDP, his friendships with Kofi Annan and Sergio Vieira de Mello and his approach to the UN system helped to foster the change in atmosphere that facilitated the progress described in the rest of this chapter. It was his misfortune that his move in January 2004 to become Kofi Annan's chief of staff, and later deputy Secretary-General, was in response to a desperate cry for help from the Secretary-General, confronted with the unrelenting fall-out from the Iraq oil-for-food scandal. That fall-out would continue right up to the end of 2006, when Annan and Malloch-Brown left office together.

Policy initiatives

An 'Agenda for Peace', published in 1992 by Annan's predecessor, Boutros Boutros-Ghali, offered a sense of what the UN should be doing, but it did not set out in any detail how it should be doing it. The final piece of the jigsaw, therefore, was the development of a new set of policies and guidance notes, which would define what the Security Council and the Secretariat could expect of each other, and how the different parts of the system were expected to work together.

Annan initiated a number of significant policy reviews. Three of these initiatives were of particular importance to the search for appropriate responses to crisis situations and helped to shape the more coherent approach that emerged between 1998 and 2000. I was privileged to work directly on two of them. I am including detailed accounts of my involvement in these two issues, in part because I am not aware that the story has been told elsewhere, but also because I think they illustrate how the United Nations can be made to work better, to respond more effectively to crisis situations than it has done in the past.

Protection of civilians

William Shawcross's *Deliver us from Evil*, published in 2000, is a sympathetic but nevertheless devastating account of the crises that confronted the UN in the 1990s. He recounts the agonies of ordinary people in Cambodia, Bosnia, Somalia, Rwanda, the DRC, Iraq, Afghanistan, Kosovo and East Timor and the often futile efforts of humanitarian workers of the United Nations, the Red Cross and NGOs to do something to help. Time and again peacekeepers were present in the countries where atrocities were taking place, but were unable to do anything to stop the killings or the ethnic cleansing, either because their mandates did not authorise them to, or because they did not have adequate personnel or equipment.

When Vieira de Mello took over as Emergency Relief Coordinator in 1998, part of his job was to brief the Security Council on the humanitarian situation in countries on the Council's agenda. During his first year in office, he found that he was repeatedly making the same points. So, the idea developed that he might address the Council, not on the situation in one country, but on the whole issue of the nature of humanitarian assistance and its linkages to the role and responsibility of the Security Council for maintaining peace and security.

On 21 January 1999, Vieira de Mello gave the Security Council an impassioned account of the appalling situations facing civilian populations and the humanitarian aid workers trying to help them. In doing so, he introduced most of the themes that were to become the elements of the debate on 'the protection of civilians in armed conflict'. He spoke about unchecked violations of international humanitarian law in which civilians were the targets of military action; he deplored the reluctance of the Security Council, in the wake of the debacle in Somalia, to authorise the peacekeeping operations that were required; he stressed the need for access for humanitarian workers to places where civilians were in need of help; he talked about the need to control 'hate media', which fomented violence against civilian populations; he reminded the Council of the humanitarian impact of sanctions and the need for 'smart' sanctions that target individuals rather than entire communities; and, finally, he emphasised the terrible risks now being faced by humanitarian aid workers.

On 12 February, Lloyd Axworthy, Foreign Minister of Canada, presided at a public session of the Security Council on the topic of 'protection of civilians in armed conflict', at which Cornelio Sommaruga, President of the ICRC, Carol Bellamy of UNICEF and Olara Otunnu, Special Representative of the Secretary-General for Children and Armed Conflict, introduced the debate. The meeting attracted so many member states and international organisations to speak that it had to be continued for a full second day.

Sommaruga confronted the Security Council with its responsibility to provide the political solutions to the conflicts that were causing such unimaginable suffering. Carol Bellamy and Olara Otunnu presented shocking accounts of the consequences of modern conflicts for children. The enormity of the atrocities being committed against children in countries in conflict could not be denied.

The presidential statement of the Security Council issued on 12 February expressed the Security Council's dismay at the situation and promised to address the problems. But the phrasing of the Council's request to the Secretary-General reflects the extent to which members recognised that there had to be more they could do, but also their genuine confusion about what that should be:

> The Security Council considers that a comprehensive and coordinated approach by member states and international organisations and agencies is required in order to address the problem of the protection of civilians in armed conflict. To this end, the Security Council requests the Secretary-General to submit a report containing concrete recommendations to the Council by September 1999 on ways the Council, acting within its sphere of responsibility, could improve the physical and legal protection of civilians in situations of armed conflict.
>
> *Extract from Security Council presidential statement of*
> *12 February 1999*

OCHA's policy branch, which I headed, was tasked with coordinating the preparation of the report. The report would have to describe the context in a succinct but comprehensive way; identify clearly the links between the situations being described and the Security Council's responsibilities, and be completely authoritative. The recommendations would have to be both innovative and practical and have the whole-hearted support of all the key players, including Secretariat departments, UN humanitarian agencies, the ICRC and key NGOs.

The whole OCHA policy team was involved. We worked with the UN departments and agencies individually and in groups, as well as with the Red Cross, to develop the text relating to each of the eleven areas of concern, and we drafted 40 specific recommendations. The areas covered were: conflict prevention; confidence-building; humanitarian access; special measures for children and women; targeted sanctions; small arms and anti-personnel landmines; peacekeeping; separation of combatants and armed elements from civilians in camps; disarmament and demobilisation; humanitarian zones, security zones and safe corridors; and intervention in cases of systematic and widespread violations of international law. The last two issues in the report were the most contentious. Every word was chewed over. Claude Bruderlein, a lawyer and former ICRC delegate, was our in-house expert on these issues.

'Safe areas' was a concept that had gone disastrously wrong in Bosnia. The Security Council had designated Gorazde, Srebrenica and Zepa as 'safe areas', but the safety of people there depended on the cooperation of the parties to the conflict, in this case the Bosniac and Serb armies, since the members of the Council were unwilling to back their designation with the necessary force. Since the parties to the conflict were not willing to abide by the Council's conditions, the tragic result had been the massacre at Srebrenica.

The lesson was that a clear distinction had to be made between areas which would be 'safe' because the parties to the conflict had agreed as much, and areas which would be 'safe' because the international community, in the shape of the Security Council, had decided that they should be, and had dedicated the necessary force to protect them from attack. In view of the tragic history of the 'safe areas' concept, it was decided to propose instead the terms 'humanitarian zones' for the areas declared safe by the parties, and 'security zones' for the areas made safe by the international community.

The text of the recommendation reads:

I [the Secretary-General] recommend that the Security Council:

39. Establish, as a measure of last resort, temporary security zones and safe corridors for the protection of civilians and the delivery of assistance in situations characterized by the threat of genocide, crimes against humanity and war crimes against the civilian population, subject to a clear understanding that such arrangements require the availability, prior to their establishment, of sufficient and credible force to guarantee the safety of civilian populations making use of them, and ensure the demilitarization of these zones and the availability of a safe-exit option.
Report of the Secretary-General on the Protection of Civilians in Armed Conflict, S/1999/957, 8 September 1999

The Security Council has not designated any 'safe areas', or humanitarian or security zones, since the report was presented.

While the issue of 'safe areas' was difficult, the issue of 'humanitarian intervention' was certain to be controversial. Some colleagues argued that the issue should not be addressed in the report, for fear of alienating support for the other recommendations. Others, and they eventually prevailed, felt that a comprehensive report on the protection of civilians in armed conflict simply had to address this question. The Secretary-General had to set out his view of when military intervention could be justified in defence of the rights of civilians. This is the recommendation which was finally agreed:

I [the Secretary-General] recommend that the Security Council:

40. In the face of massive and ongoing abuses, consider the imposition of appropriate enforcement action. Before acting in such cases, either with a United Nations, regional or multinational arrangement, and in order to reinforce political support for such efforts, enhance confidence in their legitimacy and deter perceptions of selectivity or bias toward one region or another, the Council should consider the following factors:

(a) The scope of the breaches of human rights and international humanitarian law including the numbers of people affected and the nature of the violations;
(b) The inability of local authorities to uphold legal order, or identification of a pattern of complicity by local authorities;
(c) The exhaustion of peaceful or consent-based efforts to address the situation;
(d The ability of the Security Council to monitor actions that are undertaken;
(e) The limited and proportionate use of force, with attention to repercussions on civilian populations and the environment.
ditto

This section foreshadowed both the Secretary-General's speech to the General Assembly of 20 September 1999 and the report of the International Commission on the Responsibility to Protect (2001).

The report on the Protection of Civilians in Armed Conflict was published on 8 September 1999, when the Netherlands was presiding over the Council. 'Experts' from the 15 delegations met frequently in the early days of September to discuss the Dutch draft resolution. The

133

Dutch invited OCHA to one of the meetings to answer questions about what some phrases in the report were intended to mean. It was clear that the last recommendation, on intervention, had stirred the most debate.

In the end the lack of agreement on that recommendation meant that the Council did not 'welcome the report's recommendations', but 'welcomed the report and took note of the recommendations'. Such distinctions may seem meaningless, but diplomats and UN officials got the message.

On 17 September, the Secretary-General formally presented the report to the Council. The 15 members of the Council each delivered a statement, and then member states not serving on the Council were given a chance to speak. Most welcomed the report and supported its recommendations, but Egypt and India both expressed strong reservations about the recommendation on intervention. Finally, the resolution was adopted unanimously. If the Egyptian and Indian statements had put any doubts into the minds of some delegates on the issue of intervention, they obviously felt it was too late for them to change the position they had adopted during the negotiations.

Inevitably, the resolution has a cautious tone. It contains indignation at the wickedness of warring factions, but few hard decisions about what the Council would do about it. The key issue of what to do when civilians are targeted was addressed in two short paragraphs:

10. [The Council] expresses its willingness to respond to situations of armed conflict where civilians are being targeted or humanitarian assistance to civilians is being deliberately obstructed, including through the consideration of appropriate measures at the Council's disposal in accordance with the Charter of the United Nations, and notes, in that regard, the relevant recommendations contained in the report of the Secretary-General;

11. [The Council] expresses its willingness to consider how peacekeeping mandates might better address the negative impact of armed conflict on civilians.

Security Council Resolution 1265, 17 September 1999

Just three days later, the Secretary-General chose 'intervention' as the theme of his opening statement to the general debate of the General Assembly. His remarks were considered 'courageous' by the West, but 'provocative and inappropriate' by some countries in the developing world. Several leaders used their General Assembly speeches to reaffirm the concept of national sovereignty and reject Annan's position. In the atmosphere prevailing after 20 September, the resolution on the protection of civilians in armed conflict would probably not have been adopted. It had sneaked through with three days to spare.

What did resolution 1265 actually achieve? Did it make any difference at all to the people suffering in brutal conflicts? I believe it made a difference in at least five ways.

First and foremost, it made a difference in the drafting of Security Council mandates for UN peace operations. It obliged the Council to be specific in defining the responsibilities of peacekeeping forces when confronted with situations in which the lives of civilians were being threatened. The mandates for peacekeeping missions in the DRC and Sierra Leone reflected this. And the tougher mandates made a real difference to the way that peacekeepers operated.

Secondly, the resolution launched a series of thematic debates in the Council, notably those on children and women, which led to changes in how peacekeeping operations are resourced. To take just one example, child protection officers are now routinely deployed as part of peace operations.

Thirdly, it confirmed that all peacekeepers must be trained in appropriate provisions of international law. Fourthly, the Council agreed to consider the humanitarian consequences of sanctions regimes, before they are imposed. And finally, it launched a process, which continues to this day, of regular joint reflection by governments, the United Nations, the Red Cross and NGOs to identify better ways of protecting civilians caught up in armed conflict.

By the end of 2006, the Council had issued four resolutions and five presidential statements on the issue of protection of civilians in armed conflict. It had agreed on one resolution and four presidential statements on the issue of 'women and peace and security'. And on the issue of 'children and armed conflict', it had issued no fewer than six resolutions and four presidential statements. The Council held debates and issued resolutions or statements on small arms, sanctions, landmines and the protection of UN personnel. Most of these resolutions referred back specifically to resolution 1265.

In March 2011, I wrote that it had been fascinating, and satisfying, to watch the process by which the Security Council had used the doctrine of the responsibility to protect, often abbreviated as R2P, which had been endorsed in the World Summit Declaration of 2005, as justification for resolution 1973 authorising the use of force in Libya. With its emphasis on the protection of civilians in armed conflict, the resolution seemed to have learned from the lessons of earlier conflicts. The R2P doctrine had gradually taken shape over the previous 12 years, but its basic principle – that the Security Council had an obligation to intervene with force in situations where the lives of large numbers of civilians were at risk, and all other means of bringing the slaughter to an end had been exhausted – echoed the conclusion in paragraph 40 of the Secretary-General's report in 1999 on the protection of civilians in armed conflict. After years of military interventions not authorised by the Security Council, this was refreshing.

How quickly things change. As I write in 2014, the Security Council has done nothing to stop the atrocities taking place in Syria. Indeed, the permanent members of the Council are lined up on opposite sides of the conflict. It feels very much like the proxy war in Afghanistan in the 1980s. Who will protect the civilians now?

The 'Brahimi report'

UN peacekeeping grew slowly between 1948 and 1990, constrained by the inability of the Security Council to agree during the Cold War. The massive expansion of activities in the early 1990s placed an intolerable strain on an organisation that was not adequately prepared or resourced. International staff were recruited in large numbers and sent to work in field missions with few background checks and no prior training or orientation.

Although Ambassador Lakhdar Brahimi never headed one of the UN Secretariat departments, his influence on the UN's response to crisis was greater than most of those who did. Brahimi had been Algeria's foreign minister from 1991 to 1993. He was the UN Secretary-General's Special Representative in South Africa during the elections in 1994 that brought Nelson Mandela to power. From there he went as SRSG to Haiti from 1994 to 1996, and then became special envoy to Afghanistan from July 1997 to October 1999, during the time of the Taliban.

In March 2000, Annan asked Brahimi to chair a panel to look into the management of peacekeeping operations. The report of the panel has defined the UN's approach to peacekeeping since it was published.

When the panel began work in early 2000, they were inundated with ideas for change. Within six months, they had put together detailed recommendations about almost every conceivable aspect of peace operations. The topics included preventive action, peacebuilding, doctrine and strategy, mandates, information and strategic analysis, transitional civil administration, deployment guidelines, mission leadership, military personnel, civilian police personnel, civilian specialists, logistics support and expenditure management, funding headquarters support, mission planning and support, structural adjustments in DPKO and strengthening other relevant Secretariat departments.

The huge range of issues and the specificity of the recommendations, put together in such a short space of time, reflected the fact that there was broad agreement over what needed to change. The failures of the 1990s had been marked by mutual recriminations. Governments had blamed 'the UN', by which they meant 'the bureaucracy in New York'. UN staff blamed the members of the Security Council for lack of 'political will'. What the report showed above all was that the relationship between the Security Council and the Secretariat was not working.

From all the report's recommendations, there are ten which are critical for understanding its significance and measuring its impact. They can be summarised crudely as follows:

1. UN peacekeeping operations cannot be expected to succeed, and must not be asked to try, in places where there is no peace to keep.
2. The Secretariat should put forward a strategy to strengthen its capacity to support peacebuilding.
3. The elements that make up the core of a peace operation need to be integrated from the planning stage. These include policing, human rights, confidence-building, disarmament and demobilisation, electoral assistance and quick impact projects.
4. Missions must have robust mandates, with which to confront spoilers.
5. An Information and Strategic Analysis Secretariat should be established to gather and process the information (intelligence) that any military operation requires.
6. Doctrine and guidance, and the leadership of missions, must be improved.
7. The UN Standby Arrangements System needs to be capable of deploying the essential components of a mission within 30 days of a Security Council resolution. To achieve this will require a $50 million pre-commitment authority.

8. The capacity of headquarters in New York to plan and support missions must be significantly strengthened.
9. Integrated mission task forces should bring together all relevant parts of the UN system to plan new operations.
10. To achieve all this, the personnel management system must be reformed and streamlined, and must be able to reward competent staff members and get rid of incompetent ones.

The recommendations spelled out the mechanics of the new approach, but extracts from two paragraphs capture the overall sense of the revolution that Brahimi was calling for:

> [M]andates should specify an operation's authority to use force. It means bigger forces, better equipped and more costly but able to be a credible deterrent. [...] Moreover, United Nations peacekeepers – troops or police – who witness violence against civilians should be presumed to be authorized to stop it, within their means, in support of basic United Nations principles.
>
> We see a Special Representative of the Secretary-General ending a mission well accomplished, having given the people of a country the opportunity to do for themselves what they could not do before: to build and hold onto peace, to find reconciliation, to strengthen democracy, to secure human rights.
>
> *Report of the Panel on UN Peace Operations, S/2000/809,*
> *21 August 2000*

Looking back now, after significant successes for UN peacekeeping in places like Burundi, Kosovo, Liberia, Sierra Leone and Timor Leste, it is encouraging to see what improvements can be made to the management of UN operations when the people and the circumstances are right.

I watched Brahimi's team, some of whom I knew from UNMIBH in Bosnia, putting the report together from across the street in OCHA. As the reference to 'integrated missions' suggests, a core principle of their thinking was that peacekeeping could no longer be done in isolation from the rest of the UN system. Although the panel had sought the views of humanitarian and development specialists, their report was not intended to be a consensus document. That would require one more step.

Perhaps the greatest tribute to Brahimi's long-lasting influence at the United Nations was the number of times I heard people discussing who could be sent to manage a particularly difficult assignment and saying, 'We need to clone Brahimi!'

Working together

One of the issues that bedevilled UN work in countries affected by conflict in the 1990s was the relationship between the political, humanitarian and development arms of the UN. In the chapters on Afghanistan and Bosnia, I have described the multitude of *ad hoc* arrangements that were dreamed up in those countries. In general, political representatives of the Secretary-General thought they should be in charge of everything; humanitarians thought that they should be completely independent of everybody else; and the development agencies, who had often been in the country for 20 years, wondered what on earth these cowboys from the political and humanitarian agencies thought they could achieve by jetting in for six months, acting as though they owned the place and then departing as quickly as they had come, expecting that everything would be fine.

In talking with colleagues in New York about my experiences in Afghanistan and Bosnia, I discovered that they had been quite typical. There was no clear understanding about how political, humanitarian and development components of the UN system should relate to each other in crisis or post-conflict countries. Surely, that gap could be filled by an instruction from the Secretary-General.

After we had reached agreement among OCHA's senior managers that this was a priority for us, Vieira de Mello asked his political, peacekeeping and development colleagues to join OCHA in preparing a first draft of what the Secretary-General would be asked to promulgate. He asked me to represent OCHA in the discussions. To my delight, I found that the other three departments had designated highly congenial colleagues, Michael Møller from Political Affairs, Chris Coleman from Peacekeeping and Omar Bakhet from UNDP. We agreed to spend a day together in the offices of the International Peace Academy, with our mobile phones switched off. By the end of the day, we had produced a first draft.

The common theme running through the document was that the SRSGs, resident coordinators and humanitarian coordinators were always expected to talk to each other, to meet regularly, to share information and to share with each other key documents that they sent to, or received from, their own headquarters. In multi-dimensional peace missions, where the UN was responsible for supporting the implementation of a comprehensive peace agreement, there should be only one UN, united under the authority of the SRSG. In such cases, the posts of resident coordinator and humanitarian coordinator should, wherever possible, be held by the same person, who should also be a deputy SRSG.

However, where the conflict was still ongoing, and there was no peace agreement, the UN humanitarian coordinator would not work under the SRSG, but the two should still consult regularly. All situations in which the three arms of the UN were working together required the support of a headquarters-based task force or working group. Although the team on the ground was expected to resolve policy differences among themselves, whenever possible, there had to be a headquarters body to which they could refer disagreements.

When the four of us presented the draft to our bosses, we were all chided for having conceded too much. More fine-tuning was required, but there were few major changes in the text that went to the Executive Committee on Humanitarian Affairs. In spite of the reservations of some humanitarian agencies concerned with preserving the independence of humanitarian action from the clutches of the peacekeepers, the draft was agreed and went up to the Secretary-General's office. It was issued by the Secretary-General on 11 December 2000.

The Note of Guidance was reviewed in 2005 and a new text, relating specifically to integrated missions, was issued on 9 February 2006. The Note left unchanged the guidance that applies in situations where there is no integrated mission, but it includes negotiated agreements on several issues that could not be resolved in 2000.

From relief to development, and the Peacebuilding Commission

While working in Afghanistan in 1995, I attended a meeting at the UN Staff College in Turin about the 'relief to development continuum', part of a long-running effort to ensure that people being assisted to recover from conflict are not abandoned by the humanitarian agencies before rehabilitation and development programmes are in place to provide them with sustainable livelihoods. By the time I arrived in New York in 1998, the idea of a 'continuum' had been discarded, but the High Commissioner for Refugees, Sadako Ogata, had taken up the issue by describing the gap that almost invariably appeared when her agency had helped refugees to return home with an initial settlement package, but there was no agency ready to provide help for reconstruction or even basic income-generation. Within the UN, the issue became known as 'Mrs Ogata's gap'.

Many culprits for this perennial problem were identified, including the excessively sharp divide between humanitarian and development funding within donor governments. Many solutions were proposed, including the idea, taken up at a modest level by both the US government and the World Bank, of so-called 'third window' funds, neither humanitarian nor development, but specifically for transitional situations. These funded rehabilitation activities using approval and disbursement procedures borrowed from humanitarian practice. Although these initiatives were helpful in a few places, they did not herald a new dawn, and Mrs Ogata's gap is, unfortunately, as much of a challenge for her successors as it was for her.

In many countries, the gains so painfully and expensively made could still easily be reversed. Improvements in the design, planning and implementation of peace operations have yet to be matched in the area of peacebuilding. The 'gap' between humanitarian and peace-keeping operations on the one hand, and concerted international support for economic recovery and reconstruction on the other, remains. The birth of the Peacebuilding Commission in 2006, the major success of Annan's second-term reform efforts, has focused welcome attention on the problem, but the Commission has tended to concentrate on smaller countries like Burundi and Sierra Leone, where relatively modest injections of funds can have a significant impact. The Commission has not been able to close the basic gulf between humanitarian and development funding streams; nor has it yet provided the quick access to high quality technical and country-specific expertise that we felt in 2005 could be its key contribution to UN country teams in post-conflict countries. Fragile states still face massive challenges of governance, insecurity, poverty and disastrous levels of youth unemployment.

Kofi Annan's impact

To what extent did the initiatives described in this chapter improve the performance of the UN in the places where it matters, the countries emerging from devastating armed conflict?

On the plus side, it is undeniable that the Security Council has issued more robust and realistic mandates. In Burundi, the DRC, Kosovo, Liberia, Sierra Leone, Sudan and Timor Leste long-running conflicts have been brought to an end. The concept of integrated missions and the clear guidance on how SRSGs, resident coordinators and humanitarian coordinators should work together, have led to improvements in the coordination of operations and in cooperation among political, humanitarian and development partners in the UN system. There have also been improvements in procurement, logistics and the speed with which military contingents are deployed. The headquarters capacity of DPKO has also been strengthened, providing better support to missions in the field. The reforms of the humanitarian system in 2005, and particularly the introduction of the Central Emergency Response Fund, discussed in Chapter 9, have improved response times and coverage of humanitarian aid.

On the negative side, member states blocked Brahimi's proposal for an information and analysis secretariat. Why? It seemed like a Cold-War-style effort to maintain intelligence-gathering as a purely national activity. This has constrained the UN's ability to gather and analyse information and therefore plan effectively.

The contention that the United Nations provides excellent value for money in international peacekeeping received backing from an unlikely source in 2005. James Dobbins, a retired US ambassador, led a study of UN- and US-led peace operations for the Rand Corporation, a think-tank with impeccable ties to the US establishment. In a final chapter that compared UN and US efforts at nation-building, Dobbins concludes that:

> Assuming adequate consensus among Security Council members on the purpose for any intervention, the United Nations provides the most suitable institutional framework for most nation-building missions, one with a comparatively low cost structure, a comparatively high success rate, and the greatest degree of international legitimacy. Other possible options are likely to be either more expensive [...] or less capable.
>
> *Dobbins, James et al, The UN's role in Nation-building,*
> *Rand Corporation, 2005*

It is because the UN can offer such a good deal that it is worth the effort to make it even better. There are still plenty of areas where improvements are urgently needed, and Chapters 9 and 10 identify some of them. This chapter has tried to show that inspiring leadership and intelligent collaboration between the Security Council and the Secretariat provide a potent framework for progress.

It was a tragedy that Kofi Annan was unable to maintain this momentum into his second term as Secretary-General, which began in January 2002. But by then, 9/11 had happened in our city, the scandal of the Iraq Oil-for-Food Programme was breaking and the US-led invasion of Iraq was on the horizon. There were many casualties, but perhaps none was more relevant to this story of UN reform than the collapse of Annan's efforts to reform the Security Council and make it more representative of the modern world. That effort awaits another Secretary-General.

Figure 7 Landmines come in many shapes and sizes.

7

LANDMINES
The hidden mutilators

'Anti-personnel' landmines are designed to maim, but not kill, an individual soldier – a wounded soldier is a bigger burden on his unit than a dead one. The larger 'anti-vehicle' mines are designed to destroy a vehicle. But landmines are indiscriminate; they cannot tell whether the person standing on them is a soldier or a child, or if the vehicle driving over them is a tank or a bus. And most landmines do not have an expiry date; they can remain active, hidden underground, for decades.

During the last quarter of the twentieth century, in Laos, Afghanistan and Bosnia, and also in Angola, Cambodia, Colombia, DRC, Eritrea, Ethiopia, Iraq, Lebanon, Mozambique, Somalia, Sudan and Yemen, and a dozen other countries, thousands of people were killed and maimed every year by landmines left over from conflicts which had already ended. Thousands more people were also killed or maimed by unexploded cluster bombs and other forms of unexploded ordnance.

When I visited a stark cold hospital ward in Kabul in mid-winter, and looked into the eyes of an Afghan father sitting with his child lying pale on the bed with one leg missing, I knew I was witnessing an individual human tragedy, but that the family would represent for me the countless numbers of silent victims of these terrible weapons. There are about 800,000 disabled Afghans today. If that boy is still alive, he will be in his mid-twenties.

Landmines and their impact on people had been a constant feature of my career, from the unexploded cluster bombs on the Plain of Jars in Laos in 1975, the Cambodian landmine victims crossing into Thailand in 1980, the mine-fields around Jalalabad in Afghanistan preventing refugee return in 1992, to the mined areas on the outskirts of Sarajevo in 1996. When, in 2000, the position of head of the United Nations Mine

Action Service (UNMAS) in New York was advertised, I had to apply. UNMAS is responsible for coordinating the UN's efforts on all aspects of the fight against landmines.

The humanitarian sector of activity now known as mine action has four core components: mine clearance (including survey); mine risk education; victim assistance; and advocacy. What follows is a personal account of my time at UNMAS. It is not comprehensive. It says virtually nothing about mine risk education or victim assistance. It is presented, after a brief history, as a series of self-contained vignettes.

Mines: the historical context

Mines have been used since at least the American Civil War. They were used extensively during World War II. Prisoners of war were often forced into clearing mines. Many, inevitably, were killed or injured.

The use of very large numbers of anti-personnel mines was a feature of conflicts in the late 1970s and 1980s in Afghanistan, Angola, Cambodia and Mozambique. The weapons were cheap to make, easy to use and required no maintenance. The Soviet forces in Afghanistan used them both as perimeter protection for small fixed military positions and in huge belts around major towns. They also made large quantities available to the governments or resistance groups they supported in different parts of the world.

The town of Jalalabad in Afghanistan was a classic example. When the *mujahideen* finally entered the city in 1992, they had to negotiate their way through three huge belts of landmines laid almost all around the town, in gardens, fields, orchards and in the open desert.

Cluster munitions were used extensively by American forces in Indo-China in the 1960s. Large metal canisters containing some 200 individual bomblets, each about the size and shape of a soft-drink can, were dropped from aircraft. The canisters opened up as they fell, releasing the bomblets, which scattered over a wide area. Most were intended to explode on hitting the ground, but depending on the height and speed at which the aircraft was flying, wind and other conditions, a proportion of the cluster bomblets would fail to explode. This proportion could be between 5 and 30 per cent. So, if an aircraft dropped ten canisters in a single run, between 100 and 600 bomblets would fail to go off, and would remain on or just beneath the surface, waiting for someone or something to set them off. Cluster munitions were also used extensively by US and allied forces during both invasions of Iraq, during the 2001 campaign to drive the Taliban out of Afghanistan and by Israel in their attack on South Lebanon in August 2006.

In Chapter 4, I have described how the UN's initial reaction to the landmine problem in Afghanistan was to offer training and equipment to thousands of Afghan volunteers and encourage them to return home and clear the mines in their villages. As the scale and complexity of the problem became clearer, and as the expected rush of people returning to their villages in Afghanistan after the Soviet withdrawal failed to materialise, this approach was abandoned and replaced by a structured professional programme, entirely funded by international contributions. Once that happened, local initiatives by individuals and communities to clear mines themselves, without outside support, were generally discouraged. This happened in almost every country where the UN and international NGOs set up mine clearance operations.

Faced with the apparent urgency to start clearing mines, it was easy to spend insufficient time learning to understand the problem in depth before identifying the best solutions and the highest priorities. That this was so often the case was perhaps partly because there is no military doctrine of mine clearance for civilian needs, and so many of those involved in mine clearance operations (also known as 'de-mining') were ex-military. The military treat minefields as barriers to be crossed or avoided. A civilian mine clearance operation has to find all the mines in an area that will be used by civilians and then destroy every last one of them.

The campaign to ban anti-personnel landmines

The story of the movement that resulted in 1997 in the adoption of an international treaty to ban anti-personnel landmines (the Ottawa Convention) is a remarkable one. I believe that its success owed much to two people whose role in making it happen is not always recognised: Cornelio Sommaruga, president of the International Committee of the Red Cross (ICRC), and Princess Diana.

As Cambodia finally opened up to the world in 1993, and international organisations moved in, including a huge United Nations peacekeeping operation, doctors working with the ICRC were outraged by what they found – thousands of ordinary villagers missing limbs and more new casualties arriving in the hospitals every day. In impassioned messages, they urged the leadership of the ICRC to denounce these inhuman weapons. When these messages reached Geneva, the ICRC's legal team argued that it was not the role of this neutral organisation to take a public position on the morality or legality of a particular type of weapon. But Sommaruga over-ruled them and began to speak out publicly in support of the growing call from NGOs for a ban, emphasising the idea that any military utility which these weapons might have was far outweighed by their indiscriminate and indefinite threat to the civilians whose rights the ICRC was charged with protecting.

I am often asked what impact Princess Diana had on the landmine issue, usually by people who seem to expect me to say that she had little or none. In fact, she had a dramatic impact, and it had a lot to do with timing.

The picture of Princess Diana walking through a minefield in Angola in January 1997, wearing a suit of protective clothing, her subsequent campaigning on the issue and her visit to minefields in Bosnia just a few weeks before her death, helped to create the momentum that led to the adoption of the Anti-Personnel Mine Ban Treaty in December the same year. When the picture in Angola was taken, Diana was quoted as saying she hoped that the mines that mutilate children would be banned. She was publicly criticised by members of the British government of the time for overstepping her authority and for speaking against British government policy, which was to retain the mines. The Labour Party opposition naturally seized the opportunity to attack the Conservative government and speak against the use of mines. On 1 May 1997, the Conservative government was defeated at the election by Labour, which over-ruled military advice and accepted the idea of a mine ban treaty. Britain was then joined by France. However, while over 150 countries have ratified the treaty, the other three permanent members of the Security Council (China, Russia and the US) have still not done so. If Britain had not supported the treaty, France might well not have done so and other European countries would have hesitated. The effort could well have failed.

It was ironic that Diana was wearing the HALO Trust logo in the famous picture, because, of all NGOs involved in the mine clearance business, HALO was the least supportive of the push for a mine ban treaty, probably because of their close ties to the British military and the Conservative Party.

While Cornelio Sommaruga and Princess Diana played critical roles in creating the atmosphere in which the Ottawa Treaty could be adopted, the hard work behind the treaty itself was done by a coalition of NGOs which came together to form the International Campaign to Ban Landmines (ICBL), with the support of a small number of key governments, notably Canada, Norway and Belgium. It was the ICBL, and its ambassador, Jody Williams, who were awarded the Nobel Peace Prize in 1997 for this remarkable achievement.

In all this, the UN Secretariat and agencies had not played a major role, in spite of their involvement in mine clearance and mine awareness operations in Afghanistan, Cambodia and Mozambique. This lack of participation in the campaigning work may have been due, in part, to the fact that in the early years of UN mine action operations, most senior staff involved were former military officers.

The campaigning community of government officials and ICBL activists was rightly proud of their achievements. Some of its members felt that the UN Secretariat and agencies, having played little part in obtaining the ban, should have little or no role in putting the ban into effect. This was the situation when I took up my new job with UNMAS in December 2000. The challenge was to work out how the UN could support the ICBL movement without seeking to take it over, while at the same time helping mine-affected countries to rid themselves of this terrible legacy of war.

The Ottawa Treaty of 1997, more formally known as the Convention on the Prohibition of the Use, Stockpiling, Production and Transfer of Anti-Personnel Mines and on their Destruction, has forced governments and armed groups to change their military doctrines and eliminate a significant weapon from their arsenals. It is hard to overstate the enormity of this achievement. It has rightly been held up as a model for civil society seeking to convert outrage into real change. The Oslo Treaty on Cluster Munitions of 2008, and also the Convention on the Rights of Persons with Disabilities of 2006, can both trace their heritage back to that remarkable movement.

Should all mines be cleared?

Good intentions and a successful campaign do not necessarily produce practical legislation. While the provisions on production, sale, transfers and the destruction of stockpiles are sensible and practical, the treaty's key provision on clearance of mined areas is, in my view, flawed. Article 5 of the Convention states:

Each State Party undertakes to destroy or ensure the destruction of all anti-personnel mines in mined areas under its jurisdiction or control, as soon as possible but not later than ten years after the entry into force of this Convention for that State Party.

This provision is unambiguous. It contains no wiggle room. But it was not subjected to a risk assessment or a cost benefit analysis.

Clearing mines is risky. Taking into account the terrain, the weather, the types of landmines being cleared, the equipment being used and the experience of the de-miners, the level of risk to the de-miners in any given situation can be assessed. Put simply, the likely risk to de-miners can be compared with the likely risk, over a given time period, that somebody might inadvertently enter the mined area if it was marked, fenced and sealed off.

Compliance with the Convention does not allow for this kind of comparison. Advocates for the text of Article 5 point out that the ban on AP mines is not simply intended to save lives; it is also there to prevent the mines from being used as a weapon of war. In other words, if left in the ground, a mine may still have a military utility.

The Geneva International Centre for Humanitarian Demining (GICHD) provides administrative and secretarial back-up to what is known as 'the Ottawa process'. It hosts regular meetings of states parties to the convention, and offers an excellent venue for both formal and informal debates around the key issues relating to the convention.

I vividly recall an informal meeting convened by the GICHD at which Article 5 of the Convention was the topic for discussion. Three people involved in the effort to clear landmines in poor countries, Bob Eaton of the Survey Action Centre, Sara Sekennes, then of Norwegian Peoples Aid and myself, representing UNMAS, found ourselves surrounded by many of the successful mine-ban campaigners, lawyers from the ICRC, representatives of the ICBL, officials of key governments such as Canada and Norway and staff of GICHD itself.

For more than two hours we deployed every argument we could think of to try to persuade the group that the text of Article 5 would have to be either changed or be subjected to an agreed re-interpretation. Poor countries could simply not be expected to implement it as it stood. In Afghanistan, Soviet forces had set up bases on remote mountain tops to give them a commanding view over the land below. They had protected the perimeter of these posts with landmines. After the war, nobody was going to go up to those deserted posts. They no longer served any military purpose. They could be marked or fenced and left there. If Afghan de-miners were obliged to go up and clear them, they might well suffer casualties. Indeed, the chances of a de-miner being killed or injured during the clearance operation were far higher than the chances of an Afghan civilian being killed or injured there in the next 100 years.

'Landmine impact surveys' had been done in almost all the worst affected countries and had identified areas where mines had a high, medium or low impact on the social and economic life of nearby communities, so that governments could set priorities for clearance operations that would reduce casualty figures as quickly as possible. This programme was showing some notable successes. It was also identifying mined areas which, at present, posed no threat whatsoever to the civilian population, and which were no longer of any military value to anybody. Why should de-miners risk their lives to clear these areas?

Even wealthy Britain was faced with a problem. There were a number of minefields on the Falkland Islands in the South Atlantic, left over from the war with Argentina. The islanders had asked that the mines not be cleared, because they feared that de-miners might be killed or injured in the task; they had no use for the land, and they knew very well to avoid going near the contaminated area. If the land was fenced, even the sheep would be safe.

We argued that the feasibility of clearance operations was determined in part by the limitations of current technologies. Specifically, mines with very low or no metal content remained hard to detect and therefore especially dangerous. However, research was in progress that might soon produce new technologies that would greatly reduce the risk to de-miners, by making the detection of non-metallic mines much easier.

Our arguments fell on deaf ears. Member states had signed up to the Convention; they should implement it. If one re-interpreted or amended the text, it would encourage member states to cheat, to leave in place minefields in remote areas, ostensibly on the grounds that they posed no threat to the civilian population, but in fact because they still had a military value in the country's dispute with its neighbours or with rebel groups in the country.

We emerged from the meeting dejected. It seemed so short-sighted to insist upon an impossible standard.

In the months and years that followed, we and others thought up more 'brilliant' ideas. Simon Conway of Landmine Action in the UK visited the Falklands and suggested that the UK should be allowed to fulfil its obligation to clear the mines on the islands, not by clearing them but by donating the money that the clearance would have cost to poor countries that still had many high or medium impact areas to clear. This would have brought infinitely greater 'bang for the buck'. It could have worked like carbon trading. It was rejected, too.

Surveys

The general term used for assessing the scale and scope of the problem posed by landmines and unexploded ordnance is 'survey'. This was sub-divided initially into two: 'general survey', in which local people were asked to point out areas they suspected of being mined and 'technical survey', which tried to identify the boundaries of a mined area before a clearance operation began. Neither of these surveys offered an effective way of working out which contaminated areas needed to be given priority for clearance either because they were causing casualties or because they were a significant impediment to normal social and economic activities.

The landmine impact survey was born out of a frustration with mine clearance operations that did not seem to respond to an objective assessment of priorities. Bob Eaton, then at the Vietnam Veterans of America Foundation, encouraged by NGO colleagues in Europe, notably Jean-Baptiste Richardier at Handicap International and Per Nergard at Norwegian Peoples Aid, came up with a survey format and protocols that assigned points to a hazardous area based on how many people had been killed or injured and the level of economic losses caused to the communities through not being able to use the land. These points contributed to an overall score that defined the area as either high impact, medium impact or low impact. In order to enhance the credibility of these surveys, Bob established a Survey Working Group bringing together NGOs and UN agencies involved in mine action, to discuss the process and its application in different countries. He also proposed that a Certification Committee, chaired by the director of UNMAS, should review each survey to confirm that it had correctly followed the survey protocols.

The first of these surveys, for Yemen, was completed just as I joined UNMAS in 2000. It would not be an exaggeration to say that the impact surveys revolutionised the mine action sector. Even if the surveys had to use information that was often not totally reliable or verified, the results provided a substantially improved basis for setting priorities and allocating resources. Landmine impact surveys were completed in Cambodia and Mozambique in 2002, in Bosnia and Lebanon in 2004, in Afghanistan in 2005 and in Angola in 2007.

Locating the mines

As survey techniques gave only a rough idea of where the mines were hidden, it was important that the techniques for detecting the actual mines in the ground should be rapid and reliable. Unfortunately, they were neither.

Since the world's militaries had not been interested in mine clearance, but only in 'breaching' or moving through minefields, they had invested little in improving the technology of mine detection. The standard tool was a hand-held metal detector not significantly improved since World War II, and not much superior to those used by people searching farmland for Roman coins. As the name implies, these instruments detect metal in the ground. That means they detect all the metal fragments that are the by-product of military engagement, but it also means that they cannot detect landmines that do not have any metal content.

During the years I was involved in mine action, I listened to many enthusiastic salesmen extolling the virtues of their revolutionary mine detection technology. These can be grouped into three categories: animals, mainly dogs, rats and bees, able to detect the presence of explosives in the soil; mechanical clearance systems that detected the mines by setting them off as they passed – these included flails, backhoes, fuel-air explosions and high-power hoses; and finally, detection systems that could 'see' through the ground and identify the mine by its shape – these were mainly ground-penetrating radar systems.

The basic hurdles that all these systems had to overcome were reliability and practicality; that is, were they able to find all the mines in a given minefield, and could they operate at affordable cost in remote and harsh locations? Most of the proposed systems fell at the first fence; high-powered hoses were not a very practical solution in environments where there was little water and no electricity.

We gave an extended trial in Afghanistan to the Aardvark flail system, but it was prone to mechanical breakdown and it was difficult to be sure that it had covered every inch of the terrain. Modified backhoes proved effective in very specific situations, but the two detection methods that have offered the greatest improvement on the metal detector are dogs and ground-penetrating radar.

After the success of the first group of Thai-trained dogs in Afghanistan, German shepherd dogs bred in Belgium became an important component of many programmes, but they could not be used everywhere. In recent years, ground-penetrating radar systems, particularly when mounted on vehicles to detect mines planted in roads, are beginning to offer major savings in time over other methods.

For years, in mine clearance programmes all over the world, the only technique for detecting buried anti-personnel mines involved teams of de-miners painstakingly inching forward down a marked lane, waving their metal detectors back and forth over the ground in front of them.

When the detector indicated something metallic, the operator got down and carefully prodded the ground, gradually removing the soil to uncover the object. If it proved to be a mine, the task of destroying it was simple and quick. Often, the mines would be collected in a pit, and then, at the end of the day, or when visitors came to observe the work, fuse-wire would be laid, everybody would move out of range and a satisfying explosion would announce that a few more hidden instruments of mutilation had been destroyed.

Excitement in Eritrea

Everybody was frustrated by the slow pace of mine clearance operations. One political leader who found the UN and NGO operations in his country particularly exasperating was the president of Eritrea, Isaias Afeworki.

In August 2002, I was enjoying a summer holiday in Europe when I received a call. The government of Eritrea had decided to expel all the de-mining organisations. Over the following couple of days it was decided that I should travel immediately to Asmara and attempt to change the government's mind.

After several days of discussion with middle-level officials of the Eritrean government, as well as with colleagues in the UN family, ambassadors of donor countries and NGOs running the projects, we were led to understand that the government might be ready to reconsider. I was due to fly out the following evening. We were told to expect news of the decision in the morning.

At half past seven in the morning, the phone rang. It was the UN's resident coordinator. The President himself would see us at eleven. Now, I am as vain as the next UN official. When a country's president asks to see me, I usually feel a little more self-important. But this time I knew at once that the call could mean only one thing; that we had failed in our mission. The President would not call us in to tell us that he had been swayed by the brilliance of our arguments and that he had changed his mind. It could only be that he wanted to give us a piece of his mind. And so it was.

President Isaias Afewerki has led Eritrea since it split from Ethiopia and was formally established as an independent state in 1993. Eritrea is said to have the worst record on press freedom of any country in the world. President Isaias runs a one-party state in which he takes all major decisions.

On that day in August 2002, he treated us to over an hour of fierce criticism and insults. We were not interested in clearing his country of landmines. If we were, we would not be proceeding at this snail's pace. We were only interested in spinning the work out as long as possible so that we could pocket our fat UN salaries and live in luxury in the West. The work would be done far more quickly and at a fraction of the cost if he was allowed to deploy his military in the area (the border zone had been de-militarised and was off-limits to his troops).

As is sometimes the case with mad tyrants, amid all the bluster and nonsense, there was a worrying kernel of truth. Our operation had been going very slowly, and this was not solely the fault of Eritrean bureaucratic delaying tactics.

As I flew back home, I wondered: had de-mining become the victim of a 'health and safety' culture, in which speed and effectiveness were sacrificed for fear of being sued? Were we at risk of becoming a costly irrelevance, as ordinary people were obliged to get on with their lives, while we poked around, maintaining our standards? We urgently needed more effective techniques to prioritise the work, and much faster ways of detecting the presence of individual mines. The landmine impact surveys, dogs, ground-penetrating radar and, later, a process called 'area reduction' or 'land release' would all play a part.

Coordinating mine action

By the time I left UNMAS in 2005, the sector of humanitarian activity known as 'mine action' was just 15 years old. In spite of the rants of President Afewerki, the sector has the reputation of being one where governments of affected countries, donor governments, NGOs and the UN family work effectively together. On several occasions I have been asked by colleagues working in other sectors within the UN family for an insight into how that was achieved.

Perhaps the biggest obstacle facing the United Nations in trying to develop a coherent programme in a particular sector of activity is the presence of overlapping mandates and turf wars. This happens in many fields. If UNHCR helps refugees, and UNICEF offers health-care services to mothers and children, how should UNHCR and UNICEF work together to provide health care to refugee children? I use this example not to highlight a particular problem area, but to illustrate how easy it is for mandates to overlap. Mine action was not immune to this problem.

Many of the working arrangements developed within the mine action sector were intended to address this.

The main forum for developing a common UN approach and for avoiding turf wars was the Inter-Agency Coordination Group on Mine Action. This is the forum in which 14 separate entities within the UN system meet regularly to discuss both policy issues and specific mine-affected countries.

The most important documents negotiated in this forum were the UN policy on mine action and the UN strategy on mine action. I felt strongly that the best way to ensure that we all knew what we were trying to achieve was to develop a single UN policy, every word negotiated by the senior people actively involved in mine action from each agency or department, and then formally approved by their executive heads. The best way to agree how we were going to implement the policy was to develop a shared strategy with Specific, Measurable, Achievable, Realistic and Time-bound ('SMART') objectives. Within the group, members accepted responsibility for leading the effort to achieve each objective.

UNMAS started life in the Department of Humanitarian Affairs (DHA), and then in 1997 was transferred to the Department of Peacekeeping Operations (DPKO). Both departments agreed that it should be called the UN Mine Action Service, and not just the Mine Action Service of DHA or DPKO, and all parts of the UN system accepted that UNMAS had the responsibility to coordinate the UN's overall effort in the mine action sector. The head of DPKO authorised me to print two different business cards, one of which did not mention DPKO, which gave more credibility when dealing with humanitarian partners wary of our association with peacekeeping.

To have credibility in the rest of the system, the coordinator of UN mine action, in this case the director of UNMAS, needed to be the most senior person in the UN system with full-time responsibility for mine action. In any sector of activity, the role of inter-agency coordinator cannot be fulfilled effectively on a part-time basis, or from a position of less seniority than other full-time players.

Since UNMAS's main potential competitor for pre-eminence within the UN system was UNDP, it helped that the two people who headed UNDP's mine action unit during my time at UNMAS, Ian Mansfield and Sayed Aqa, had both worked with me in the Afghanistan operation.

The development of the International Mine Action Standards (IMAS), which was well underway before I arrived at UNMAS, was a joint effort between the UN family, the Geneva International Centre for Humanitarian De-mining (GICHD) and a number of NGOs. The exercise of defining what constituted good practice, and the fact that the UN was recognised as the body that could ultimately validate these standards, was an important factor in getting all the very disparate actors on the same page. Different organisations led the development of each standard; so, for instance, UNICEF, with one of the NGOs, led the development of the mine risk education standard.

It is important that the coordinating office has control over the principal public relations tool, so we modelled the Electronic Mine Information Network (E-MINE) website (www.mineaction.org) on reliefweb (www.reliefweb.int), the comprehensive public information site, established and maintained by OCHA, which we felt had played an important part in cementing recognition for OCHA as coordinator of humanitarian operations within the UN system and beyond.

It was important too that we engaged the other UN partners, especially UNDP and UNICEF in the drafting of the UN Secretary-General's annual report to the General Assembly. As coordinator of UN mine action, it was essential that we recognised the contributions of other parts of the UN system in all our communications.

Regular meetings of states parties to the Mine Ban Treaty were held, mainly in Geneva. Some representatives of member states delighted in trying to play one part of the UN system off against the others, so our colleagues in UNDP, UNICEF and the Department of Disarmament Affairs would sometimes be encouraged by diplomats not to bother coordinating their participation with UNMAS. But once the UN strategy had clearly identified the division of labour among the UN bodies, we began to prepare our participation together, and member states rarely managed to put daylight between us after that.

The partnership between UNMAS and the GICHD was a key element of the international mine action architecture. Established by the Swiss government and directed by a succession of Swiss ambassadors, the GICHD was co-funded by a number of other governments. The centre hosts meetings of the states parties to the Mine Ban Treaty and undertakes research on mine action issues. They provide the secretariat for the International Mine Action Standards and they also host and fund what for me was the most important meeting of the year, the annual week-long meeting of the national directors of mine action programmes. While they host and fund the meeting, they have always accepted that it is an UNMAS-led event.

For most of my time at UNMAS, the director of GICHD was Ambassador Martin Dahinden. We became known as the two Martins. We signed a memorandum of understanding in which the GICHD recognised UNMAS's role as UN coordinator and Dahinden unfailingly respected the agreement and supported our role, in spite of pressures from some of his board members to take GICHD on a more independent path.

Shortly after I joined UNMAS, we were able to negotiate a multi-year core funding agreement with the UK's Department for International Development (DfID), which put the office on a sound financial footing, and which also emphasised to the British NGOs working in the mine action sector that the British government saw the role of the UN in the overall coordination of the international effort as important and worth supporting. This was another example of extremely fortunate timing. We took advantage of an initiative at DfID led by Mukesh Kapila, the head of DfID's humanitarian team, with the support of Clare Short, the then secretary of state, to provide predictable core funding to OCHA and a number of other components of the UN system's humanitarian effort.

These were some of the key elements of what is seen as a successful formula. However, if I have given the impression that all ran smoothly, and that everybody accepted the importance of UNMAS as a coordinating body, that would not be correct. Throughout my time at UNMAS, a representative of one donor country did not hide his dislike of UNMAS and tried quite hard to undermine us. Although I never fully understood the reasons for his opposition, and it did not seem to reflect his government's position, it may have derived from a belief that the Ottawa Treaty process should play the coordinating role. There were also others, who harboured similar feelings, although not so vigorously. Moreover, UNDP were often tempted to interpret our coordinating role more narrowly than we did.

There was also one major British de-mining NGO, the HALO Trust, that thought UNMAS was a complete waste of time and did not shrink from telling anybody who would listen.

International de-mining NGOs

When I went to Pakistan for the first time in 1988 on behalf of the UN coordinator for Afghanistan, the scale of the landmine problem facing Afghanistan gradually became clearer. The UN had no ready-made solutions. It had never confronted this sort of situation before.

As we asked around, we heard that a retired British Army officer had set up a new charity called the HALO Trust. It had just opened its first field office in Kabul. Perhaps we could work with them. So, when I returned to London to prepare for the move to Islamabad, I made contact with Colonel Colin Mitchell and went to see him and his colleague, Guy Willoughby, in the colonel's London flat.

I was cordially received, but it was clear that they did not see HALO as a partner of the United Nations. They would 'do their own thing'.

HALO have been in Kabul ever since. They employed a succession of enthusiastic young ex-British Army officers who had finished their short-service contracts and came out to manage teams of Afghan de-miners, predominantly on the road north from Kabul. These young men were not professional de-miners from the Corps of Engineers, but mainly infantry and cavalry officers. Guy Willoughby would give them intensive training at HALO headquarters in southern Scotland before they flew out to Afghanistan.

HALO was the first Western NGO to specialise in mine clearance. After Afghanistan, they started operations in the three other most affected countries – Angola, Cambodia and Mozambique – and in 2014 they were still very much in business, operating in a dozen countries.

Soon after HALO came the Mines Advisory Group (MAG), founded in 1989 by Rae McGrath and his brother, Lou. Where Guy Willoughby and HALO focussed on clearance, MAG conducted surveys and lobbied. They were to be one of the core partners in the international campaign to ban landmines.

HALO and MAG were 'purpose-built' de-mining NGOs, created by their energetic founders specifically for this task. Once the international community sought to tackle the landmine problem in Cambodia, two years after the start of operations in Afghanistan, they were joined by two existing NGOs, Handicap International of France and Norwegian People's Aid, which began to do mine clearance alongside their other humanitarian work. Although a number of other NGOs, including World Vision, tried their hands at mine clearance, no others would commit to it over extended periods in several countries, except for Danish Church Aid, later to be joined by the Danish De-mining Group. These six NGOs, two British, two Danish, one French and one Norwegian, would constitute the quasi-totality of the international de-mining NGO world. Why did so few NGOs enter the field, and what were the consequences of that choice?

There were probably three reasons why the mainstream NGOs were reluctant to get into mine clearance. Firstly, they were concerned about possible liability claims. Although HALO and the others had managed to negotiate insurance cover, they still worried that their personnel might be killed or injured in accidents, or that they might be sued if somebody was blown up on a mine left over after clearance operations had finished. Secondly, clearing landmines is an activity normally carried out by armies or specialised units of police. For many NGOs, de-mining was simply not part of what they had been set up to do – they would not think of getting involved in it in their own countries, so they were not willing to do it overseas. Finally, I suspect that some NGO managers were just not comfortable around the ex-military officers who made up the bulk of the de-mining NGO personnel.

While NGOs were reluctant to become involved, several commercial companies were interested. Both USAID and the World Bank preferred to contract companies rather than provide grants to NGOs. While USAID began a quite successful commercial partnership with RONCO, the World Bank's effort to promote the growth of local de-mining companies in Bosnia faced all kinds of difficulties. During the first five years of the twenty-first century, a pattern began to emerge in which NGOs and companies worked together on several programmes, the choice of partners depending in part on the source of the funding and in part on the preferences of the host government.

But there was to be no repeat of the Afghan experience with national NGOs. A couple of the Afghan NGOs won contracts to do surveys or mine clearance in other countries, but the major mine clearance operators in Angola, Cambodia, Mozambique and Sudan have been international NGOs and commercial companies. Once the six international NGOs based in European countries came on the scene with their core staff of ex-military officers, many donor governments preferred to channel their money through them. Most UN programme managers were also ex-military and did not have the skills to nurture the development of local NGOs in the countries where they were assigned. In an early comparative study of mine action in Afghanistan, Angola, Cambodia and Mozambique, commissioned by the UN Department of Humanitarian Affairs, the Afghan model of using local NGOs was rated highly successful.

I have discussed this issue already in Chapter 4, and I will return to it in Chapter 10, because for me this failure to develop genuine local capacity is symptomatic of the arrogant and patronising approach adopted by far too many purveyors of humanitarian assistance.

Peacekeeping and mine action

My arrival at UNMAS in late 2000 coincided with the surge in UN peacekeeping activities. UNMAS had been working in Kosovo since 1999. Within days of my arrival, we had sent a team to Eritrea as part of the start-up of the UN Mission in Ethiopia and Eritrea. Over the following four years, UNMAS introduced mine action components into peacekeeping operations in Burundi, Democratic Republic of Congo, Lebanon and Sudan, and took over the operation in Afghanistan in 2002. These were hybrid operations, in that they operated as part of a peacekeeping mission with funding from the mission's budget, but also in partnership with local organisations and international NGOs, supported by funding from donor governments.

Peacekeeping operations are funded from 'assessed contributions', meaning that if the Security Council approves an operation, then member states are obliged to pay for it, according to a scale of assessments, under which the United States pays 23 per cent of the bill, Japan 9 per cent and other countries lower percentages in accordance with the agreed scale. Humanitarian operations, on the other hand, are funded entirely from 'voluntary contributions', which means that governments contribute only as much as they wish.

In order for UN budget committees to allocate funding from peacekeeping budgets for mine action, UNMAS had to ensure that the mandate of the UN mission adopted by the Security Council included a reference to the landmine problem and what the mission would do to confront it. Initially, we had to work with our colleagues from DPKO's Office of Operations and the budget officers to develop the concept of 'one foot in, one foot out'. This allowed the UN Mine Action Centre to be both inside the peacekeeping mission – to document the affected areas and advise and support the mission in planning its operations taking the mine problem into account and clearing essential access routes – while also operating outside the mission to carry out humanitarian work with voluntary funding to clear areas that would enable displaced people to return to their homes.

One part of the world where, fortunately, landmines were not part of the weaponry of conflict was West Africa. In Liberia, Sierra Leone and Cote d'Ivoire, mines had not been used and there was virtually no demand for our services when UN peacekeeping missions were sent to those countries.

De-mining as an element of a development project

Funding from humanitarian and peacekeeping budgets, and special operations funded by the World Bank, was still inadequate to meet the demand for mine clearance. In Afghanistan, as the major international funding agencies embarked on the reconstruction process, beginning in 2002, another source emerged. USAID had agreed to fund the reconstruction of a major part of the ring road, linking Kabul with Kandahar and Herat. They approached UNMAS to ask if we could clear the route of landmines, so that they could start the work. In the politest terms we could think of, we told them that they had to be joking. Where did they think we would get the money? In the end it was agreed that the cost of the mine clearance operation would be factored into the budget for the road construction. This funding mechanism became known as 'cost recovery' and is, of course, a principle that applies to all sorts of major development projects, from archaeological remains to environmental impact studies.

So, when the government of Egypt approached UNMAS to fund the clearance of mines left over from World War II, to enable the development of new resort towns along the Mediterranean coast west of Alexandria, they received the same polite answer as USAID had received in Afghanistan. Mine clearance operations are the responsibility of the affected country. If developers want to build on mined land, they need to include the cost of clearance in their project costs. Scarce voluntary funding for mine clearance should be used to enable people in poor countries to move around safely.

The government of Egypt had also tried, for many years, to argue that the countries which had laid the mines during World War II should be responsible for clearing them. So far, however, no country has successfully argued before an international court that the forces that laid the mines should be obliged to remove them.

Releasing land

As I approached the end of my time at UNMAS, I was still troubled by two related ideas. One was that there must be a way of reducing the size of the suspected hazardous areas, which even many landmine impact surveys had clearly over-estimated, and the other was that we might have underestimated the capacity of individuals and small groups of local people to de-mine their own villages by themselves.

My vague ideas on the first topic received a welcome boost from a visit to Lebanon in 2004 where Chris Clark was the manager of the UN

Mine Action Coordination Centre (UNMACC). Chris had worked with John Flanagan on the operations in Kosovo, where clearance operations had been quick and effective, and had then gone to Sudan.

In Lebanon, Chris had enlisted the support of Staffan de Mistura, the Personal Representative of the Secretary-General, who had understood the importance of mine clearance operations at both a symbolic and a practical level, for encouraging the return of people and businesses to the south of the country after the departure of the Israeli forces in 2000. Together, Staffan and Chris had persuaded the United Arab Emirates to fund an extremely effective clearance operation carried out by two commercial operators under contracts that gave local responsibility for oversight of the work to the UNMACC, headed by Chris, with the participation of liaison officers from the Lebanese Army and the UAE.

After showing me the impressive work that was underway, Chris talked about ways of reducing the area that had to be cleared of mines by introducing more sophisticated survey techniques, including by statistically sound sampling methodologies, rather than blanket clearance involving unnecessary time and expense. I was hooked. Why were we not doing this everywhere? One of the last things I did before leaving UNMAS was to write to Bob Eaton at the Survey Action Centre and ask him to follow this up. This would become known first as 'area reduction' and then as 'land release'.

General or landmine impact surveys identify land perceived by the local population to be dangerous, and which is therefore not used. This is not necessarily the same as the area actually contaminated by mines. In many countries, the areas identified by surveys as hazardous have been carefully recorded in a national database. The surveys have also often been used to estimate the scale of the de-mining task that still remains. But when technical survey teams come and take a closer look, they invariably discover that the area actually contaminated is smaller. In some cases communities discover that they have been avoiding land that they could have been using. In others villagers may learn that an area has been classified as hazardous, even though they have been using the land for several years without suffering casualties.

Bob Eaton and the Survey Action Centre, spurred on by Norwegian Peoples' Aid and Handicap International, and joined by UNMAS and GICHD, have been leading an effort to come up with procedures that can be adopted by national governments to cancel or reduce in size hazardous areas on national databases, where all the evidence is that the area is not, or is no longer, contaminated.

'Village de-mining'

In Afghanistan in 1989, the UN's first inclination, supported by its major donors, was to provide a helping hand to the longstanding approach of self-help. The basic training for thousands of Afghan volunteers, supplemented with a simple kit, was intended to reduce risk to those who would volunteer to do this dangerous work in their home districts. We did not imagine then that we would be involved in professionalising the activity of mine clearance and even actively discouraging the volunteer spirit that we had initially tried to promote. Were we right to change course so completely?

There have been many discussions of what came to be called 'village de-mining', although this is a misnomer. We are talking mainly about private, unregulated initiatives by individuals to clear mines, either to make land usable, or to profit from the sale of the components. Discussions of 'private de-mining' have revolved around questions of how, if at all, the work should be recorded on national databases of hazardous areas, and whether private de-miners should receive technical help and equipment from government programmes. The debate has not seriously tackled the idea that, in some circumstances at least, private de-mining might be more appropriate than the professional approach.

The arguments against private de-mining can be persuasive. I have used them myself. They point out that private de-miners do not work systematically. The de-miners cannot guarantee that they have cleared all the mines from a given area. Indeed, they may not be able to say exactly where they have worked. In order to be sure that the area is really free of mines, a professional team will need to come in and do the job again.

Nevertheless, land release may provide an opportunity to recognise, indirectly at least, the work of private de-miners. If observations show that mines are not impeding normal life in a community, which is making unrestricted use of its land, the designation of a hazardous area can be cancelled.

So, perhaps it is time to revisit the official attitude to private de-mining. In Laos, along the mountainous border with Vietnam where the Ho Chi Minh trail ran, private de-miners continue to unearth bombs dropped 50 years before by American planes. The government's UXO programme focusses on contaminated areas of higher economic importance. But slowly, but surely, Laos is being decontaminated by the initiative of private enterprise. Lives are lost, but profits are made, families are fed and the land becomes safer.

Sometimes, I wonder if the history of humanitarian de-mining might have been different, if the detectors given to the Afghan volunteers in 1989 had not been pink.

Global champions

After Princess Diana's death, other global champions of the landmine cause emerged. Perhaps the most persistent and articulate advocate was Jody Williams, laureate, along with the International Campaign to Ban Landmines, of the 1997 Nobel Peace Prize. She spoke passionately at the meetings of states parties to the Ottawa Convention, and at other events whenever she had the chance. She and her husband, Steve Goose of Human Rights Watch, made a formidable partnership.

Queen Noor of Jordan took up the cause as well. Jordan was the leading advocate for the Convention in the Arab world, although they faced opposition particularly from Egypt, which was still waiting for the parties to World War II to come and clear up its ordnance-polluted deserts.

One of the most original and inventive advocates for the cause is Heidi Kuhn, founder of an NGO, Roots of Peace. Heidi was a journalist in California, who became obsessed with this issue and mobilised her whole family and corporate California behind her efforts. She had great slogans – she turned 'mines into vines' in Croatia and Afghanistan; she sponsored a permanent 'swords into ploughshares' exhibit in the peace garden opposite the entrance to UN headquarters; she went to Angola to try to save the elephants that were getting blown up by landmines left over from the civil war; and she and her daughter started a 'penny campaign' that has raised over 50 million pennies by encouraging school children to learn about landmines and contribute pennies to support projects.

Baghdad

In early 2003, the US State Department approached UNMAS to work with them on the development of a plan for mine action in post-invasion Iraq. They told us that they wanted mine action efforts in a future Iraq without Saddam Hussein to be coordinated by the United Nations. This approach was part of US engagement with the UN system as a whole to plan for the international follow-up to an inevitable and imminent invasion by a US-led coalition.

We worked on the outline plan and dispatched colleagues to Cyprus where the UN family deployed its forward planning team. And then, of course, the US administration scrapped the State Department plan and handed responsibility for the post-invasion effort to the Pentagon, which did not have a plan.

As Samantha Power recounts in her excellent biography of Sergio Vieira de Mello, once it was clear that Iraq without Saddam would not stabilise automatically, President Bush looked for international support and persuaded Secretary-General Kofi Annan to release Sergio from his job as UN High Commissioner for Human Rights and send him as his special representative to Baghdad. Our contacts in the US administration encouraged UNMAS to dust off the plans we had made and start an operation in Basra. Bill Van Ree, an Australian retired colonel, who had succeeded Ian Mansfield as programme manager in Afghanistan, got things going there with admirable speed. The Americans had identified qualified Iraqis to run a national mine action centre in Baghdad and regional centres in the Kurdish north and in Basra. UNMAS set up a small support team in Baghdad, and the time seemed right for me and a small group of colleagues to visit.

We arrived in Baghdad from Amman on the morning of 18 August 2003. In the arrivals lounge, I greeted Arthur Helton and Gil Loescher, former colleagues from my days working on refugees. They had come to look at the situation of people displaced by the war.

That afternoon, we had arranged an appointment with Sergio to discuss our mission. He greeted me warmly, but he seemed tense. The security situation was bad. I told him of our plans to visit Basra and the north, and to give a press briefing the following day about our visit. I asked him what I should say.

Sergio told me that the country was awash with explosives, in small and large stores in every town and city, and that the ground was polluted by vast quantities of unexploded ordnance. He asked me to tell the media that the United Nations was committed to supporting a huge national and international effort to help Iraq dispose of this terrible legacy. He also promised to help arrange meetings for me with key Iraqis in the security sector, with whom we should develop plans for decommissioning explosives. I agreed to return the following afternoon to discuss those plans in detail with his chief of staff, Nadia Younes, after the press briefing.

The next day we had an extended meeting with the new UNDP representative, Henrik Kolstrup, and other members of the UN family in

Baghdad. Kolstrup had just arrived from five years in Bosnia, where he had been closely involved in the mine action programme after my departure. He was full of enthusiasm for our mission in Iraq. Then we drove back into the UN's Canal Hotel compound for our meeting with the press. There was a good attendance including two film crews. I made my introductory presentation, focussing, as Sergio had requested, on the UN's commitment to helping Iraq get rid of the pollution of unsecured explosives. The UNMAS programme manager in Baghdad, Salomon 'Solly' Schreuder, talked about the work of our teams in the country. The briefing seemed to interest the journalists and there were several questions. And then the bomb went off. There was a deafening explosion, the room went black, except for the camera lights, and plaster fell from the ceiling. There was a moment of silence, and then screaming from outside the room. Twenty-two people were killed, including Sergio, Nadia Younes and Arthur Helton. Many more were injured, some very badly, including Henrik Kolstrup and Gil Loescher.

None of those who had been in the press briefing was hurt, thanks to the fact that it was held in an internal room with no windows. Many of those who died or were badly injured were hit by flying glass. Younger colleagues, especially those with military training, rushed off to help. For a time I stood outside the main entrance to the building, as the bodies of my dead colleagues were brought out and laid on the ground. Then a colleague led me out to the area behind the building where those with minor wounds were being treated. After a while, we were told that a fuel tank might explode and that we should move to a vacant open area at the back. I sat on the ground next to Benon Sevan, my former boss from Afghanistan and the head of the ill-fated Iraq programme during the sanctions regime. He, too, was in town on a short visit. It was hot in the sun and a young Australian working with UNHCR gave me his wide-brimmed Australian bush hat. I still use it.

When our team returned to New York, we found the place in shock. This had been the worst attack on the UN in its history. Sergio Vieira de Mello, the man widely seen as a future secretary-general had died. Some extraordinarily talented young people, attracted to work with a charismatic leader, died with him. There were calls for 'accountability', mainly from long-serving New-York-based staff, who were not known for their willingness to serve in dangerous duty stations. The Deputy Secretary-General offered her resignation, which was rejected. Gerald Walzer, a former Deputy High Commissioner for Refugees, was asked to chair a committee of investigation. The committee identified failures in the security management. Tun Myat, who had only recently taken over from Benon Sevan as UN security coordinator in New York, was fired. Ramiro Lopes da Silva, who had been designated official for security in Baghdad, was reprimanded and barred from holding security-related functions in the future.

I was deeply uncomfortable with these developments. It seemed to me that everybody was forgetting that the UN had been deliberately targeted, and was looking for scapegoats, as if the deaths were the result of building management failure and not the appalling action of a ruthless terrorist organisation. If individuals in the UN were to be held accountable, surely the person who had decided that the UN should go to Baghdad, against the advice of many of his staff, was the Secretary-General. And the most senior official in Baghdad who had insisted that the UN should be accessible to Iraqis and not hide behind concrete walls like the American administrators did, was Sergio himself. It seemed deeply unfair to blame Tun Myat and Ramiro.

I regret that I did not speak out more clearly about this at the time. It seemed to me that the Secretary-General was poorly advised. He himself was understandably in shock, having obliged one of his closest friends to take a job that he did not want, and that had killed him. I eventually found my voice a few months later at an open meeting at the UN on post-traumatic stress. My argument clearly struck a chord; several people came up to me in the following days to say that they had been waiting for somebody to say this.

Military discipline and humanitarian principles

In spite of all the difficulties and constraints that the UN has faced in addressing the problems posed by landmines, the humanitarian sector of activity now known as 'mine action' has developed from scratch, starting in 1990, to become a respected component of the international crisis response architecture. It has done it by combining military approaches to standards and discipline with humanitarian principles and policies. It has brought ex-military personnel together with mainstream aid workers to build effective teams. It has pioneered methods of data collection, surveying, coordination, funding and priority-setting that have been copied by other sectors. It has cleared large areas of contaminated land in over 20 countries and enabled thousands of families to return to their homes and live productive lives in safety.

Whatever the critics say of the UN's work in mine action, and some of them have been shrill and unrelenting, I am proud to have been part of the effort.

As I handed over at UNMAS and retired from the UN, I thought how fortunate I had been to have had such a varied and fascinating career, and to have survived – if the bomber had been 20 minutes later, I would have been in Nadia Younes's office, next to Sergio's. I had reached the end of my career in the United Nations with my sense of pride and privilege at being part of the world's only global organisation as strong as it had been on the day I had joined UNHCR 30 years earlier.

UNITED ARAB EMIRATES

FOREIGN AID

2009

مكتب تنسيق المساعدات الخارجية لدولة الإمارات العربية المتحدة

UAE Office for the Coordination of Foreign Aid

Figure 8 First annual report of the UAE's foreign aid, issued by the UAE's Office for the Coordination of Foreign Aid (OCFA) in 2009.

8

AID FROM ARABIA
Lessons for the West?

In July 2009, a friend at OCHA Geneva called to ask if I would like to go to Abu Dhabi 'for a few days'. OCHA was helping the government of the United Arab Emirates (UAE) to establish a small office to 'coordinate' the aid that the UAE provides to other countries. They were looking for somebody to help them develop their first strategic plan.

I had never lived or worked in the Arab world and this sounded like an interesting short assignment. In the end I stayed for more than three years. That assignment would open my eyes to an important and widely misunderstood component of the international aid effort in the twenty-first century.

Abu Dhabi, the capital of the emirate of the same name and also of the UAE, has grown from a village of a few hundred people around a fort in the 1950s into a city of 2.5 million, of whom 90 per cent are foreign nationals. High-rise apartment blocks and shiny malls with every major international brand have replaced the huts and dusty souk of 60 years ago. Many people commute from Dubai, a distance of 150 kilometres, on the eight-lane highway. Men of my generation, the fathers and grandfathers of my new colleagues, had grown up in the desert with camels and falcons. A more rapid and complete transformation would be hard to imagine.

The Office for the Coordination of Foreign Aid (OCFA) had been set up by the UAE federal government in 2008 when ministers realised that there was no central record of the aid that the country was giving to other countries and that estimates of the amount being spent were not based on accurate figures.

In March 2013, shortly after I left Abu Dhabi, OCFA became part of a new Ministry for International Cooperation and Development (MICAD).

I went to Abu Dhabi with an open mind, ready to be told that aid from an Arab point of view was very different from our Western model. What I found was a fascinating and complex set of ideas and practices that owed much to the country's social and political history, but was also influenced by the desire of the country's leaders to be recognised by their friends in the West as an important international donor. I was greeted with great warmth and quickly became engaged in intensive debates about goals, targets and methods. These discussions forced me to re-examine some long-held assumptions.

The UAE

In 1971, seven emirates in the Gulf region, previously known by the outside world as the Trucial States, and of which Abu Dhabi is by far the largest and Dubai the most well-known internationally, joined together to form a new independent state, the United Arab Emirates (UAE). Bahrain and Qatar might have joined, but decided to go it alone. The UAE's immediate land neighbours are Saudi Arabia and Oman. The Islamic Republic of Iran lies just across the waters of the Gulf.

Of the countries in the Gulf region, Saudi Arabia is by far the largest and wealthiest and Yemen by far the poorest. Bahrain, Kuwait, Oman, Qatar and the UAE are the others. With the exception of Bahrain, which has a Shi'i majority, the Gulf states are predominantly Sunni Muslim tribal societies. Their religion, Islam, and their social and political organisation based on an ancient tribal system are key to understanding how these societies work.

In the 1950s, before the discovery of oil, the emirates that now make up the UAE were sparsely populated territories of settled and nomadic desert communities, reliant on camels, date palms, fishing, trade from the ports on the Gulf coast and diving in the Gulf waters for pearls, a once vibrant industry which had not recovered from the invention of the cultured pearl in Japan, the global depression in the 1930s and World War II.

Each of the seven emirates recognises an emir, or ruler, the head of the tribal family that traditionally provides the emirate's rulers. In its simplest form, the role of the ruler and his family is to mediate among the tribes, to represent their interests in dealings with neighbouring emirates or foreigners, to levy taxes on the activities of the wealthier tribes and on foreigners doing business on their territory, and then to redistribute the resources in subsidies to the poorer tribes.

The discovery and exploitation of oil from the 1960s onwards had dramatically transformed the economy of the UAE, but it has not led to major changes in the compact between the tribes that governs national politics. The emirate of Abu Dhabi has provided the first two presidents of the UAE, Sheikh Zayed Bin Sultan Al Nahyan, a man of legendary vision, strength and charisma, regarded as the founder and father of the nation, who served from 1971 until his death in 2004, and his eldest son, Sheikh Khalifa Bin Zayed Al Nahyan, the president since then.

Although Sheikh Zayed was such a dominant personality, the UAE was established as a decentralised state, in which each emirate exercises a high degree of autonomy. This has implications for the way in which it organises its foreign aid.

The UAE as a donor of foreign aid

For Sheikh Zayed, the wealth that oil brought to his country had to be shared with those less fortunate, both at home and abroad, without discrimination as to race or religion. He saw this as an obligation imposed by his faith and he communicated this vision regularly to his people. He endowed hospitals and schools from North Africa to Indonesia and frequently provided cash grants to visiting heads of state from impoverished countries.

Even before the birth of the UAE as a nation, Sheikh Zayed had endowed the Abu Dhabi Fund for Development, a sister organisation to the Kuwait and Saudi Funds for Development. In the 42 years of its existence, the Abu Dhabi Fund has spent over $4 billion on loans and grants to 59 countries, mainly for infrastructure projects – all formally requested by governments – such as roads, bridges, dams and ports. The Abu Dhabi Fund cooperates on major projects with the eight other members of the 'Coordination Group' that includes the Saudi and Kuwaiti funds, as well as the Islamic Development Bank and the OPEC Fund for International Development.

In 1983, Sheikh Zayed set up the UAE Red Crescent Authority as a way of channelling private contributions of UAE residents for humanitarian relief operations and charitable projects. Many private Arab donors want their money to help orphans. In the Muslim world an orphan has lost one or both parents and needs help, either in an institution or in the community, to get a basic education. So, the Red Crescent, while working with other Red Cross and Red Crescent societies on traditional relief operations, also supports programmes for orphans in more than 20 countries.

During his lifetime, Sheikh Zayed endowed a number of specialised foundations to undertake charitable and social work within the UAE and abroad. In 1992, he founded the Sheikh Zayed Humanitarian and Charitable Foundation and this example has been followed by his son, Sheikh Khalifa and by the Ruler of Dubai, Sheikh Mohammed Bin Rashid Al Maktoum, who have each endowed several foundations. One of the most interesting of these is Dubai Cares.

Dubai Cares focusses on the promotion of high-quality primary education in poor countries. It gives as much importance to school sanitation as to textbooks, on the principle that preventable disease is the most common reason for absence from school among both pupils and teachers. Dubai Cares's proactive approach contrasts with the more reactive approach of most other UAE donor organisations, which prefer to react to the priorities of their individual donors and to specific requests from recipient countries.

This helps to explain why, in spite of its long history of providing foreign aid, the UAE has not developed an 'aid programme' as a Western aid ministry would understand the term. The UAE provides budget support to friendly countries, gives funding for infrastructure projects through the Abu Dhabi Fund, supports projects submitted for funding to individual ministries, foundations or NGOs and responds to humanitarian emergencies through the Red Crescent or one of the foundations.

In 2010, the Red Crescent and two of the UAE's largest foundations responded separately to the Haiti earthquake, but in 2011 they came together as the UAE Relief Team, with logistical and technical support from the UAE Armed Forces, to respond to the exodus of people fleeing the violence in Libya. This operation was well received by the UN and other international organisations and was seen as a possible model for future action by the UAE in major humanitarian operations.

Altogether more than 40 governmental or non-governmental entities in the UAE are recognised by the government as donors of foreign aid. At OCFA, our job was to document the aid of these entities, improve the skills of their staff, advise them on standards and promote their activities to the public and the media.

Documenting the UAE's aid

OCFA's first task was to document all the aid provided by the UAE since its foundation in 1971. Although impressive numbers of paper records describing a huge volume of aid were located in archives and made available by different government entities, it became clear that much aid had been handed out either without being recorded or that the records that had been made had since been lost or destroyed. OCFA therefore put to one side the work on the historical record and focussed on the immediate past. Beginning with the year 2009, OCFA has published an official annual report on the country's foreign aid.

What is foreign aid?

In setting up the system for documenting the UAE's aid, we encountered several questions that have parallels in Western thinking about aid. The first and most interesting of these was, how should we define 'foreign aid'?

In its account of the UAE's aid, OCFA included any contribution made to any other country for the purposes of its development or for humanitarian or charitable purposes. Within that overall total we identified the elements that qualified to be considered as 'Official Development Assistance' (ODA) under the definition of the Development Assistance Committee (DAC) of the OECD. Elements of the UAE's aid which did not qualify as ODA included aid that was not 'official', meaning that it was not given by a government entity; aid to 'high-income' countries that were not eligible to receive ODA, and aid that fell outside the sectors of activity considered as ODA, including notably 'activities with a religious motivation'.

The distinction between 'official' aid, as defined by the OECD for the purpose of ranking governments according to the volume of their aid as a proportion of Gross National Income (GNI), and 'non-official' or 'private' aid, including everything that falls outside the definition of 'official', raises the question of whether this distinction is now useful. In the UAE it obliged us to distinguish between aid given 'by the decision of a ruler', which was considered official, and aid given by the decision of another sheikh or wealthy individual, which was not.

More generally, this definition of ODA means that the aid of the Bill and Melinda Gates Foundation, which for some developing countries is among the most significant aid that they receive, does not appear in the reports of the OECD, and that aid provided by Oxfam is included when the funds come from the British or another government, but not if the money was raised from private contributions. Similarly, donor governments that are not members of the DAC, such as the Gulf states and the BRICS countries (Brazil, Russia, India, China, South Africa) for the most part do not report their aid to the DAC. Recipient governments need to know what aid is coming into their countries. Reports that include only ODA contributed by members of the DAC no longer provide a realistic picture.

Countries cease to be eligible to receive ODA when the World Bank records their Gross Domestic Product (GDP) as having exceeded a specified amount for a period of three years. Under this formula, Oman ceased to be eligible for ODA in 2011. This was unlucky for the UAE, which made a grant of $1 billion to Oman in 2011, which would have been ODA in 2010, but was not in 2011. Instead of an ODA/GNI ratio for 2011 of 0.52, which would have put the UAE in the top ten of donors for that year, the actual ODA/GNI ratio was 0.22, which put it outside the top 20.

This discussion may seem rather academic, but when aid is reaching developing countries from an increasingly bewildering number of sources, governmental and private, it is more important than ever that those governments receiving aid have a clear picture of what is coming in. Since the DAC records only aid to ODA-eligible countries from official sources in countries that have accepted its reporting system, that view of foreign aid has become increasingly partial, and less useful than it should be.

So, why did the UAE, in 2010, decide to report its aid to the DAC, at a time when no other country that was not a member of the DAC did so? The simple answer was that the UAE wanted its aid to be taken seriously and therefore it was willing to play by the rules of the donors' club. The exercise promoted transparency among donor organisations in the UAE and provided useful benchmarks.

If it is ever possible to recover the figures for the UAE's gross national income during the 1970s and to estimate reliably the volume of the UAE's aid during that period, I have no doubt that the ODA/GNI ratio for those years will be far above the 1 per cent of today's most generous donor. But, while the UAE's GNI has grown at a phenomenal pace, the increases in the volume of its foreign aid have inevitably been less spectacular, faced with demands for investment at home. Nevertheless, for 2009, the UAE gave over $1 billion in ODA and was ranked 14th in the world on the OECD rankings with an ODA/GNI ratio of 0.36.

Charity and aid

Charitable giving is an important feature of Islam, but it is a private activity – 'the left hand does not know what the right hand is doing'. Similar thinking motivates many people who give to Christian NGOs. So, are charity and aid the same thing?

We think of aid as an activity of institutions, intended to have a beneficial impact on the recipient country or community. Aid is about 'them' – the recipients, not about 'us' – the donors, or is it? It was only in December 2011 that the international language of development cooperation finally shifted from a focus on 'aid effectiveness', with its implication that we should be evaluating the donor, to 'development effectiveness', which obliges us to look at what is happening to those receiving the aid.

Perhaps the Arab approach is more honest. They are quite open about the idea that private giving is a personal religious act. If the giver of charity asks for his money to be used in a specific way, he is not pretending that he knows what the people he is helping need most; he is deciding what he wants to give. Of course, the charitable giver may also contribute to an appeal for an emergency relief operation, but that is a different action.

This thought took me back to an incident I described in Chapter 2, when one of the largest US NGOs came to help Cambodian refugees in Thailand and could offer only medical teams, which were not needed, but was unable to help with sanitation, which was desperately required.

In turn, that reminded me of the work that we had done at OCFA looking at the aid policies of Western European governments in 2011. They almost all identified sectors of activity, such as governance, the environment or human rights, which they, as donors, prioritise, without reference to the particular needs and priorities of the recipient country. These are all donors deciding what they want to give, rather than asking the recipients what they need.

Western donors and NGOs can be quite patronising about the aid activities of Arab donors, suggesting that the Arab organisations are not sufficiently professional, that the motivation is primarily religious and that most of their aid goes to fellow Muslim countries. I found these comments irritating and often hypocritical. Quite apart from the fact that most Arab donors work through implementing partners who are expected to be professional, and that a focus on their own region, which includes countries like Afghanistan, Pakistan, Somalia, Sudan and

Yemen, makes perfect sense for Gulf countries, this attitude begs the question of the motivation of Western governments and NGOs. As demonstrated above, the answers to that question are not as straightforward as some of them would like us to assume.

One international donor that was successful in developing a meaningful partnership with the UAE aid sector, was the UK's Department for International Development (DfID). Ministers and officials were frequent visitors, and they stationed a representative in the British Embassy in Abu Dhabi. In the context of the UAE/UK Task Force on a range of foreign policy issues, cooperation on aid issues in specific countries became a regular feature. It took time for DfID to understand that the UAE did not have a similar set-up to theirs and that decisions about aid, and the organisations that implemented them, were highly decentralised. But, when DfID began to know the UAE aid world better, they identified ways of engaging collaboratively.

Transparency through better documentation

The UAE is probably the only major government donor which provides most of its foreign aid from its local governments, the emirates, rather than from the federal government. In 2014, the country's leadership had yet to reach an agreed national policy position on aid issues. However, they are committed, at the highest levels of government, to the ideals of transparency and accountability. This is translated into two ideas that dominated my time at OCFA: transparency through documentation; and accountability through improving standards of performance and effectiveness.

Among the more than 40 donor entities in the UAE, there were wide variations in 2009 in the way they documented what they were doing. While the Abu Dhabi Fund for Development, for example, was able to give OCFA considerable detail about their activities, some other donors had difficulty initially in giving us much more than the amount spent and the country that benefited. As OCFA introduced reporting formats, based on the standards of the DAC, these donors were encouraged to insist on more detailed reporting from their partners. Several of them subsequently thanked OCFA staff for insisting on the new standards, because it enabled them to learn more about what their money was being used for.

Improving performance

From the moment I arrived in Abu Dhabi, I heard senior officials express concern about the effectiveness of the UAE's aid. This was not so much because they had heard of any particular problems, but more that they had no way of knowing whether it was effective or not. Within the mandate assigned to OCFA, there were three components that seemed designed to address this: training and capacity-building of aid workers; coordination of field operations; and monitoring and evaluation. I will not describe OCFA's programmes in these areas in any detail, but have picked out a couple of issues from each of these components which seem to me of general interest.

OCFA offered a monthly series of training events open to the staff working for the donor organisations. These events ranged from one-day roundtables on policy issues to a nine-day training-of-trainers course on the SPHERE humanitarian standards. Three things quickly became apparent: several UAE donor organisations might be working in the same sector and country, but were not aware of each other's activities; there was a dearth of relevant materials in the Arabic language; and the impact of the training was substantially increased if it was delivered in Arabic and not through translators.

Even before OCFA was established, a senior adviser to Sheikh Hamdan Bin Zayed Al Nahyan, the president of the UAE Red Crescent, and later the president of OCFA, had asked OCHA to provide a simple manual in Arabic for aid workers responding to emergencies. Soon after I arrived, OCHA sent us a draft to look at. We edited it into three self-contained booklets, all in both Arabic and English, the first on mobilisation, the second on assessments and the third on coordination. We agreed the final version with OCHA and offered to print it. The text was a UN text, but it had both UN and UAE logos. Some months after distributing copies around the region, we commissioned a simple evaluation. It produced several interesting observations: in some countries the manual was the UN logo that people looked for while in others it was embraced because of the UAE logo; the availability of both Arabic and English texts in the same volume was of real help to Arabic speakers who knew some English and were working in an environment where English was the language of coordination; and the manual was so popular that at a meeting to introduce it to aid workers in Yemen, a fight had broken out over the last available copy.

OCFA made Arabic translations of several other documents that would not otherwise have been available. Perhaps most strikingly, this included the outcome document of the 4th High-Level Forum on Aid Effectiveness in Busan, Korea in December 2011. On discovering that neither the OECD nor the UN had any plans to translate it into Arabic,

OCFA did it. The Arabic text of this seminal document is now on the OECD/DAC website only because a small federal office in the UAE government took the initiative to translate it.

During my time at OCFA, our role in supporting a coordinated response by UAE donors to humanitarian emergencies was generally limited to providing good quality information in Arabic and English. After a lot of debate, OCFA settled on a portfolio of three regular products: a monthly 'humanitarian flash', featuring early warning information about a wide range of potential and ongoing crises; a series of 'humanitarian country profiles', providing detailed background information on vulnerable countries like Afghanistan, Somalia and Yemen; and, 'emergency in focus', giving up-to-the-minute information about a crisis.

Monitoring and evaluation was an important part of OCFA's mandate. We held workshops with senior evaluators from the Islamic Development Bank and the African Development Bank, we translated DAC standards on evaluation, and we talked about it whenever we could. But progress was slow. Why? Some organisations did not feel they could justify the cost of commissioning evaluations. Donors expect that their funds will go directly to the beneficiaries. Some organisations, such as the Abu Dhabi Fund for Development, felt that it was up to the recipient governments to commission evaluations of the projects they had supported. But in several organisations one could sense anxiety about the consequences of commissioning evaluations. The people who took the decisions about what to fund were not full-time staff members. They were very senior people who had very high expectations; their staff were careful to ensure that they received only the most positive reports. An independent evaluation sounded risky. And then there was the language; the Arabic term for 'evaluation' is the same as that used for appraising the performance of individual staff members. People worried that they might be criticised personally in an evaluation, and that their jobs could be at risk.

These concerns will be familiar to readers from any cultural background. In the UAE, one organisation, Dubai Cares, had embraced monitoring and evaluation. Their example will hopefully be contagious over time.

The UAE and multilateral aid

Visitors from European governments, UN agencies and international NGOs, all asked essentially the same question: how can we persuade the

UAE to put some of its money into our programmes? Some of these visitors, seeking to be more delicate and diplomatic, would invoke one of the new aid buzz-words 'partnership', but the partnership always seemed to involve the visitor's organisation providing the people with technical expertise, while the UAE would provide money. Hardly any of them stopped to think that they were in a country that had achieved the most astonishingly rapid transformation from poverty to wealth, where, for example, malaria had been eliminated, and where women were already on average better educated than men. The idea that they might seek to learn something from the UAE experience did not seem to have occurred to them.

So, perhaps it is not entirely surprising that the UAE remained cautious about contributing aid through UN agencies. Except in a very few cases, UAE contributions to the UN tended to be at modest levels, or large one-off grants which did not get repeated and, in some cases, were not completed to the satisfaction of the UAE donor organisation.

The reasons most often cited by UAE officials for reluctance to fund multilaterally were that UN administration was expensive, that different UN agencies sometimes came asking for the same thing, that the donor had little say over what the money was used for, and, perhaps most importantly, that the UAE did not receive appropriate recognition for multilateral contributions. This reaction was sometimes justified – it is easy for UN agencies to take donors for granted, but it also reflected another problem: in gratitude for a generous donation, a UN agency might invite the UAE to take a seat on a UN group or committee, or to nominate a candidate for a senior position, but the government often did not take up these offers.

This problem, and the misunderstandings it could cause, was neatly illustrated at a seminar organised by OCFA for health programme managers. A director from the WHO Regional Office in Cairo bemoaned the lack of senior UAE doctors on the WHO staff. One UAE manager replied that there were plenty of highly qualified doctors who would be suitable for senior WHO positions. Why did WHO not select them? The WHO director replied that working for WHO or another UN agency required not only experience in one's own country, but also significant periods of professional experience in other countries. Very few UAE doctors had that, and, he might have added, if they did, they were often not attracted by the UN's conditions of employment, which were generally less favourable than the UAE's.

Humanitarian and development funding

Although the Abu Dhabi Fund for Development concentrates on development, and the Red Crescent responds to humanitarian emergencies, there has been no attempt, fortunately, in the UAE to make any rigid distinction between humanitarian and development funding. The Red Crescent may be asked to manage long-term projects, and most of the foundations can use one stream of funds to support both humanitarian relief operations and infrastructure development. Observing how helpful such flexibility can be made me wonder how Western donors had got themselves into this apparently insoluble problem of how to bridge the gap between humanitarian response and the start of recovery and development programmes.

Lessons from Arab aid

After three years in Abu Dhabi, I have a very different and far more nuanced impression of Arab aid. The Abu Dhabi, Kuwait and Saudi development funds, the Islamic Development Bank and the five other partners in the Coordination Group have made possible the construction of essential infrastructure in many developing countries, at a time when Western donor governments' efforts to promote good governance and human rights have not always managed to reduce corruption in the targeted countries. If the comparison may seem unfair, it is no more so than the selective criticism by Western donors of their Arab counterparts.

The Busan conference on aid effectiveness in 2011 attracted over 3,000 delegates to a wide range of plenaries, panels and workshops. In an effort to attract 'emerging donors', the organisers had invited representatives of the BRICS countries to take part in many of the panels; we heard a lot about the aid from Brazil, China and India. But the Gulf donors, who certainly provide far more aid than the BRICS, were almost invisible. Why? Part of the reason may be that the Gulf donors, with their reactive approach to requests for aid, have not articulated policies on aid which they could speak about at such conferences. But, invitations to take an active part at such events, rather than simply to attend, can stimulate the internal work necessary to have a policy position on a particular issue approved. When OCFA's Executive Director spoke on the UAE's reporting framework to an international conference in Beijing in January 2013, this attracted great interest from other non-Western donors.

The UAE's decision to establish a Ministry for International Co-operation and Development in 2013, absorbing OCFA, and to appoint an experienced minister, Sheikha Lubna Al Qasimi, is a major step on the road to better recognition and representation of Arab donors in the top international aid forums.

This kind of move from the Arab world, and the emergence of the BRICS and other middle-income countries as donors of international aid, requires a redesign of the international architecture of development cooperation. The forum that emerged from Busan, the Global Partnership for Effective Development Cooperation, should get the process started, but the complete absence of Arab governments from its initial Steering Committee was not a good start. The Western donors of the DAC need to recognise the distinctive value of Arab donors, make use of their experience in rapidly transforming their economies, and ensure that they are represented at the high tables of policy-making forums.

During my farewell calls before leaving Abu Dhabi in 2013, one senior adviser in a large UAE donor said that in its short life so far, OCFA had 'raised the level of the debate about aid matters in the UAE'. That was gratifying, but it would be doubly satisfying if our work was also recognised as having raised the levels of respect and recognition among Western donors for the important aid work of the UAE and other Gulf countries.

On 20 June 2014, the OECD posted the following notice on its website under the heading, "United Arab Emirates' Development Cooperation:

> In 2013, total net ODA of the United Arab Emirates (UAE) reached USD 5.1 billion, representing an increase in real terms of 375% over 2012. The ratio of ODA as a share of GNI also rose, to 1.25%, up from 0.27% in 2012. Multilateral ODA accounted for 1% of the country's total ODA.

This put the UAE at the top of the world rankings for ODA as a share of GNI in 2013 – a remarkable achievement.

9

PULLING IT ALL TOGETHER
Coordinating the humanitarian response

Some people hate talk of 'coordination'. It can produce loud protestations of independence or groans of boredom and frustration. But for me, there is nothing more fascinating than to watch how people work together in different institutions on a common enterprise. I have had the extraordinary good fortune to have been involved in coordination in the UN, NGOs and a national government, on refugees, humanitarian aid, peacekeeping, mine action and development, in Vientiane, Bangkok, London, Islamabad, Kabul, Sarajevo, New York and Abu Dhabi. I hope that some of the excitement of coordination has come across in earlier chapters.

Since 1991, the world has looked to the United Nations Secretariat, and specifically to an official bearing the title of Emergency Relief Coordinator (ERC), to pull together the efforts of governments, the Red Cross/ Red Crescent movement, NGOs and UN agencies in response to humanitarian emergencies, when the government of the affected country is unable to cope. In that year, General Assembly resolution 46/182 assigned the task unequivocally to the UN, created the post of ERC and mandated an Inter-Agency Standing Committee (IASC) as the forum of UN agencies, with the Red Cross movement and NGOs, to support the ERC's efforts to achieve a coordinated response to humanitarian needs.

In 1992, UN Secretary-General Boutros-Ghali appointed as the first ERC Jan Eliasson, a Swedish diplomat who had been the principal architect of the very resolution (46/182) that had established the post. Boutros-Ghali gave Eliasson the additional title of Under-Secretary-General for Humanitarian Affairs and put him in charge of a new Department of Humanitarian Affairs (DHA), with its headquarters split between New York, where the ERC had his office, and Geneva, where

DHA absorbed the existing UN Office of the Disaster Relief Coordinator (UNDRO).

Eliasson's senior colleagues in DHA New York were drawn mainly from other parts of the UN Secretariat and had little or no firsthand experience of managing humanitarian operations. This set the tone for a New York office focussed heavily on its role as a secretariat department, interacting with other parts of the New York bureaucracy, rather than trying to become the focus for coordination of field operations. The appointment by Kofi Annan of Sergio Vieira de Mello as ERC and head of the re-branded Office for the Coordination of Humanitarian Affairs (OCHA) in 1998 (described in Chapter 6), and of his successor Jan Egeland, would change that – Sergio's career in UNHCR had included plenty of field operations and Egeland had a strong background in the Red Cross – but these appointments would only briefly interrupt the selection of career politicians and diplomats to the post responsible for coordinating relief operations around the world.

Perhaps this offers a clue to the essential ambiguity with which governments perceive this and so many other UN enterprises. Donor governments insisted that the Red Cross movement and the major international NGOs should take part in the Inter-Agency Standing Committee, but they left themselves out of it. Two of the largest international providers of emergency relief are USAID and ECHO, the European Commission's humanitarian office; they are not part of the IASC. Of course, if they were, other government bodies might try to insist on being members too, which would make the system unworkable, but such pressures could be resisted.

The ideas discussed in this chapter are based on the assumption that the United Nations is likely to remain the same kind of organisation that it is today. The Secretary-General will not be given more powers over the agencies; agency mandates will remain unchanged; micro-management by member governments in UN committees will continue to make decision-making difficult and administration tedious; but reforms remain possible if their architects recognise these constraints.

Coordinator, not commander

One of the definitions of 'coordination' in the *Compact Oxford Dictionary* is 'the ability to move different parts of the body smoothly and at the same time'. I like that. If you think of the United Nations as a body, that's a pretty good description of what characterises a good coordinator. The daily task is to persuade different parts of the body to move in the direction you want it to go and in a way that will not tear the body apart. But perhaps the analogy is not really such a good one because, of course, these arms and legs have minds of their own.

Since my earliest days in the business of coordination, I have spent many long evenings discussing with colleagues whether an office or an individual can successfully play the roles of coordinator and operational manager at the same time. Another way of looking at the same question is to ask whether the international response to a humanitarian crisis will be organised more effectively by an office dedicated to the task of coordination or by a 'lead agency'. There was never a clear conclusion to these debates, but as the following paragraphs illustrate, the issue has not gone away.

In previous chapters I have described my experiences working for UNHCR in Thailand, when UNHCR was the lead agency for the response to the refugee crises; then for the British Refugee Council, where we coordinated NGO operations for refugees coming to the UK but also managed support programmes ourselves; for UNOCHA, where we coordinated the UN humanitarian operations in Afghanistan, from offices in neighbouring Pakistan, while ourselves running a mine action operation and managing aircraft and radio communications; in Bosnia, where as part of a UN peacekeeping mission, I helped to coordinate the work of UN lead agencies for humanitarian and development operations; and finally in UNMAS, where the coordination model was similar to those I had experienced with UNHCR, BRC and UNOCHA; as the coordinator of UN mine action, UNMAS also managed operations itself. In all these cases, the offices I worked for operated like a lead agency, fulfilling both a coordinating and an operational role.

In 1997, when Kofi Annan was preparing his first major reform package as UN Secretary-General, he decided to propose to the General Assembly that the post of Emergency Relief Coordinator, created six years earlier and established in New York as the head of the Department of Humanitarian Affairs, should be moved to Geneva and combined with the post of UN High Commissioner for Refugees. When the heads of UNICEF and WFP heard about this, they were outraged, not because they opposed the lead agency concept, but because they did not want UNHCR to play that role. So, they lobbied the US government to intervene with the Secretary-General to amend his proposal. The US State Department intervened as requested, fearing perhaps that the plan would shift the UN's centre of gravity too decisively to Geneva. Just 48 hours before publication of his proposals, the Secretary-General dropped the UNHCR/ERC combination and replaced DHA with the Office for the Coordination of Humanitarian Affairs (OCHA), its headquarters remaining split between New York and Geneva and its operational responsibilities, for mine action and the Iraq programme, removed. The lead agency idea had lost out, in part because there was no consensus on which agency should lead, and in part because of the diverging interests of member states over the roles of New York and Geneva in relation to humanitarian affairs.

This story offers a healthy reminder that politics is the art of the possible, and that the coordination of global humanitarian relief operations is as much about politics as it is about efficient and effective management. The structure had to accommodate the insistence of member states that the ERC should be available to the Security Council in New York with the demand of Geneva-based institutions and their government supporters that Geneva should remain the world's humanitarian capital.

It is perhaps worth recalling that the operations that the ERC is charged with coordinating do not actually take place in New York or Geneva. It would be quite legitimate to ask why all the fuss is about activities in those two wealthy cities. Seen from the offices of UNICEF or WFP in Kinshasa or Kabul, and even from the offices of OCHA itself in those cities, the OCHA headquarters in New York and Geneva can easily seem remote and out of touch, endlessly demanding reports and updates but offering little in return. How has it come to this, and what can be done about it? Does it even matter?

To dispose of the last question first, it certainly matters. The success of a major humanitarian operation, like any other complex and demanding human enterprise, requires effective leadership and management at all levels. If those delivering the assistance feel they are not being effectively led, that affects the quality of their work.

UN humanitarian operations in a specific country are led by an official with the title of humanitarian coordinator (HC), who is accountable to the ERC. The HCs are appointed in consultation with the heads of UNDP, UNICEF, UNHCR and WFP. Most frequently, the HC also serves as UN resident coordinator, in charge of development programmes, although in some cases the local head of one of the humanitarian agencies such as UNICEF may be designated. In multi-dimensional peacekeeping operations, the HC/RC may serve at the same time as the Deputy Special Representative of the UN Secretary-General (DSRSG) in an arrangement known as triple-hatting. Occasionally, the ERC may appoint the head of an OCHA field office as HC. Whichever arrangement is chosen, OCHA provides the HC with a small team of support staff.

So why is it all so complicated? Why can a humanitarian relief operation not be run more like a military operation under a single commanding general? The answer lies in the nature of the United Nations system. The UN is a collection of almost wholly autonomous bodies, set up as distinct entities, each with its own mandate and governance structures. They are all overseen by the same 193 governments, but by different representatives of those governments, each with their own agenda and priorities.

In these circumstances, the principles defining successful coordination, and even the meaning of the word 'coordination', are different from those applying to situations in which the coordinator is a commander.

Principles of effective coordination

The principles that follow are not taken from an official document, although several of them are reflected in the standard job description of humanitarian coordinators. They identify what I feel are essential elements of a mutually beneficial understanding between the coordinator and the agencies involved in a humanitarian operation run by the United Nations. In light of the detailed guidance emerging from the humanitarian reforms of 2005 and the IASC's Transformative Agenda protocols of 2011, these principles may seem very basic, but I think it is worth recalling the nature of the essential compact between coordinator and agencies.

The coordinator should:

1. Provide a service that the agencies recognise as being helpful to them in doing their job.
2. Collect and make available to the agencies information about the situation of the people they are assisting, as well as about developments relating to the political, economic and security context in the areas they are working in.
3. Collect and process information provided by the agencies about their programmes and funding needs and present that information to potential donors.
4. Ensure the availability of a safe and reliable air service, if required, and of a communications network, as well as decent and safe accommodation for agency personnel on mission in the country.

5. Represent the interests of the agencies in negotiations with the authorities of the countries concerned, as well as with opposition groups when required.
6. Provide a forum for policy debate, strategic and operational planning and monitoring of operations.
7. Develop with the agencies a joint media strategy and use the most effective means to get out the key messages.

For their part, the agencies should agree to:

1. Provide all the information required to the coordinator.
2. Take an active part in the forums for planning and policy debate.
3. Support and implement the common strategic and operational plans.
4. Use the agreed media strategy to 'speak with one voice'.

In 2005, the then ERC, Jan Egeland, introduced a package of humanitarian reforms, including two initiatives – the 'cluster system' and the Central Emergency Response Fund (CERF) – which have transformed the way that coordination of humanitarian response to major crises is organised.

The first of these is the so-called 'cluster' system. Under this system, UN agencies have agreed to play the role of global coordinator for a specific sector of activity. WFP is the 'cluster lead' for food aid, and also for logistics, while UNICEF is cluster lead for water and sanitation, and so on. This means that WFP and UNICEF have similar roles vis-à-vis other members of their clusters as OCHA has overall in relation to them. But, whereas the cluster lead agencies are playing the dual roles of coordinators and operators, OCHA itself has been stripped of any operational functions, even those like aircraft operations and communications, which are a direct support for coordination.

The second major reform was the creation of the Central Emergency Response Fund (CERF), a central pot of funding of up to US$450 million annually, made available for the ERC to distribute to the UN agencies, both in situations of sudden-onset emergencies and in cases where a particular emergency response is seriously underfunded. The ERC takes decisions on the use of this fund on the basis of recommendations from humanitarian coordinators in the field. This development is worth examining in more detail, since it has fundamentally changed the relationship between the coordinator and the operational agencies.

'Pooled' funds

In 2005, the ERC, Jan Egeland, an energetic Norwegian politician with a strong humanitarian background, mounted an extraordinary campaign to fill the hole in the coordination architecture left by the absence of a reserve fund which the ERC could call on when disaster struck, or when donors had failed to provide resources for programmes which the ERC believed were essential. Egeland got this through the UN General Assembly by forming an alliance with a small group of government ministers favourable to the idea, including notably Hilary Benn, then secretary of state for international development in the UK, and by selling the change as an overdue adjustment to an existing mechanism, rather than the seismic shift that it actually was.

Before 2006, UN coordinators of humanitarian operations had quite a few tools with which to keep the UN humanitarian agencies on the same page, but money was rarely one of them. Coordinators may have had some success in persuading donors to support certain programmes, but they did not get to decide. That all changed with the passage of General Assembly resolution 60/124 on 15 December 2005, which transformed the Central Emergency Revolving Fund into the Central Emergency Response Fund. Egeland had persuaded the General Assembly to add a major grant component to what had been, until then, a small loan facility. The decision appears as paragraph 15 of the annual resolution about the work of OCHA, almost as though it was an after-thought. It was actually a revolution. And it was one that I had thought so unlikely that I had not realised how badly it was needed.

When people asked me in Afghanistan how we expected to coordinate an operation without control over the purse strings, I would reel off all the reasons why I was quite happy not to have responsibility for distributing the funds: it might destroy the team spirit in the UN family; the UN agencies could not blame me if their projects were not funded; a coordinator can often persuade a donor to fund something really important anyway; and so on.

In 2008, OCHA asked me to lead a team of consultants to evaluate the first two years of operation of the CERF, as required by the General Assembly resolution. To my surprise, we found that the reaction to the introduction of this new fund had been overwhelmingly positive. Granted that some of its most notable successes had been in speeding up the response to sudden-onset natural disasters, which I had rarely been involved with, it had also allowed humanitarian coordinators in post-conflict situations to direct funds at the sectors they felt were in most urgent need of support. It had certainly heightened tensions in some UN country teams, but that had been a small price to pay for a facility which allowed the team to plan with some confidence that funds would be forthcoming, rather than in the knowledge that the selection of projects for funding would be decided by donor preferences.

Donor governments like the CERF because it allows them to be seen to respond quickly to every major emergency anywhere in the world, without having to do more than write one large cheque every year. The host governments like it because humanitarian coordinators can no longer explain to them that they would love to help but have no money. And the UN agencies somewhat grudgingly admit that it has helped to speed up the response and has enabled them to fund activities in countries where they had been chronically under-funded, but they worry that donors are now less likely to fund their own programmes, and some NGOs complain that the UN agencies are using all this new money, some of which would previously have come to them, to fund their own programmes, sometimes in situations where the NGOs are better placed to deliver quickly and effectively.

There is merit in these criticisms, and the recommendations we made sought to address them, but they also highlight what for me has been one of the most important lessons from my career in this business: the more the system demands of coordinators, the more important the selection of the people who fill those posts becomes. In a word, it's all about leadership. The humanitarian coordinator who receives $10 million from the CERF to respond to a natural disaster, and gives $2 million each to UNDP, UNICEF, UNHCR, WFP and WHO is not a leader. The UN agency representative who uses that agency's $2 million to fund its own operations, even if an NGO is better placed to react quickly, is not a leader. I will return to this point.

In addition to the CERF, major donors also began to support two other types of 'pooled' funding, both made available to humanitarian coordinators in the field. One, the 'Common Humanitarian Funds' (CHFs), was launched initially in DRC and Sudan, where, and this was not a coincidence, the UN had deployed its two most effective humanitarian coordinators. The CHFs allowed a small number of donors to pool their resources to support programmes for humanitarian operations and early post-conflict recovery. The other facility, given the name 'Emergency Response Funds' (ERFs), consisted of small, country-specific funds in a dozen countries facing emergencies, which allow humanitarian coordinators to make small grants to NGOs for vital relief activities for which there is no other source of money.

I must admit that this belated conversion to the idea of money for coordinators has shaken my confidence somewhat. It shows how easy it is to be lulled by familiarity into laziness and a reluctance to challenge assumptions. In the final chapter looking at 'blind spots', I identify some of the other issues where I believe that deep-rooted assumptions need to be challenged.

Coordination services

In Afghanistan, I fought hard, and successfully, to retain control, as humanitarian coordinator, over the aircraft operation. However, my successors were obliged to accept a global deal which saw the creation under WFP of Humanitarian Air Services.

Throughout the 1990s, the small aircraft operations run by the UN and the ICRC provided the only means for international aid workers to reach all parts of Afghanistan. From Islamabad we flew regularly to Kabul, Herat, Kandahar, Mazar-i-Sharif and Jalalabad, and less frequently to other provincial centres. My critics told me that we could set the rules for the operation, but that the management should be in the hands of the logisticians. I was not convinced. We could not foresee the unpredictable circumstances which would require an immediate decision. The aircraft were the lifeline of the whole operation. It was not a responsibility I felt able to delegate.

So, why is Humanitarian Air Services not managed by OCHA? Once again, it comes down to the nature of the UN system and the ambivalence of member states and the UN agencies over what sort of organisation they expect OCHA to be. To put it as simply as possible, is OCHA a department of the UN Secretariat, or is it the coordinator of all major humanitarian relief operations? Of course, it is supposed to be both, but it cannot perform the latter role effectively with the administrative mechanisms of the former.

The administrative rules and procedures of the UN Secretariat were not designed to support emergency relief operations in remote parts of the world. In UNMAS, we knew that we would never be able to administer mine action operations in Africa and Asia from the UN Secretariat building in New York, so we contracted the UN Office for Project Services (UNOPS) to administer our field operations. UNOPS had been set up for exactly this purpose and operates on procedures more attuned to the commercial world than to the demands of an old-world civil service bureaucracy.

I proposed on several occasions, including in 2008 in the evaluation of the CERF, that OCHA should contract UNOPS to administer its field operations, but then somebody would tell a story about how badly UNOPS had administered a project of a UN agency in a particular country, and people would throw up their hands and say, 'we can't hand our operations over to them'. I would respond, in vain, that any such relationship needs to be managed constantly. If UNOPS did not perform, you could tell them to put new people on the project, which you could not do with OCHA's own non-performing personnel, who are protected from dismissal for incompetence. For UNMAS, the arrangement with UNOPS worked perfectly well. If OCHA did the same, they would be in a much better position to manage the coordination services that major operations require.

Coordination meetings

When the heads of the local UN agency offices start sending their deputies or other more junior staff to OCHA's coordination meetings, you know you have a problem. Carl Bildt, the High Representative in Bosnia, never had this problem. Aside from the effortless authority and gravitas that he exuded, the 'principals' knew that the NATO commander might come prepared to share, in confidence, some sensitive information. But, of course, that was a political–military operation. How do you create the same sense of excitement and anticipation for a weekly meeting of humanitarian agencies? The answer lies in the quality and relevance of the information that the coordinator, or another key member of the team, can provide, or the significance for the agencies of decisions to be taken. Meetings of the agencies working in Afghanistan would be better attended if I had just returned from a meeting with Gulbuddin Hekmatyar in Kabul or Peshawar, or if we had a high-level visitor, than if we had spent the week in the office working on the annual report.

Information exchange is the most basic component of the coordination bargain. You tell me what the state of Afghanistan's children is, and I'll tell you which donor expressed interest in receiving a project proposal on maternal and child health. There must be a sense that both sides are giving and receiving useful information.

Division of labour

In Thailand in 1980, UNHCR built five new camps for refugees from Cambodia in the space of just a few months. The large piece of paper on the wall of the UNHCR office in Bangkok had columns with the names of the camps or sections, while the rows across read Education, Health, Sanitation, Social Services, and so on. In the boxes created by this matrix we put the names of UN agencies and international NGOs that had agreed to provide the services in a particular camp. Some horse-trading went on, which we encouraged. This practice of dividing up the work remains at the heart of the coordinator's role to this day, but it can often be fraught with difficulty.

In Chapter 4 I told the story of efforts in 1989 to identify one UN agency to lead the work on irrigation systems in Afghanistan and how we ended up with seven agencies doing it. In 2008, when I was reviewing the use of the CERF in the DRC, NGOs complained vociferously that an ineffectual WHO office had swallowed up all the money allocated from the CERF for health, whereas in its capacity as 'cluster lead' for health, WHO should have divided the funds among the agencies best placed to provide vital health coverage in the areas of greatest need.

With more and more NGOs trying to attract donors to believe that they are the right organisation to provide help to those in need, my impression is that it is less easy today than it was in 1980 to persuade organisations to operate in the places where the need is greatest, and not only in the places where they will get the most media attention or most easily bring their celebrity visitors for a photo-op. The CERF and the cluster system both offer ways to help reverse this tendency, but both need to be used creatively and with firm leadership.

OCHA also has to get the balance right between too much and too little coordination. If the OCHA office in a crisis situation is well staffed and funded, but the aid operation is starved of resources, OCHA is accused of prioritising coordination over the provision of aid. If the humanitarian coordinator feels unable to do his/her job because of inadequate support, the whole operation can suffer. It is a delicate balancing act.

Talking to everybody

Shortly after I arrived in Pakistan in 1988 as head of the local UN office for the coordination of assistance to Afghanistan, I was having coffee with a brigadier from Pakistan's Inter-Services Intelligence (ISI), which was managing the US-funded operation to support the *mujahideen* in Afghanistan, when he asked me whether I had some particular link with Thailand. No, I said, I had worked there in the past, but I had no links now. The conversation moved to other topics, but we both understood what had been said. My wife is from Laos, and the Lao language is similar to Thai. The brigadier's operatives listening to our nightly telephone conversations in Lao were having trouble with the translation.

A key function of a coordinating office is to be in regular contact with all parties that are in a position to help or hinder the operation, however unsavoury they may be, and however hard governments may try to suggest that it is not your role. When I visited the UN operations in Afghanistan after 2001, I was concerned to see that the links with the ISI in Pakistan were not being kept up. You cannot run a humanitarian operation in the hope that parties to the conflict will not interfere with it. You have to keep lines of communication open all the time.

In order for humanitarian coordinators to fulfil this negotiating role, they need the authority, training and necessary support staff. If the personnel of other UN agencies are to be involved in such negotiation, it must be because they have been mandated by the coordinator to do it, and not because they want to obtain an advantage for their own agency.

Security

These contacts and negotiations with parties to a conflict are all about finding ways to achieve a secure environment for the delivery of humanitarian assistance and for the people employed by the UN and NGOs to manage and monitor the deliveries. This issue has become extraordinarily complex and highly charged, particularly as a result of events in Iraq and Afghanistan and, more recently, the passage of anti-terrorism laws in several countries that criminalise contacts with some armed groups controlling areas where people are in desperate need of humanitarian aid. Tragically, the first decade of the twenty-first century has seen a steady rise in the numbers of UN and NGO humanitarian aid workers being killed, wounded and kidnapped in the course of their work.

In 2011, OCHA published an outstanding independent study entitled *To Stay and Deliver: Good Practice for Humanitarians in Complex Security Environments*, by Jan Egeland, Adele Harmer and Abby Stoddard. Based on over 250 interviews with aid workers in Afghanistan, Pakistan, DRC, Somalia, Sri Lanka and Sudan, the study identifies the practices that give aid agencies the best chance of being able to carry out their work safely, as well as those practices of governments, including donor governments, and the aid agencies themselves that are most likely to compromise the security of humanitarian operations and put the lives of aid workers at risk. What the study brings out is that the politicisation and militarisation of humanitarian aid compromises the status of humanitarian aid workers trying to operate according to humanitarian principles of humanity, impartiality and neutrality. Once those principles are abandoned, it becomes far more likely that parties to the conflict will see aid workers as assets or allies of a foreign power that has taken sides in the conflict. The core message of the study is the importance of a renewed focus on humanitarian principles and on applying tried and trusted techniques of risk management.

It all begins with an assessment of risks. Agencies have to invest in expert assessments of the risks they face and measure them against the potential benefits to the people they are trying to help. Providing aid in insecure environments is a job for professionals, using techniques whose risks and benefits are now well understood. Egeland's team correctly concluded that the best strategy in most insecure environments is what they call an 'acceptance-based approach', in which humanitarian organisations explain their role and activities to all sides in the conflict and seek their acceptance. The organisation that has most consistently used this approach is the world's original humanitarian agency, the International Committee of the Red Cross (ICRC).

In Afghanistan in 2014, the SRSG and his deputies are protected around the clock by teams of armed guards. UN staff members are restricted to their heavily fortified offices and approved accommodation. They cannot walk on the streets or go to restaurants. And still, in recent years groups of UN international staff have been murdered in their accommodation in Kabul and in their offices in Mazar-i-Sharif. I can see no justification for continuing UN political and development operations in these circumstances. There has to be a point at which the Secretary-General decides that the conditions for safe and effective UN operations with international staff are simply not present. In those circumstances, an assessment needs to be made as to whether a minimum presence of international staff to manage humanitarian relief operations is still possible, or whether national staff can safely manage the humanitarian operation, with remote support from international staff based in neighbouring countries, or whether all UN operations should simply cease, until all parties to the conflict are agreed on the need to invite the UN to resume operations, and are ready to give assurances of safety and security for UN staff. As Jan Egeland and his team put it in their study, 'There is little point in an aid agency being present in a country if its staff remain behind compound walls or cloistered in safe areas and capital cities, unable to work with the people in need.'

Speaking with one voice

Among Prince Sadruddin's early efforts as coordinator for Afghanistan in the winter of 1988–89 was an appeal for emergency relief items to assist the people of Kabul. He decided we would open an air-bridge from Pakistan amid a fanfare of publicity. We were informed of a planeload of medical supplies that would arrive in Islamabad and then fly on to Kabul with its load. Finally, the flight arrived at Islamabad airport and discussions took place with the captain and crew about the flight to Kabul. The next morning everyone was ready. The only problem was that the captain had not relished the prospect of flying into Kabul and had flown home instead.

This incident reinforced for me a principle that I had already learned in Laos and Thailand: never tell the press about an operation until it has actually happened.

Equally important is to persuade all the UN partners in an operation to speak with one voice. This is an area where real progress has been made in recent years. Many more UN officials are authorised to speak to the media now than used to be the case, provided that they keep to the facts of the work that they are themselves involved in. The ERC issues regular 'Key Messages' on different country situations which are widely disseminated within the UN system and which provide the basis for interviews by senior officials of all agencies.

Integrated missions

As if it was not difficult enough to make all the parts of the humanitarian body move smoothly and in the same direction, the humanitarian coordinator almost always has to work alongside development colleagues and sometimes with UN peacekeepers as well.

In Chapter 6, I describe how I arrived in New York from Bosnia in 1998, concerned that there was no clear guidance from the Secretary-General about how the humanitarian, development and political arms of the UN were supposed to work together. I had discovered immediately that my experience was by no means unique. Not only was there no guidance, but each part of the UN had very different ideas about how these relationships should work. These disagreements were playing out in UN operations all around the world.

The first Note of Guidance on relationships between representatives of the Secretary-General, resident coordinators and humanitarian coordinators was issued in December 2000, and a more detailed note on the relationships in 'integrated missions' was issued in 2006. Integrated missions are those in which the entire UN family is integrated under the leadership of a Special Representative of the Secretary-General, with one of his or her deputies being 'triple-hatted', that is taking on the roles of resident coordinator (development) and humanitarian coordinator, as well as deputy SRSG.

This arrangement has come in for considerable criticism from humanitarian organisations which complain that it compromises the neutrality, impartiality and independence which the humanitarian coordinator must have in relation to all parties to a conflict. Here is the root of what is becoming a serious problem for the UN. The concept of 'integrated missions' was designed for post-conflict situations, where there would no longer be 'parties to the conflict'. The management of a humanitarian operation in peacetime poses very different challenges from the same task during a conflict.

In Afghanistan at the end of 2001, and in Iraq in 2003, it was everybody's hope that the conflicts were over and the UN presence in both countries was designed on that basis, with integrated missions incorporating peacekeepers, development experts and humanitarians. But of course, hopes for peace were soon blown away, particularly in Afghanistan, and it took too long for the UN system to recognise that, in these changed circumstances, the humanitarian operation no longer belonged with the political mission.

A structural challenge to coordination

The architecture that defines the way the international community responds to emergencies was put in place in 1991. As we have seen, the structure was adjusted in 1997, but the essential components of a post of Emergency Relief Coordinator, combined with that of UN Under-Secretary-General for humanitarian affairs, and the Inter-Agency Standing Committee, have remained. While this structure has clarified much, it inadvertently caused a problem for those involved in trying to reduce the vulnerability of countries and cities to major disasters, and those involved in getting ready to respond to the disaster when it strikes.

The government of a country vulnerable to natural disasters has to consider three distinct questions when planning for the worst: how to reduce the chances that an extreme event will cause a disaster; how to be ready to respond in case of disaster; and how to manage the actual response. In the jargon of humanitarian action, we refer to these three elements as 'disaster risk reduction', 'preparedness' and 'emergency response'. Reducing vulnerability to disasters is, in most countries, a responsibility of national and city planners, who need to ensure that construction does not take place in flood plains and that flood defences are constructed where required, and maintained.

The tasks of being prepared to respond and actually responding are in most cases the responsibility of a single authority or group of organisations working together. In many countries this is done by a civil defence or equivalent authority working with the national Red Cross or Red Crescent society. These are the people who make sure they have stocks of relief items and are in a position to mobilise search-and-rescue teams, and so on.

So, if the government wants to seek help from the UN, either for advice on reducing risk and vulnerability, or for support with its disaster response preparedness, it will naturally turn to the UN resident coordinator in its capital, who then might expect to find support organised along the same lines within the UN system. Unfortunately that is not the case.

UNDP and UN Habitat (UN Centre for Human Settlements) are the agencies most obviously concerned with planning for development, and the ERC and OCHA are obviously responsible for responding to emergencies, so you might think that governments and RCs should approach UNDP and UN Habitat for advice on risk reduction and OCHA for response preparedness. But that would be to reckon without the capacity of the UN system to get tied in knots by historical accident.

When DHA was established in 1992, it took over the Office of the Disaster Relief Coordinator (UNDRO) as its Geneva office, with its teams of technical specialists in disciplines such as urban search and rescue and telecommunications. They provided support to RCs and governments in countries vulnerable to, or affected by, natural disasters. When UNDRO was absorbed into DHA, UNDP took advantage of the change to claim that it would be better placed to assist governments of countries vulnerable to disasters with issues of risk reduction, mitigation and preparedness.

UNDP had a good case in relation to risk reduction, but taking preparedness away from the ERC was like making Oxfam responsible for procuring tents, but making the Red Cross responsible for delivering them – a recipe for confusion and mutual recriminations. So, how did this happen?

It seems that UNDP was able to argue that, unlike UNDRO, which was all about support for national governments in partnership with UNDP country offices, DHA/OCHA would be coordinating the response to complex emergencies and that it would not be working with national governments in the way that UNDP does. This has turned out, in my view, to be a most unfortunate argument that has led to conflict and confusion, which continued up to the time of writing in 2014. As OCHA exercises responsibility for coordinating the international support for governments confronted by huge natural disasters, it needs to rediscover UNDRO's approach to partnerships with national governments for preparedness.

And then, to make matters worse, in 2000, at a time when 'resilience' was not yet the buzz-word that it became in the 2010s, and when UNDP had given little priority to developing its new responsibility for risk reduction, a new UN office came into being, called the International Strategy for Disaster Reduction (ISDR), whose head was asked to report not to UNDP and UN Habitat, which would have been logical, but to the ERC.

In summary, preparedness is part of the system of response and should be with OCHA, while risk reduction is part of planning for development and should be with UNDP and UN Habitat. So, what is to be done? It looks simple – a nice swap, with no loss of face for anyone – responsibility for 'preparedness' returns to OCHA, and ISDR, combined with UNDP's risk reduction team, could become a joint project of UNDP, UN Habitat, OCHA and the World Bank, administered by UNDP, in the same way that Roll Back Malaria is a project of WHO, UNICEF, UNDP and the World Bank, administered by WHO.

There would be many advantages to this arrangement: clarity for governments, civil society, RCs and agency staff; a logical, coordinated approach to disaster risk reduction; and a recognition that being prepared is a pre-condition for effective response.

How could this be made to happen? Changes like this need to be championed by sympathetic governments and supported by relevant senior UN officials and civil society groups. As my account of the introduction of the Central Emergency Response Fund demonstrated, this combination of key governments with activist UN insiders can make things happen.

Leadership

Structural reforms in the UN system are of limited value in the absence of effective leadership. Leadership is also the most difficult topic to talk and write about, because any illustrations inevitably relate to real people.

Human resources departments in the UN system have made progress in adopting modern methods to identify the required skills and competencies for thousands of posts throughout the organisation, and then selecting, theoretically at least, the best candidate – except at the top, where it matters most. A government puts forward one of its top diplomats for a post for which they seem well qualified. The Secretary-General tells the candidate that the post their government has proposed them for has already been filled by a candidate from another country, but there is another post, with a completely different set of responsibilities, which is still vacant. The candidate tells the Secretary-General that they have no experience in this field. They are told that they will learn quickly and are duly appointed. Surely, that couldn't happen, could it? It did, in 2007, and Sir John Holmes recounts the story in his refreshingly honest and comprehensive account of his time as Emergency Relief Coordinator in his book, *The Politics of Humanity*.

John Holmes did learn quickly, as his book illustrates, and the general view seems to be that, in the circumstances, he performed remarkably well; this may even have convinced some observers that these top jobs can be done by anybody with a track record of success in any field, however unrelated. Unfortunately, in the last year of his time as ERC, Holmes was confronted with the most devastating natural disaster of recent memory, the Haiti earthquake of January 2010.

Among the dead in the Haiti earthquake were the head of the UN Mission, Hedi Annabi of Tunisia, and his deputy, Luiz da Costa of Brazil, both good friends from my days in peacekeeping. Along with many other UN insiders, I expected to hear within the first 48 hours that Ross Mountain, or one of the two or three other most experienced coordinators of UN relief operations, had been flown in to take over the role of humanitarian coordinator. It did not happen. The official who was already there, and who had been personally traumatised by the disaster, stayed on to coordinate the response. Sadly, but in my view all too predictably, the UN was criticised for an unacceptably poor performance in the coordination of one of the most difficult and complex relief operations ever mounted.

In his book, Holmes courageously describes the process through which he decided not to send in one of the most experienced humanitarian coordinators, in spite of the advice he received from colleagues to do so. While one can always argue the merits of a specific decision, I am one of those who believe that it would have been better for Haiti and the reputation of the United Nations if he had listened to his advisers; and that an experienced humanitarian in the role of ERC would have listened to that advice.

In Mark Malloch-Brown's fascinating book, *The Unfinished Global Revolution*, he describes how, as chief of staff and then deputy Secretary-General, he worked with Kofi Annan to change the culture that allowed governments to nominate unqualified candidates for the most senior positions and expect that the Secretaries-General would appoint them. They published job descriptions for senior posts, encouraged applications and engaged head-hunters. Even for posts, such as the head of peacekeeping, where it had already been decided that the selected candidate should be French, they asked the government to submit three names and then interviewed them. Unfortunately, Kofi Annan's successor, Ban Ki-moon, seems to have reverted to the old approach when making senior appointments.

In Chapter 2, I described how my boss had insisted that I needed a mentor when I was put in charge of UNHCR's operation to assist Cambodian refugees arriving in Thailand after the Vietnamese intervention in 1979. In Afghanistan, although I did not have a dedicated mentor, we employed a number of experts on Afghan society and politics, including Michael Barry, Jean-José Puig and Didier Leroy, on contracts of varying lengths to advise and assist us in working in this unfamiliar territory.

Whatever their background and experience, nobody can be fully prepared for their first assignment as humanitarian coordinator for a complex disaster or as Special Representative of the Secretary-General in charge of a multi-dimensional peace operation. Routinely providing a mentor for new leaders in these situations would quite simply improve the effectiveness of the operation. For leaders in a highly stressful job, having an experienced individual who is not part of the operation and not involved in evaluating their performance, would help them through the difficult first six months. While working on this manuscript in 2013, I was pleased to learn that OCHA had recently begun to offer the services of a mentor to new humanitarian coordinators.

So, who were the effective leaders, and what was it that made them so? Prince Sadruddin at UNHCR, Kofi Annan in his first term as Secretary-General, Sergio Vieira de Mello as Emergency Relief Coordinator, Jean-Marie Guéhenno at the Department of Peacekeeping Operations and Mark Malloch-Brown in the Cambodian refugee camps in Thailand and at UNDP in New York were all strong leaders who I observed in action. But the selection suggests two observations: they all put together strong teams to support them – a complex operation needs more than a single leader, it needs a balanced leadership team; and some of them went through periods in their careers where their leadership was less successful, suggesting that effective leadership needs a minimally favourable context. If the cards are stacked against them, the best leaders can trip up.

The politicisation of humanitarian coordination

In every chapter of this book, we have seen evidence of how the humanity, neutrality and impartiality of humanitarian action have been 'politicised' in one way or another, since 1975. However, there have been three new ways in which humanitarian principles have been compromised since 2000. The first has been the emergence of armed groups in certain countries which have declared humanitarian organisations to be legitimate targets of attack. The second is the role adopted by international military forces in Afghanistan and Iraq, for example through 'provincial reconstruction teams', which have delivered humanitarian aid to communities, not on the basis of need, but as an incentive to support the presence of international military forces. And the third is the politicisation of the role of the Emergency Relief Coordinator.

The first two of these new developments have been widely discussed by others. Suffice it to say here that they have made the task of humanitarian aid workers considerably more difficult than it already was.

In creating the post of Emergency Relief Coordinator in 1991, the General Assembly of the United Nations, while specifying that the new position would be a senior official in the United Nations, did not actually include the letters UN in the proposed job title. Valerie Amos, the UN Under-Secretary-General for Humanitarian Affairs in 2014, was not the UN ERC. She was *the* ERC. This is an important distinction. As chair of the Inter-Agency Standing Committee, she coordinates the activities not only of the UN system, but also the Red Cross (although the ICRC participates as an observer), the International Organisation of Migration and three NGO consortia. None of these bodies would readily have accepted being coordinated by an Under-Secretary-General without the ERC designation.

From 1992 to 2006, there were six ERCs – a Swede, a Dane, two Japanese, a Brazilian and a Norwegian. Note that none of these was from a country that is a permanent member of the Security Council. The post was excluded from the group of posts, which includes the heads of political affairs and peacekeeping, that have in recent years been divided up among the five permanent members. By giving the post to the UK, and by appointing to it first John Holmes, a diplomat who was a candidate for the political affairs post, and then Valerie Amos, who although better qualified was nevertheless another British diplomat and politician, Ban Ki-moon showed that he considered the post to be a political one and effectively made it impossible for the incumbents to play the role of ERC as it had been understood in the humanitarian aid community since 1992.

In his book, John Holmes admits that some of his interlocutors in countries like Sri Lanka saw him as much as a British diplomat as a UN official. He also recounts situations in which he accepted instructions from the Secretary-General with which he did not agree. While previous ERCs certainly did the same, the admission reinforces the idea that the Secretary-General has deliberately politicised the role. If this position does not change with the next Secretary-General, the whole rationale behind the architecture agreed in 1991 will be called into question.

A brief agenda for action

It may seem presumptuous in a memoir of this kind, published almost ten years after leaving full-time employment in the UN, to offer recommendations. But, I should like those following a similar career path to mine to be able to work in an environment where lessons from the past have been learned and acted on. So here are some simple suggestions for the UN Secretary-General and the Emergency Relief Coordinator that derive from the discussion in this chapter. If the SG and ERC discuss these ideas with their advisers, in the IASC and with member states committed to effective humanitarian action, progress can result.

Firstly, the SG and ERC should recognise the dual functions of the Emergency Relief Coordinator and the Under-Secretary-General for Humanitarian Affairs, as global coordinator of international relief operations and head of a department of the UN Secretariat, by appointing as deputy ERC in Geneva an experienced humanitarian coordinator, who would have day-to-day responsibility for managing

OCHA's field operations and liaison with UN, Red Cross and NGO partners.

Secondly, they should invite USAID and ECHO to join the Inter-Agency Standing Committee, making it clear that other government bodies will only be invited to join if they can match the size and reach of those two organisations.

Thirdly, they should contract UNOPS to administer OCHA personnel and offices outside New York and Geneva, and to procure the coordination services that OCHA should offer.

Fourthly, they should arrange for the International Strategy for Disaster Reduction to become a project of UNDP, UN Habitat, OCHA and the World Bank, administered by UNDP (along the lines of Roll Back Malaria's relationship to WHO), and arrange for responsibility for preparedness for response to disasters to be transferred from UNDP to OCHA.

Fifthly, they should strictly limit the use of 'integrated missions' to post-conflict situations. If conflict breaks out again in a country where an integrated mission is operating, or if there are groups that have not accepted the peace deal, then the humanitarian coordinator should not be part of an integrated mission.

Sixthly, they should introduce a mentoring service for new ERCs, and for all new SRSGs and humanitarian coordinators.

Finally, the Secretary-General should remove the post of ERC from the list of posts held by representatives of permanent members of the Security Council and apply best practice to the selection of candidates for the post.

These initiatives would gradually transform the attitudes of governments, UN agencies and NGOs to OCHA. Then the ERC would be in a position to deliver the kind of coordination that the UN system needs and the people receiving humanitarian aid deserve.

10

BLINDED BY HUMANITY?

In Dubai in March 2011, a speaker at a conference on humanitarian aid reported seeing a poster in Haiti after the earthquake reading, 'The solution to this country's problems is not on the screen of your laptop'.

Sadly, the solutions to the problems faced by aid workers are often not to be found in the places where we have tended to look for them. Here I return to some of the themes that have recurred all the way through this book and which have filled a lot of my spare thinking-time during a long career. All of them can be characterised in one way or another as 'blind spots', either because they are not recognised as problems, or because resolving them is not considered practical or a priority. But they all have a corrosive effect on the UN system and on the wider aid community.

Each one of these seven issues has caused me frustration and a feeling of helplessness, as if confronted by something inevitable. But, in fact there is nothing inevitable about any of them. They derive either from a short-sighted decision that became embedded as standard practice, or from a misguided sense that they offer an easier option. For each of them I have heard colleagues say, 'Oh, we can't do anything about that', to which my reply is: if the campaigners against anti-personnel landmines had listened to the military officers who told them that the mines were an essential part of an army's weaponry, those mines would still be in general use today. Fortunately, the campaigners didn't listen to the pessimists or those with vested interests, and neither should we assume that 'nothing can be done' about these insidious problems.

1. *Brain drain* – aid agencies poach the best personnel from the governments of developing countries.
2. *Short tours* – international personnel involved in humanitarian and peacekeeping work spend too little time in each assignment to become effective.
3. *Election madness* – most elections are destabilising, not peacebuilding.
4. *No substitute for political action* – humanitarian aid can prolong conflict unless it is accompanied by political initiatives.
5. *Reform of the UN* – reform should not be held up on the grounds that we might end up with something worse.
6. *Power to the people* – aid organisations must empower the communities they are working among.
7. *Good intentions are not enough* – good intentions do not justify bad policies or programmes.

The paragraphs below give the background to these ideas. Taken together the failure to address these issues condemns the international response to crisis to being less honest, less principled and less effective than it can and should be. These things need to be fixed.

Brain drain

In 2006, I led a team conducting an inspection of a major UN agency working in Afghanistan. In the agency's office in Kabul, I was introduced to an energetic and articulate Afghan woman, a lawyer, recently recruited by the agency to work on their capacity-building programme in support of an Afghan government department. Most days, she travelled across town from the UN agency's office to the ministry, where she advised the staff of the department that she herself had just left. Her salary had multiplied several times, she spent less time in the ministry since she had to travel to and from the UN office, but it would be fair to say that she was doing much the same job that she had been doing for the government before she was recruited by the UN.

This is just one among countless such stories familiar to every UN official who has worked in a field assignment. I cite it not to blame the UN agency in question. It is quite possible that this was the only way to retain the services of the talented individual for the government. In the climate prevailing in Kabul at the time, she would have had little difficulty in finding a well-paid post with an embassy, NGO or private company.

All across the developing world, governments are deprived of their best talent by the ability of foreign organisations to pay far more. The inevitable consequence is that governments become less competent and more corrupt. Foreign donors are duly outraged at the government's poor performance and decide that they cannot afford to channel their assistance through the government, but will have to make grants to international NGOs instead. And how will these NGOs make use of these grants? By recruiting any remaining competent government officials, paying them five times the salary they are used to receiving and condemning the government to even greater incompetence than before.

This vicious cycle of decline in the quality of government in poor countries 'enjoying' a substantial foreign aid programme is a scandal. So why is it allowed to continue? While there is no easy answer, decades of living under conditions set by the International Monetary Fund, and low commodity prices, are both contributing factors. This phenomenon promotes dependency on foreign aid, reduces the value for money of the foreign aid that is received, and condemns millions of people in poor countries to living under governments that are more corrupt and less competent than they need to be. So, how can this be ended?

This is not a problem created by the United Nations, although the International Civil Service Commission (ICSC), which fixes the salary scales of UN personnel, both international and local, is complicit in the scandal. But the United Nations could provide the forum and the vehicle for a solution. Ministers of donor countries and chief executives of international agencies should commit themselves to working it out. In most cases, the solution will involve encouraging governments to increase civil service pay as part of an overhaul of employment practices. This is what the Afghan government was beginning to do during my visit in 2006. But it will also require an understanding among donor governments, UN agencies and the ICSC that salaries of national staff of international organisations will have to be restrained in some situations. The funds made available to UN agencies for their work in poor countries are contributed by parliaments on the understanding that they will benefit the country. If the ICSC sets salary scales for national staff, which international NGOs then follow but the national government cannot match, that is not in the interests of the country. Ironically, there are a few countries where the ICSC is not given free rein in setting salary scales and national governments insist on the right to negotiate what the UN will pay. These countries include China and Laos. If the UN and the ICSC will not address the issue, perhaps other developing countries should follow their example.

Short tours

In recent years the number of assignments undertaken by internationally recruited UN staff, particularly in humanitarian and peacekeeping operations, seems to have increased, while the length of time spent in each job has decreased correspondingly. Many CVs are packed with short assignments.

Because people stay in each assignment for less time and because, in the high-risk duty stations, they spend a high proportion of their time on leave or travelling to and from their duty station, most people spend less time getting to know the history, language and culture of the country where they are working than was the case 30 years ago. During my early career, I would often take vacations in the country where I was working, or else in the immediately neighbouring countries. Now, international travel is so easy and cheap, that many young staff travel back to their home countries several times a year. One consequence of this is that international staff are less likely to speak the language of the country where they are working, more likely to misunderstand the messages being communicated to them and more likely to be misunderstood by those they are working with than was the case 30 years ago.

Staff today are expected to have a very detailed knowledge of the policies, project management systems and other internal regulations of their agency – much of which simply did not exist 30 years ago, but they know less about the people they are working with. This has led to a decline in the quality of the interaction between international staff members of United Nations agencies and the people of the countries where they work. Young staff often seem to be encouraged by their organisations to imagine that a project designed for one country that ticks all the boxes about gender, environmental impact and child protection can simply be rolled out in another country. This breeds arrogance and fuels mistrust. After I had been in Laos for a few years, I used to impart a little folk wisdom to newcomers. It went like this: 'When I had been here six months, I thought I knew everything; after a year, I realised I knew nothing; after 18 months I realised I had learned something.'

The answer should be simple. The top leadership of the UN system needs to tell their human resources departments that they want to introduce a new culture into their agencies, one where short assignments are discouraged and are a barrier to promotion; one where knowledge of local languages is expected; and one where managers are encouraged to work with people, both nationals of the country and international academics who have worked there for years, about the design and content of their programmes.

The problem of turnover in personnel is even more acute in peacekeeping or peace enforcement operations. In Bosnia, on the shortest assignment of my career – just under two years – I welcomed four different individuals as my counterpart in a military function. Inevitably, my briefing to the fourth eager newcomer lacked a bit of the enthusiasm that I had shown to the first two. Imagine the situation of the Afghan district governor welcoming the tenth or twelfth different foreign military officer to serve as his counterpart.

In his book, *Cables from Kabul: The Inside Story of the West's Afghanistan Campaign,* Sherard Cowper-Coles, Britain's ambassador to Kabul from 2006 to 2008, writes that each new British brigadier commanding the force in Helmand seemed to feel obliged to mount a big attack on some Taliban positions soon after arriving in the country, whether there was any real political or military justification or not.

Intervening in another country, whether with military force or humanitarian assistance, is a deeply serious matter. If it is to be done at all, it should be done properly and with genuine humility and commitment. That should mean minimum two-year assignments for virtually everybody involved.

Election madness

First negotiate a ceasefire agreement; then send out a peacekeeping operation; then organise some elections. This was the UN Department of Political Affairs's unvarying prescription for ending wars in the second half of the twentieth century, in spite of mounting evidence that elections, and particularly presidential elections of the winner-takes-all variety, do not secure the peace, but are destabilising and likely to provoke further bouts of conflict.

In Chapter 4, I described the disastrous decision at the Constitutional Loya Jirga in Kabul in 2003 to opt for a highly centralised executive presidency. This was just one in a long line of decisions proposed by urban elites in developing countries, beginning in Angola in the 1980s, which 'experts' from the United Nations and donor governments supported, against the evidence of previous disasters and even their experience in their own countries.

The folly of this approach was well described by Roland Paris in his book, *At War's End: Building Peace after Civil Conflict*. More recently Paul Collier, in *Wars, Guns and Votes*, has shown, on the basis of empirical research, that elections in countries emerging from conflict are not, as is so often claimed, a force for peace and reconciliation or even for the achievement of democracy, but rather a source of instability.

So, why do the major powers and the United Nations continue to promote and support this failed approach? Could it be because it appears to offer quick 'closure', 'success' and an exit strategy? If the elections produce a corrupt dictatorship, then perhaps we can argue that the Afghans or the Angolans have only themselves to blame. If this is indeed the rationale, it is not only shameful but also counterproductive.

In his book, *Fixing Fragile States*, Seth Kaplan contrasts the French and Swiss models of democracy and asks why it is that the international community almost always ends up supporting versions of the over-centralised French system, of which a very senior French diplomat once observed to me, 'It doesn't even work in France. We have an executive monarchy!', when the Swiss model of decentralised, local, bottom-up democracy would seem far more appropriate to most developing countries emerging from conflict. One reason for choosing the French model is that the urban elites, who speak to us in English or French, love it. When they persuade UN advisers to support the idea, they can hardly believe their luck.

The irony is that France is almost the only country in the West to adopt such a system, and in spite of all the checks and balances to presidential power that a mature democracy such as France offers, the French still complain about it. Yet we encourage countries with weak democratic institutions to adopt a system that puts all power into the hands of one man (they are nearly always men), and frequently leads to life-long dynastic dictatorships of the type that the Arab Spring sought to overthrow. Is it too much to hope that the UN could, with the support of governments, embrace a new norm of democratic governance, based on a Swiss-style, bottom-up approach?

There is now a remarkable example of how the UN can help to bring about this kind of change. In 2007, Kenya held elections which led to terrible inter-communal violence. Secretary-General Ban Ki-moon asked his recently retired predecessor, Kofi Annan, to lead a commission which also included Graca Machel and Benjamin Mkapa of Tanzania, to help the Kenyans. As Annan recounts in his book, *Interventions: A life in War and Peace*, they persuaded President Kibaki to accept a power-sharing deal with his rival Raila Odinga, and to embark on a process of constitutional change to adopt a more decentralised political structure. That is, of course, what Afghanistan and many other countries have needed all along.

No substitute for political initiatives

Readers may be tempted to ask what this discussion of electoral systems has to do with the provision of humanitarian assistance. The answer is that, unlike the humanitarian aid given after natural disasters, humanitarian aid provided to the victims of conflict is never a solution. It can provide space for people to survive with some vestiges of dignity while a political solution is found, but it is not part of the solution. What frequently worries humanitarians is that their work is used as an excuse to avoid a serious search for political solutions, and even that it can make a political solution more difficult when it enables warlords and spoilers of political dialogue to keep on fighting because their population base is being fed by the international community. Humanitarian aid, so the accusation runs, can prolong conflicts.

Is that a valid accusation? In a literal sense, of course it is. However, it is also meaningless, since humanitarians have no choice but to assist those in need. It is up to the politicians to find solutions that do not involve starving parts of the population or depriving them of the most basic services. But when the politicians turn away from conflict resolution because it is too difficult, or when they propose solutions which play into the hands of a small elite and lead to another round of conflict, and yet more work for the humanitarian aid community, then we should make our voices heard.

Reform of the UN

In 1996, as Boutros Boutros-Ghali's campaign for re-election as UN Secretary-General spread despondency among UN staff around the world, I wrote a two-page paper entitled *Don't Reform the United Nations – Start Again (DRUNSA)*. It started from the premise that the United Nations had been founded in 1945, had achieved great things in the 50 years of its existence, but that the approach of a new millennium offered a great opportunity to design a new global body from scratch. It proposed a worldwide consultation among governments, parliaments, civil society groups and ordinary people to define what we would expect a global organisation to do in the twenty-first century and how it should be structured to do it. Once the new design was ready, it could be launched to run in parallel to the UN for an initial period before replacing it. The initiative would not affect the agencies and funds of the existing UN system, like WHO and UNICEF, but would replace the General Assembly, the Security Council and the Secretariat with new structures and arrangements. I shared *DRUNSA* with a few friends in Sarajevo and some visitors too. The overwhelming reaction was, 'Interesting idea, but you would be bound to end up with something worse than the UN.'

This was the very same argument that I had heard in the 1980s at the British Refugee Council when I suggested that it might be time to renegotiate the 1951 UN Convention on the Status of Refugees, since governments had long since ceased to apply it (see Chapter 3).

Faith in the wisdom of our predecessors, and lack of confidence in the wisdom of our own generation, are deeply engrained in many cultures. Personally I find these ideas depressing and misplaced. We should not imagine that our forefathers could see into the future and know what would be right for us, and we should not be so afraid of ourselves and of each other in our efforts to design institutions that are right for our time.

A reverence for history is not a problem when the institutions created by previous generations seem still to be working. But a UN Security Council without India, Japan or any country from Africa or South America among its permanent members, cannot work. A General Assembly, in which a country with 50,000 inhabitants has the same number of votes as China, cannot work. And a Secretariat that is encumbered with the kind of operating regulations that have been abandoned years ago in modern organisations cannot deliver the best results.

Recent initiatives, substantially driven by civil society groups, show that grassroots activism can create good international law. The 1997 Ottawa Treaty banning anti-personnel mines, described in Chapter 7, was followed by the Convention on Persons with Disabilities (2006) and the Oslo Convention banning cluster munitions (2008). I realise that redesigning the United Nations may be a more ambitious task than legislating against anti-personnel mines, but that does not have to be a barrier. The Mine Ban Treaty was inspired by the International Campaign to Ban Landmines (ICBL). Perhaps we need an international campaign to redesign the UN.

DRUNSA died when Boutros-Ghali's campaign failed and Kofi Annan was elected Secretary-General, the first UN insider to get the top job, bringing new hope to a battered UN staff. While Chapter 6 describes some of the important achievements of his tenure, he nevertheless failed to persuade member states to adopt many of the reforms which he, and other UN insiders, felt were most important. In spite of his best efforts, the Security Council remains stubbornly unreformed. Shall we try again?

Power to the people

In 1989, Graham Hancock published a fierce attack on the aid community entitled *Lords of Poverty*. Like every other aid worker, I rushed to the index to see if my name was there. It was! Imagine my relief at finding that the reference was to an observation that I had made about the public information materials of the UNHCR. I had pointed out that many of UNHCR's posters showed the refugees in a passive, even subservient position, often sitting on the ground, with the photographer looking down at them. This promoted the idea that refugees were helpless, unable to do anything for themselves and dependent on international help.

The following year, all UNHCR's posters seemed to show refugees putting a roof on their houses. The word had gone out. Look up at the refugees. It was a start, but it did not herald, unfortunately, a real change of attitude.

In this sense, people in all parts of the world are the same. They do not want to be obliged to accept help. If given half a chance, people adapt to changing circumstances in remarkable ways. But if they do have to take help, they would like to be spared the lectures and sermons that go with it. And they would like some choices over what type of help they actually get.

During the many years I spent working on Afghanistan, the projects I felt were most successful were those with the least involvement of international staff and the greatest 'ownership' by Afghans. These included a wonderful WFP programme, where wheat was given to bakeries in Kabul to turn into bread, which could then be sold to the poorest women, identified in advance and provided with vouchers, at subsidised prices. This gave work to the bakers and gave those poor women the dignity of buying their bread, even if they had to sell half of it to finance their purchase and buy other essentials. Another success was FAO's animal health project, which got trained extension workers out into the villages with the veterinary medicines required. It resulted in spectacular improvements in animal health and therefore in livelihoods.

My personal favourite, of course, was the de-mining programme and the role played in it by the Afghan NGOs, in spite of continuous efforts in some quarters to discredit them. While there were always valid criticisms to be made, what concerned me most was the implication – never far from the surface – that the Afghans could not be trusted to run something like this.

People of every society and country, if given responsibility, training and ownership of their programme, can run more effective programmes than foreign managers if they feel they are being trusted and if the structure in which they are working offers them transparent ways of demonstrating their accountability.

In Chapter 3, I describe how in the 1980s a programme supported by the European Commission helped refugee communities from a dozen different countries living in Britain to set up community-based organisations offering social services within their own communities. They provided, and some still do, a lifeline to vulnerable members of their communities at a fraction of the cost to local authorities of providing a similar service, and with a sensitivity to cultural norms that no government office could match.

In recent years, many humanitarian organisations have worked hard to improve their 'accountability' to the communities they assist. While these are valuable initiatives, they tend to downplay two issues which for me are of vital importance, the primary role of local authorities in situations where aid programmes are being implemented; and the empowering impact of providing aid through home-grown organisations. The Red Cross and Red Crescent movement has been working for generations through national societies in the countries being assisted. Power to the people!

Good intentions are not enough

Coming to the end of this book, and reflecting on my career, I find myself returning again and again to two related ideas: firstly, intervening, whether invited or not, in another country, another society, in ways that affect people's lives, should be a humbling experience, but we can too easily approach it with arrogance, even a sense of entitlement; and, secondly, things are very often not what they seem on the surface.

This is the territory of ambiguous motivations and inaccurate perceptions. As a social anthropologist, I want to understand how people view the world and how they perceive what I do. As a Buddhist, I want to understand myself. So, this final section offers a few stories from my experience, intended to reinforce the idea that we must go out into the world armed with more than good intentions. And where better to start than with an admission of failure.

For almost the whole time that I was in charge of the UNOCHA office in Islamabad, my personal assistant was a wonderful lady called Sarwar Rana. Arriving at the office one morning in a particularly cheerful mood, I greeted her with, 'Comment ça va?', which most readers will recognise as the French for 'How's it going?' I don't know why I said it, but during the years that followed, I would use the same greeting from time to time. As far as I recall, Sarwar always smiled politely.

Years later, when I returned for a visit, Sarwar admitted that what she had thought I was saying was, 'Come on, Sarwar!' She had been mystified about the reasons for this exhortation. I am still mortified, when I think about it, that I, who have prided myself on having more cultural sensitivity than the average, could have caused such a basic misunderstanding.

Language is so important, and far too often taken for granted. My experience in Abu Dhabi of being the only non-Arabic speaker in long meetings conducted in Arabic was almost cathartic, making up for the countless hours that I have spent in meetings conducted in English, at which people whose futures were being discussed understood little of what was being said. Truly, the English language is too often an instrument of Anglo-Saxon tyranny. I invite native English speakers to imagine how they would feel if the discussion at their local council meeting on the siting of the next wind farm was conducted in Chinese.

Hang on, I hear you say – what about interpreters and translators? Surely, they must be used when local officials don't speak English. Yes, of course, in formal discussions, they are used, and some are very good – but some are not. In quite a few countries, if a foreign visitor says something critical to a local leader, the interpreter is unlikely to translate it accurately, for fear of annoying the boss. Even with written translations, when translators have time to think and get it right, there can still be problems. In Chapter 6 I described the work I did on the Secretary-General's first report to the Security Council on the protection of civilians in armed conflict. Once the English text of the report had been approved by the Secretary-General's office, it went for translation into the five other official languages. I soon received a call from the Russian translator, 'Mr Barber, in paragraph x, what do you mean exactly by the second sentence?' I looked it up and realised that he had identified an English phrase that contained some ambiguity, which we had negotiated so that different agencies could put their own interpretation on it. But the ambiguity did not translate into Russian. I had to choose one interpretation or the other.

Throughout my career I have tried to create conditions that help those whose native language is not English to participate fully in meetings. To those readers who take part in meetings in which some participants are not native English speakers, I offer a little experiment: just make a note of how frequently and for how much time the native English speakers speak, and do the same for the non-native speakers. In my experience, all other things being equal, the native speakers will speak more frequently and for longer. It is not that they have more interesting and relevant things to say; it is simply that it takes longer to react when working in a second language. Unless people chairing meetings are aware of this, and compensate for it, meetings are less productive than they should be.

In *The Unfinished Global Revolution*, Mark Malloch-Brown chides me for not appreciating that the American policy to accept large numbers of refugees from Southeast Asia in the late 1970s and early 1980s, which fuelled the massive exodus of 'boat people' described in Chapter 2, was motivated by a conviction among liberal activists in the US that they must do something to make amends for the horrors that American policies had inflicted on the people of Viet Nam. In other words, their intentions were honourable. But what the liberal activists could not or would not see was that their programme was encouraging people to set out on journeys which many would not complete, and that the departure of the educated elites was condemning the 90 per cent who stayed to longer poverty and slower economic progress.

Almost every chapter of this book contains examples of individuals or institutions making decisions that have unintended, although not necessarily unforeseeable, consequences. From my professor diverting a medical team to assist people who were no longer there when the team arrived in Chapter 1; to the programme that put immense pressure on elderly Hmong refugees to move to the US against their will in Chapter 2; to the officials who encouraged Afghans to adopt a constitution that was virtually guaranteed to fuel conflict in Chapter 4, there are countless examples of situations in which things could have been done better, or at least less badly. In this chapter and the previous one, I have identified a few initiatives which would help to improve the chances of success.

If it seems to some that I have been too critical and not sufficiently recognised the extraordinary courage and sacrifice of so many humanitarians, I would simply say that our goal for people in need is for them to have decent lives with dignity. If we give ourselves a better chance of achieving our goal by changing some of the ways we do business, we should recognise that and act on it.

So, if there is one message that I would pass on to young people wanting to do good in the world, it is this: be passionate, but know your world. Everybody can have good intentions, and indeed, most people do. If you fail to understand the context in which you are working and the people you are working with, and if you do not assess, with infinite care, the likely impact of your actions on them, you may find that you will do more harm than good.

It has been a privilege to have been able to travel the world, to experience new cultures, to meet wonderful people, many confronting the most difficult situations, to witness their courage and spirit and to realise that the work of the United Nations helped some of them to cope with the disasters they encountered.

APPENDIX

'How can I get a job at the United Nations?'

Many young people – and some not so young – have asked me this question. If, after reading this book, you still feel you might like to work for the United Nations, this is for you. But, as you read on, please continuously ask yourself the question, 'Is this really for me?'

Firstly, there are many parts of the United Nations, and you need to decide which one you are interested in. For simplicity, I break them down into four broad categories:

1. The specialised agencies of the United Nations

FAO, ILO, UNESCO, WHO and WIPO are 'specialised agencies' in the fields of agriculture, labour law and relations, education, science and culture, health and intellectual property respectively. Other specialised agencies deal with civil aviation, meteorology, trade and so on. If you are a doctor with a specialisation in a particular aspect of global public health, or a lawyer with a background in intellectual property litigation, then you will know where to apply. If you do not have this kind of specialised knowledge, then these agencies will probably not be your main focus.

2. The Secretariat

United Nations headquarters is split between New York, Geneva, Vienna and Nairobi. New York hosts the Security Council, the General Assembly and the Secretary-General and has a political and economic focus; Geneva has the high commissioners for human rights and refugees and several humanitarian agencies; Vienna deals with crime and outer space and Nairobi hosts the work on environment and human settlements.

The Secretariat also includes the regional commissions – for Africa (Addis Ababa), Asia and the Pacific (Bangkok), Europe (Geneva) and Latin America (Santiago).

3. The United Nations for development

UNDP is at the centre of the UN development effort, with UNFPA, UNICEF, WFP, the specialised agencies, particularly FAO and WHO, and, more remotely, the World Bank. Also considered part of this component are the UN Volunteers (UNV) and UN Women.

4. The United Nations for crisis response

This is the part of the United Nations featured in this book. It includes OCHA and UNHCR, the humanitarian divisions of UNICEF and WFP, and the Department of Peacekeeping Operations (DPKO). The people working in this part of the United Nations tend to be more mobile, more transitory and perhaps a bit crazier than the staff of the first three components.

The staffing rules, recruitment criteria and personnel policies are broadly similar in all parts of the system, except for the World Bank, the UN Volunteers and some jobs in DPKO.

There are two broad types of post to which the UN recruits: professional and general service. For almost all professional posts, a Masters degree is the minimum requirement. General service posts are primarily in the area of administrative support.

How to get recruited

1. *National competitive exams*

The General Assembly has instructed the Secretary-General to retain a 'geographical balance' in recruitment to professional posts in the Secretariat. The formula for calculating how many posts each country should have is based on a combination of population and the level of financial contributions to the UN's core budget. When a country is 'under-represented', its nationals are invited to take part in the annual National Competitive Exams (NCE) in various specialisations.

2. *Advertised posts*

UN bodies that are not part of the Secretariat are not subject to the same rules on geographical balance, although all try to ensure that they recruit from a wide range of nationalities. Similarly, all parts of the UN system are committed to achieving gender balance, so preference may be given to women candidates in some cases.

All UN bodies advertise employment opportunities on their websites. For jobs in the UN crisis response agencies, the reliefweb site (www. reliefweb.int) is the central market place.

Managers seeking to recruit to vacant posts are almost always looking for somebody who will fit into the post quickly and will not prove to be a liability or a headache. Ideally they want somebody who has done a comparable job before and acquired a good reputation while doing it. They are looking for a proven track record, even at quite junior levels. Because it is now so easy to submit an application electronically, managers will normally receive hundreds of applications for each post. How can you ensure that yours stands out?

Your application needs to demonstrate, with evidence, that you have what the post requires. The statement 'I am convinced that I am the best candidate for the job' is not sufficient.

So, how do you acquire the track record and reputation that managers are looking for? The examples below focus on the 'UN for crisis response', but there are similar opportunities in the other parts of the UN.

Junior Professional Officers (JPO)

A number of governments have made agreements with different parts of the UN system to take on JPOs, usually for two years. Governments encourage some of their young diplomats to take such assignments to prepare them for a career in their national diplomatic service, but it is also an excellent way of acquiring the experience and reputation that can lead to longer-term employment in the UN, not necessarily with the same part of the system.

UN Volunteers (UNV)

Most agencies in the UN crisis response system use UNVs to do jobs for which they do not have a budget, or things which they had not thought of when preparing their annual plans.

UNV contracts range from three months to two years. Terms and conditions of employment are less generous than for regular posts, but service as a UNV can be a good way to gain some experience in the field, and can also suit older people in the later stages of their careers, who would like to 'give something back'.

Willing to go anywhere

There are the places where everyone wants to go, and then there are posts in the places where very few people apply. Naturally the competition is less intense in the latter cases.

Languages

A good knowledge of one or more languages other than English is always an advantage. Many managers will look for a knowledge of languages as an indication that a candidate has an international outlook, even if the particular post does not specifically require language skills other than English.

Managers are almost always looking for an ability to write well in English and in the working language of the office if it is not English. It is amazing how many candidates' applications end up in the bin because the application contains basic errors of English language or simple proof-reading mistakes. If you are applying for several jobs, make sure that each application reads as if it is for the only job that really interests you.

Relevant experience

Apart from service as a JPO or UNV, how can you acquire relevant experience? Many staff in the UN crisis response system started life in NGOs, the Red Cross system or in their government's aid programme. Many nationals of countries in which the UN has responded to crises have started out as locally recruited staff of a UN agency, and from there have been recruited to international posts. Several Thai nationals who joined UNHCR as national officers in the 1980s, and Afghans and Pakistanis who joined UNOCHA in the 1990s, have risen to senior positions in UN humanitarian agencies.

Being in the right place at the right time

I suppose my own story is a classic example of being in the right place at the right time. I was in Laos, speaking quite good Lao, at the time when

UNHCR was looking for people who were not from the immediate region, and were not American or French. I was on a shortlist of one.

Even if you cannot manage that, people are still being recruited after showing up in a country facing a crisis, demonstrating that they know the country well and can contribute something valuable.

Administration, finance and logistics

No agency can operate without good administrative and logistical back-up. Finance officers, human resources staff, procurement, IT and communications technicians are all essential to a successful programme. For people with those skills, the routes into the mainstream professional ranks of the UN can be the same as for others. As before, there is no substitute for relevant experience, a good reputation and a proven capacity to work well in a challenging environment.

Don't give up!

If you really want to work for the UN, be prepared for rejections and for long periods of silence. Just when you think they have forgotten about you, you get a phone call asking if you can be somewhere you have never heard of within the next week. This recruitment style has many possible causes. Perhaps the first choice candidate declined the offer. Perhaps the human resources department objected to your nationality, your qualifications, your experience or your gender, and the manager had to demonstrate that there really were no internal candidates who could do the job. If you have been shortlisted and interviewed, and several weeks have passed with no word, pick up the phone and call the person who invited you to the interview and ask politely if the position has been filled yet.

A former senior colleague at UNHCR used to recount how he had applied for over 40 posts, and that was well before computers allowed people to crank out an application in less than five minutes.

Is this really for me?

If you have reached this point and still think that the answer to this question may be 'yes', please read these final paragraphs.

As I hope will be clear from this book, I consider the opportunity to work in the United Nations an enormous privilege, but not everybody sees it like that. Some believe that they are entitled to the job and spend a fair amount of their time ensuring that they receive all the 'entitlements' that the job offers. There is an oft-repeated story of two friends walking past the UN headquarters in New York, and one asking the other, 'How many people work in there?' The reply was, 'About a third'. This is, of course, unfair.

Working in the crisis-response components of the United Nations can put tremendous strains on family life. In my whole career, I had only one posting, of two years, that was 'non-family', meaning that my family was not allowed, for security reasons, to stay with me in the duty station. Many younger colleagues have spent much more time separated from their families. The work is unpredictable, stressful, sometimes dangerous, and because of that, it tends to attract people who like that kind of life. If you want stability and not too much stress, you may want to give the crisis-response work of the United Nations a miss.

SUGGESTED FURTHER READING

This list of books and articles is arranged according to the chapters in the book to which they most closely relate. Some have provided source material for the book, others were essential reading at the time I was working on the country in question. This is not intended as a comprehensive reading list on any of the countries or topics covered.

Introduction

Mazower, Mark (2012) *Governing the World: The History of an Idea*, New York: Allen Lane History.

Myint-U, Thant, and Scott, Amy (2007) *The UN Secretariat: A Brief History (1945–2006)*, New York: International Peace Academy.

United Nations (2004) *Basic Facts about the United Nations*, New York: United Nations.

Urquhart, Brian (1987) *A Life in Peace and War*, New York: W.W. Norton.

Chapter 1 – Laos 1968–77

Burchett, Wilfred (1968) *Furtive War: The United States in Vietnam and Laos*, New York: International Publishers.

Condominas, Georges (1965) *L'Exotique est Quotidien*, Paris: Librairie Plon.

Dommen, Arthur J. (1971) *Conflict in Laos: The Politics of Neutralization*, New York: Praeger.

Le Boulanger, Paul (1945) *Histoire du Laos Français*, Paris: Librairie Plon (republished in 1969 by Gregg International, Farnborough, UK).

McCoy, Alfred W. (1972) *The Politics of Heroin in Southeast Asia*, New York: Harper Colophon Books.

USAID (1973) *Facts on Foreign Aid to Laos*, Vientiane: US Embassy to Laos.

Whitaker, Donald P., Roberts, Thomas Duval, with Barth, H., Berman, S., Heimann, J., MacDonald, J., Martindale, K., and Shinn, R. (1972) *Area Handbook for Laos*, Washington: US Government.

Chapter 2 – Thailand 1978–81

Barber, Martin (1987) 'Resettlement in Third Countries Versus Voluntary Repatriation' in Barry S. Levy and Daniel Susott (eds) *Years of Horror, Days of Hope: Responding to the Cambodian Refugee Crisis*, New York: Associated Faculty Press.

—— (1987) 'Operating a United Nations Program: A Personal Reflection' in Barry S. Levy and Daniel Susott (eds) *Years of Horror, Days of Hope: Responding to the Cambodian Refugee Crisis*, New York: Associated Faculty Press.

Clarkin, Patrick F. (2005) 'Hmong Resettlement in French Guiana', *Hmong Studies Journal*, 6: 1–27.

Cooper, Robert (2008) *The Hmong*, Vientiane: Lao Insight Books.

Fadiman, Anne (1997) *The Spirit Catches You and You Fall Down: A Hmong Child, her American Doctors and the Collision of Two Cultures*, New York: Farrar, Strauss and Giroux, pp. 183–4.

Ressler, Everett (December 1980) 'Analysis and Recommendations for the Care of the Unaccompanied Khmer Children in the Holding Centres, Thailand', Bangkok: Inter-Agency Study Group.

Robinson, W. Courtland (1998) *Terms of Refuge – The International Exodus and the International Response*, London: Zed Books.

Shawcross, William (1984) *The Quality of Mercy*, New York: Simon and Schuster.

UNHCR (1983) *Pirate Attacks on Boat People Arriving in Thailand (1981–83)*, Geneva: UNCHR.

Chapter 3 – London 1981–8

Independent Commission on International Humanitarian Issues (1985) *Famine*, New York: Vintage.

—— (1985) *Winning the Human Race?*, London: Zed Books.

—— (1986) *Refugees: The Dynamics of Displacement*, London: Zed Books.

Chapter 4 – Afghanistan 1988–96

Cowper-Coles, Sherard (2011) *Cables from Kabul: The Inside Story of the West's Afghanistan Campaign*, London: Harper Press.

Duncan, Emma (1989) *Breaking the Curfew: A Political Journey through Pakistan*, London: Michael Joseph.

Dupree, Louis (1973) *Afghanistan*, Princeton, Princeton University Press.

Marsden, Peter (2009) *Afghanistan: Aid, Armies and Empires*, London: I.B.Tauris.

Rashid, Ahmed (2008) *Descent into Chaos: How the War Against Islamic Extremism is Being Lost in Pakistan, Afghanistan and Central Asia*, London: Allen Lane.

Rubin, Barnett, Hamidzada, Humayun, and Stoddard, Abby (eds) (2003) *Through the Fog of Peace-Building: Evaluating the Reconstruction of Afghanistan*, New York: Center on International Cooperation.

Saikal, Amin (2006) *Modern Afghanistan: A History of Struggle and Survival*, London: I.B.Tauris.

Chapter 5 – Bosnia and Herzegovina 1996–8

Andric, Ivo (1994) *Bridge over the River Drina*, London: Harvill Press.

—— (1996) *Bosnian Chronicle*, London: Harvill Press (originally published in Serbo-Croat in 1945 as *Travnicka hronika*; originally published in English in 1992 as *The Days of the Consuls*).

Bennett, Christopher (1995) *Yugoslavia's Bloody Collapse*, London: Hurst.

Holbrooke, Richard (1998) *To End A War*, New York: Random House.

Maclean, Fitzroy (1991 [1949]) *Eastern Approaches*, London: Penguin.

Malcolm, Noel (1996) *Bosnia: A Short History*, London: Papermac.

Owen, David (1996) *Balkan Odyssey*, London: Indigo (originally published by Victor Gollancz, 1995).

Silber, Laura, and Little, Allan (1996) *Yugoslavia: The Death of a Nation*, London: Penguin.

West, Rebecca (1993 [1942]) *Black Lamb and Grey Falcon*, Edinburgh: Canongate Classics.

Chapter 6 – New York 1998–2000

Annan, Kofi (2012) *Interventions: A Life in War and Peace*, London: Allen Lane.

Barber, Martin (October 2009) 'Humanitarian Crises and Peace Operations: A Personal View of UN Reform During Kofi Annan's First Term', *Conflict, Security and Development*, 9: 3.

Berdal, Mats, and Wennmann, Achim (eds) (2010) *Ending Wars, Consolidating Peace: Economic Perspectives*, London: Routledge.

Cain, Kenneth, Postlewait, Heidi, and Thomson, Andrew (2005) *Emergency Sex (and Other Desperate Measures) from a War Zone*, Santa Monica, CA: Miramax.

Chesterman, Simon (ed.) (2007) *Secretary or General? The UN Secretary-General in World Politics*, Cambridge: Cambridge University Press.

Chesterman, Simon, and Franck, Thomas M. (2007) 'Resolving the Contradictions of the Office', in Simon Chesterman (ed.), *Secretary or General? The UN Secretary-General in World Politics*, Cambridge: Cambridge University Press.

Dobbins, James, Jones, Seth G., Crane, Keith, Rathmell, Andrew, and Steele, Brett (2005) *The UN's Role in Nation-building: From the Congo to Iraq*, Santa Monica, CA: Rand Corporation, p. 250.

Guéhenno, Jean-Marie (1996) *The End of the Nation-State*, Minneapolis: University of Minnesota Press.

International Commission on Intervention and State Sovereignty (2001) *The Responsibility to Protect*, Ottawa: International Development Research Centre (IDRC).

Pugh, Michael (2006) 'Post-War Economies and the New York Dissensus', *Conflict, Security and Development*, 6(3): 269–89.

Shawcross, William (2000) *Deliver Us From Evil*, London: Bloomsbury.

Traub, James (2006) *The Best Intentions: Kofi Annan and the UN in the Era of American Power*, London: Bloomsbury.

United Nations (17 June 1992) *Report of the Secretary-General: An Agenda for Peace – Preventive Diplomacy, Peacemaking and Peace-keeping*, A/47/277. www.un.org/en/ga/search/view_doc.asp?symbol=A/47/277

—— (8 September 1999) *Report of the Secretary-General on the Protection of Civilians in Armed Conflict*, S/1999/957, New York: United Nations.

—— (21 August 2000) *Report of the Panel on United Nations Peace Operations*, S/2000/809, New York: United Nations.

—— (2000) *Note of Guidance on Relations Between Representatives of the Secretary-General, Resident Coordinators and Humanitarian Coordinators*, New York: United Nations.

—— (9 February 2006) *Note of Guidance on Integrated Missions*, New York: United Nations.

United Nations Security Council (17 September 1999) *Protection of Civilians in Armed Conflict*, Resolution 1265, New York: United Nations.

—— (19 November 2003) *The Importance of Mine Action and Peacekeeping Operations*, Presidential Statement S/PRST/2003/22, New York: United Nations.

Chapter 7 – Mine action 2000–5

Bottomley, Ruth (2003) *Crossing the Divide: Landmines, Villagers and Organisations*, Oslo: International Peace Research Institute (PRIO).

Maslen, Stuart (2004) *Mine Action After Diana: Progress in the Struggle against Landmines*, London: Landmine Action and Ann Arbor Press.

Millard, Ananda, and Harpviken, Kristian Berg (eds) (2000) *Reassessing the Impact of Humanitarian Mine Action: Illustrations from Mozambique*, Oslo: International Peace Research Institute (PRIO).

Chapter 8 – United Arab Emirates 2009–13

Government of the UAE (2010) *United Arab Emirates: Foreign Aid 2009*, Abu Dhabi: Office for the Coordination of Foreign Aid (OCFA).

—— (2013) *Foreign Aid Reporting Framework of the United Arab Emirates*, Abu Dhabi: OCFA.

Heard-Bey, Frauke (2004) *From Trucial States to United Arab Emirates*, Dubai: Motivate Publishing.

Chapters 9 and 10 – Coordination

Barber, Martin, Bhattacharjee, Abhijit, Lossio, Roberta M., and Sida, Lewis (2008) *Review of the Central Emergency Response Fund (CERF)*, New York: UN Office for the Coordination of Humanitarian Affairs.

Collier, Paul (2009) *Wars, Guns and Votes*, London: Bodley Head.

Cowper-Coles, Sherard (2011) *Cables from Kabul: The Inside Story of the West's Afghanistan Campaign*, London: Harper Press.

Egeland, Jan, Harmer, Adele and Stoddard, Abby (2011) *To Stay and Deliver: Good Practice for Humanitarians in Complex Security Environments*, New York: Office for the Coordination of Humanitarian Affairs.

Hancock, Graham (1989) *Lords of Poverty: Power, Prestige and Corruption in the International Aid Business*, New York: Atlantic Monthly Press.

Holmes, John (2012) *The Politics of Humanity*, London: Head Zeus.

Kaplan, Seth (2008) *Fixing Fragile States, A New Paradigm for Development*, New York: Praeger.

Malloch-Brown, Mark (2011) *The Unfinished Global Revolution*, London: Allen Lane.

Paris, Roland (2004) *At War's End: Building Peace after Civil Conflict*, London: Cambridge University Press.

Power, Samantha (2008) *Chasing the Flame: Sergio Vieira de Mello and the Fight to Save the World*, New York: The Penguin Press.

United Nations (1991) *Resolution of the General Assembly on Strengthening the Coordination of Humanitarian Assistance*, UNGA Resolution 46/182, New York: United Nations.

—— (2005) *Resolution of the General Assembly on Strengthening the Coordination of Humanitarian Assistance*, UNGA Resolution 60/124 (Central Emergency Response Fund), New York: United Nations.

ACRONYMS

Only the most common acronyms found in the book are shown in this list.

BCAR	British Council for Aid to Refugees
BRC	British Refugee Council
BRICS	Brazil, Russia, India, China, South Africa
CCSDPT	Coordinating Committee for Services to Displaced Persons in Thailand
CERF	Central Emergency Response Fund
CHF	Common Humanitarian Fund
CIA	Central Intelligence Agency
DAC	Development Assistance Committee (of the OECD)
DfID	Department for International Development (UK)
DHA	United Nations Department of Humanitarian Affairs
DOS	Designated Official for Security (of the United Nations system)
DPKO	United Nations Department of Peacekeeping Operations
DRC	Democratic Republic of the Congo
DSRSG	Deputy Special Representative of the United Nations Secretary-General
EC	European Commission
ECHO	European Commission Humanitarian Aid and Civil Protection
E-MINE	Electronic Mine Information Network (of UNMAS)
ERC	Emergency Relief Coordinator
ERF	Emergency Response Fund
FAO	Food and Agriculture Organisation

GDP	Gross Domestic Product
GICHD	Geneva International Centre for Humanitarian Demining
GNI	Gross National Income
HC	Humanitarian Coordinator (of the United Nations)
IASC	Inter-Agency Standing Committee
ICBL	International Campaign to Ban Landmines
ICRC	International Committee of the Red Cross
ICSC	International Civil Service Commission
IDP	Internally displaced person
IFOR	Implementation Force (NATO-led force in Bosnia)
IFRCS	International Federation of Red Cross and Red Crescent Societies
ILO	International Labour Organisation
IMAS	International Mine Action Standards
IPTF	International Police Task Force
IRC	International Rescue Committee
ISDR	International Strategy for Disaster Reduction (UN)
JPO	Junior Professional Officer
KR	Khmer Rouge
LPDR	Lao People's Democratic Republic
MAG	Mines Advisory Group
MICAD	Ministry of International Cooperation and Development (UAE)
NATO	North Atlantic Treaty Organisation
NCE	National Competitive Examinations
NGO	Non-governmental organisation
OCFA	UAE Office for the Coordination of Foreign Aid
OCHA	United Nations Office for the Coordination of Humanitarian Affairs
OECD	Organisation for Economic Cooperation and Development
OPEC	Organisation of the Petroleum Exporting Countries
OSCE	Organisation for Security and Cooperation in Europe
RC	United Nations Resident Coordinator
SCOR	Standing Conference on Refugees
SFOR	Stabilisation Force (NATO-led force in Bosnia)
SMART	Specific, Measurable, Achievable, Realistic and Time-scaled objectives

SRSG	Special Representative of the United Nations Secretary-General
UAE	United Arab Emirates
UK	United Kingdom of Great Britain and Northern Ireland
UN	United Nations
UNA	United Nations Association
UNCHS	United Nations Centre for Human Settlements (Habitat)
UNDP	United Nations Development Programme
UNDRO	Office of the United Nations Disaster Relief Coordinator
UNESCO	United Nations Educational, Scientific and Cultural Organisation
UNFPA	United Nations Population Fund
UNHCR	Office of the UN High Commissioner for Refugees
UNICEF	United Nations Children's Fund
UNMACC	United Nations Mine Action Coordination Centre
UNMAS	United Nations Mine Action Service
UNMIBH	United Nations Mission in Bosnia and Herzegovina
UNMOGIP	United Nations Military Observer Group in India and Pakistan
UNOCA	Office of the United Nations Coordinator of Humanitarian and Economic Assistance Programmes relating to Afghanistan
UNOCHA	United Nations Office for Coordination of Humanitarian Assistance to Afghanistan
UNOPS	United Nations Office for Project Services
UNPROFOR	United Nations Protection Force
UNTSO	United Nations Truce Supervision Organisation
UNV	United Nations Volunteers
USAID	United States Agency for International Development
UXO	Unexploded Ordnance
VSO	Voluntary Service Overseas
WFP	World Food Programme (of the United Nations)
WHO	World Health Organisation
WIPO	World Intellectual Property Organisation

GLOSSARY

Institutions

AP Mine Ban Treaty – The 'Convention on the Prohibition of the Production, Use, Transfer and Stockpiling of Anti-Personnel Landmines and on their Destruction' (see also Ottawa Treaty).

British Refugee Council (BRC) – British NGO founded in 1983 and now known as the Refugee Council.

Central Emergency Response Fund (CERF) – UN fund set up in 2006 for ERC to provide quick responses to disasters.

Central Intelligence Agency (CIA) – US government agency that channelled funds to the *mujahideen* through Pakistan's ISI.

Department for International Development (DfID) – Department of the UK government responsible for the government's overseas aid programme.

Department of Humanitarian Affairs (DHA) – UN department established in 1992, which became OCHA in 1997.

Department of Peacekeeping Operations (DPKO) – UN department responsible for all UN peacekeeping operations.

Department of Political Affairs (DPA) – UN department responsible for the UN's political work at headquarters and around the world.

Development Assistance Committee (DAC) – This committee of the OECD established in 1961 is a forum for 27 major donors, mainly from Europe and North America.

Emergency Relief Coordinator (ERC) – Post created by the UN General Assembly in 1991 to coordinate the international response to humanitarian emergencies. The ERC is also the UN Under-Secretary-General for humanitarian affairs.

Executive Committee on Humanitarian Affairs (ECHA) – UN internal committee established in 1997 to ensure coordination among UN departments and agencies.

Executive Committee on Peace and Security (ECPS) – UN internal committee established in 1997 to ensure coordination among different parts of the UN system.

General Assembly (GA) – UN forum of all member states (193 in 2014), which adopts non-binding resolutions.

Geneva International Centre for Humanitarian Demining (GICHD) – Body established in 1998 by the government of Switzerland which 'works to eliminate mines, explosive remnants of war and other explosive hazards'.

Humanitarian Coordinator (HC) – UN official coordinating international response to emergency in a specific country or region.

Inter-Agency Standing Committee (IASC) – Forum for coordination of international response to humanitarian emergencies, established by the UN General Assembly in 1991. It includes UN agencies, the Red Cross and NGOs, and is chaired by the ERC.

International Campaign to Ban Landmines (ICBL) – Nobel Prize-winning international civil society group, instrumental in the adoption of the Anti-Personnel Mine Ban Treaty (Ottawa Treaty).

International Committee of the Red Cross (ICRC) – Geneva-based Swiss organisation which is custodian of the Geneva Conventions and provides humanitarian aid during war.

International Federation of Red Cross and Red Crescent Societies (IFRCS) – Coordinates and supports activities of national Red Cross and Red Crescent societies.

International Police Task Force (IPTF) – Part of the UN Mission in Bosnia and Herzegovina from 1995 to 2002.

Inter-Services Intelligence (ISI) – Pakistan military agency which channelled funds from the CIA to the Afghan *mujahideen*, and then the Taliban.

Khmer Rouge (KR) – Came to power in Cambodia in 1975; responsible for genocide.

Mujahideen – Groups fighting communist governments in Afghanistan in the 1980s and early 1990s.

Non-governmental organisation (NGO) – Term applied to a wide range of civil society organisations, mainly conducting advocacy or providing aid.

Office for the Coordination of Foreign Aid (OCFA) – UAE government office established in 2008, absorbed into MICAD in 2013.

Office for the Coordination of Humanitarian Affairs (OCHA) – UN office established in 1997 to succeed DHA and support the role of ERC in the coordination of humanitarian aid.

Official Development Assistance (ODA) – Term defined by DAC to identify all recognised forms of humanitarian and development aid.

Organisation for Economic Cooperation and Development (OECD) – Established by governments of developed countries in 1961.

'Ottawa Treaty' – short form for the Convention on the Prohibition of the Production, Use, Transfer and Stockpiling of Anti-Personnel Landmines and on their Destruction, signed in Ottawa in 1997.

Overseas Development Administration (ODA) – UK government department responsible for overseas aid; became DfID in 1997.

P5 – The five permanent members of the Security Council (China, France, Russia, the United Kingdom, the United States).

Resident Coordinator (RC) – UN official who coordinates UN development cooperation in a specific country.

Secretary-General (SG) of the United Nations – Chief administrative officer of the UN, elected for up to two five-year terms.

Security Council – UN forum of 15 member states, of which five permanent members have a veto; adopts binding resolutions on matters of international peace and security.

Special Representative of the United Nations Secretary-General (SRSG) – Senior official responsible for the UN's overall involvement in a specific country or region, or for a particular thematic issue.

Taliban – Name given to Afghan groups that emerged in 1994 and seized power in Kabul in 1996. They were overthrown in 2001 and have continued to mount armed opposition to the Afghan government.

Under-Secretary-General (USG) of the United Nations – Senior official in charge of a UN department.

United Nations Children's Fund (UNICEF) – UN fund focussed on humanitarian and development assistance for women and children.

United Nations Coordinator of Humanitarian and Economic Assistance Programmes relating to Afghanistan (UNOCA) – Position held by Sadruddin Aga Khan from 1988 to 1990 and by Benon Sevan from 1991 to 1992, when it became UNOCHA.

United Nations Development Programme (UNDP) – Lead agency within the UN system for development cooperation in developing countries.

United Nations High Commissioner for Refugees (UNHCR) – Official responsible for protection and assistance to the world's refugees. The office is also known as the UN Refugee Agency.

United Nations Mine Action Service (UNMAS) – UN office responsible for coordinating the UN's efforts to combat the impact of landmines and other explosive remnants of war.

United Nations Mission in Bosnia and Herzegovina (UNMIBH) – UN peacekeeping mission from 1995 to 2002, which included the IPTF.

United Nations Office for Coordination of Humanitarian Assistance to Afghanistan (UNOCHA) – UN office which operated from 1992 to 2002.

United States Agency for International Development (USAID) – Agency of the US government responsible for US overseas aid programmes.

World Food Programme (WFP) – UN body responsible for food aid programmes.

World Health Organisation (WHO) – Specialised agency of the UN system.

People

Amos, Baroness Valerie – Emergency Relief Coordinator and USG for Humanitarian Affairs (2010–); former British government minister and diplomat.

Annan, Kofi – Secretary-General of the United Nations (1997–2006); Ghanaian former senior UN official.

Ban, Ki-moon – Secretary-General of the United Nations (2007–); former foreign minister of Republic of Korea.

Bhutto, Benazir – Prime minister of Pakistan (1988–90 and 1993–6); assassinated in 2007.

Bildt, Carl – High Representative for Bosnia and Herzegovina (1995–7); Swedish diplomat and government minister (prime minister, 1991–4).

Brahimi, Lakhdar – Chair, UN High-Level Panel on Peace Operations (2000); SRSG for Afghanistan (2001–4); former diplomat and foreign minister of Algeria.

Cuénod, Jacques – UNHCR Regional Representative for Indo-China (1974–8).

Egeland, Jan – Emergency Relief Coordinator and USG for humanitarian affairs (2003–7); former Norwegian government minister and appointed Secretary-General of the Norwegian Refugee Council in 2013.

Eide, Kai – SRSG for Bosnia and Herzegovina (1997–8) and SRSG for Afghanistan (2008–10); Norwegian diplomat.

Guéhenno, Jean-Marie – UN Under-Secretary-General (USG) for peacekeeping operations (2000–8); French diplomat and writer.

Hartling, Poul – UN High Commissioner for Refugees (1978–85); former prime minister of Denmark.

Hekmatyar, Gulbuddin – Leader, Hezbi Islami party, Afghanistan.

Holmes, Sir John – Emergency Relief Coordinator and Under-Secretary-General for Humanitarian affairs (2007–10); British diplomat.

Karzai, Hamid – President of Afghanistan (2002–).

Lockwood, David – UN resident coordinator in Afghanistan (1991–6).

Malloch-Brown, Lord Mark – UNHCR field officer, Thailand (1979–81); administrator, UNDP (1999–2005); Deputy Secretary-General of the United Nations (2006); minister of state, UK Foreign Office (2007–9).

Mojaddedi, Sibghatullah – President of Afghanistan (1992–3).

Najibullah, Mohammad – President of Afghanistan (1986–92).

Ogata, Sadako – UN High Commissioner for Refugees (1991–2001); Japanese diplomat.

Perez de Cuellar, Javier – Secretary-General of the United Nations (1982–91); Peruvian diplomat and politician.

Rabbani, Burhanuddin – President of Afghanistan (1993–6).

Rehn, Elisabeth – SRSG in Bosnia and Herzegovina (1998–9); former minister of defence of Finland.

Riza, Iqbal – UN SRSG for Bosnia and Herzegovina (1996); Chef de cabinet, Office of the UN Secretary-General (1997–2004); Pakistani diplomat.

Rizvi, Zia – UNHCR Regional Representative for Southeast Asia (1980–2); Secretary-General, Independent Commission on International Humanitarian Issues; deputy UN coordinator for Afghanistan (1988–90).

Sadruddin Aga Khan – UN High Commissioner for Refugees (1966–77); UN Coordinator for Afghanistan (1988–90).

Sevan, Benon – Personal representative of the UN Secretary-General in Afghanistan and Pakistan (1989–92) and head of UNOCHA (1991–2); UN Security Coordinator (1994–2002); Executive Director, UN Iraq Programme (Oil-for-Food) (1997–2003); Cypriot UN official.

Sommaruga, Cornelio – President of the ICRC (1987–99); president of GICHD; Swiss diplomat.

Vieira de Mello, Sergio – Emergency Relief Coordinator and USG for Humanitarian Affairs (1998–2002); SRSG for Kosovo (1999); SRSG and transitional administrator for East Timor (Timor Leste) (1999–2002); UN High Commissioner for Human Rights (2002–3); SRSG to Iraq (2003); Brazilian UN official.

INDEX

This index is a list of personal names, institutions, key concepts and selected place names.

The references in **bold** (for example, Afghanistan 75–103) indicate that the topic is the principal focus of the highlighted pages in the book.